"No other guide has as much to offer... a pleasure to read."   Gene Shalit on the *Today Show*

". . . Excellently organized for the casual traveler who is looking for a mix of recreation and cultural insight."
Washington Post

★ ★ ★ ★ ★ (5-star rating) "Crisply written and remarkably personable. Cleverly organized so you can pluck out the minutest fact in a moment. Satisfyingly thorough."
Réalités

"The information they offer is up-to-date, crisply presented but far from exhaustive, the judgments knowledgeable but not opinionated."   *New York Times*

"The individual volumes are compact, the prose succinct, and the coverage up-to-date and knowledgeable . . . The format is portable and the index admirably detailed."
John Barkham Syndicate

". . . An abundance of excellent directions, diversions, and facts, including perspectives and getting-ready-to-go advice — succinct, detailed, and well organized in an easy-to-follow style."   *Los Angeles Times*

"They contain an amount of information that is truly staggering, besides being surprisingly current."
Detroit News

"These guides address themselves to the needs of the modern traveler demanding precise, qualitative information . . . Upbeat, slick, and well put together."
Dallas Morning News

". . . Attractive to look at, refreshingly easy to read, and generously packed with information."   *Miami Herald*

"These guides are as good as any published, and much better than most."   *Louisville* (Kentucky) *Times*

Stephen Birnbaum Travel Guides

Acapulco
Bahamas, and Turks & Caicos
Barcelona
Bermuda
Boston
Canada
Cancun, Cozumel & Isla Mujeres
Caribbean
Chicago
Disneyland
Eastern Europe
Europe
Europe for Business Travelers
Florence
France
Great Britain
Hawaii
Honolulu
Ireland
Italy
Ixtapa & Zihuatanejo
Las Vegas
London
Los Angeles
Mexico
Miami & Ft. Lauderdale
Montreal & Quebec City
New Orleans
New York
Paris
Portugal
Puerto Vallarta
Rome
San Francisco
South America
Spain
Toronto
United States
USA for Business Travelers
Vancouver
Venice
Walt Disney World
Washington, DC
Western Europe

CONTRIBUTING EDITORS

Frederick H. Brengelman
Patricia Canole
Kevin Causey
Wendy Luft

Thérèse Margolis
Eleanor Morris
Melinda Tang
Carol Zaiser

MAPS Susan Hohl

SYMBOLS Gloria McKeown

A Stephen Birnbaum Travel Guide

Birnbaum's ACAPULCO 1993

Alexandra Mayes Birnbaum

EDITOR

Lois Spritzer

EXECUTIVE EDITOR

Laura L. Brengelman
Managing Editor

Mary Callahan
Jill Kadetsky
Susan McClung
Beth Schlau
Dana Margaret Schwartz
Associate Editors

Gene Gold
Assistant Editor

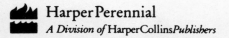

HarperPerennial
A Division of HarperCollins*Publishers*

To Stephen, who merely made all this possible.

FIRST EDITION

ISSN 0749-2561 (Stephen Birnbaum Travel Guides)
ISSN 1055-5633 (Acapulco)
ISBN 0-06-278041-7 (pbk.)

91 92 93 94 95 96 CC/WP 10 9 8 7 6 5 4 3 2 1

Contents

GETTING READY TO GO

All the practical travel data you need to plan your Mexican vacation to the final detail.

USEFUL WORDS AND PHRASES

THE CITY

A thorough, qualitative guide to Mexico's favorite resort area. This is a comprehensive report on the city's most compelling attractions and amenities, designed to be used on the spot.

DIVERSIONS

A selective guide to more than ten active and/or cerebral theme vacations, including the best places in Acapulco to pursue them.

DIRECTIONS

Major driving routes, leading from the country's most beautiful beaches to nearby cities and ancient ruins.

A Word from the Editor

My husband Stephen Birnbaum's relationship with Acapulco went back more years than he cared to confess. Suffice to say it was before the multi-lane highway was completed from Mexico City to the Pacific Coast.

He got to Acapulco's storybook harbor by boat, and tied up at a very basic marina down at the end of Caleta Beach. Steve stayed 10 days (he'd originally scheduled only 3), but even then Acapulco exerted a very strong pull on visitors that made it very hard to weigh anchor.

Each day back then was very strictly scheduled: Arise at about 10 AM for sustenance (toast and beer, as Steve recalled) and the first important rays of the day at Caleta (the "morning" beach). By about noon, and after several turnings over, the band of gringo tourists (about a dozen in all) had begun its southeastward migration toward the thatch-roofed refreshment stands (more beer) and the midday rays of Hornos Beach (the "afternoon" beach). Mid-afternoon was always nap time, with inner alarms set to allow enough time for a low-water-pressure shower and the short ride to the hammocks at Pie de la Cuesta, which was the socially correct spot from which to watch the sun fall dramatically into the Pacific Ocean at day's end (with a bottle of beer clutched in one's fist).

Acapulco's history as a transshipment port for the Spanish as far back as the 16th century meant the existence of enough bars and restaurants to sit in while filling the evening hours with heated debates on the subtleties of local margarita making, and the nighttime revelries ended when funds ran out or there was a threat that any more imbibing would jeopardize attendance at the 10 AM "Happiness Is Horizontal" meeting next morning on Caleta. It was an existence that later formed the definition of "laid-back."

My own first foray to Acapulco goes back more than 2 decades, but the city exerts no less of a pull now. Although very little of that lifestyle of a generation or so ago still exists within Acapulco's now heavily developed harbor, that doesn't seem to keep travelers away. Quite the contrary seems to be the case; Acapulco's reliable weather and nearly constant sun encourage visitors by the thousands to congregate along these shores whenever the temperatures farther north start to approach freezing. Not even the legions of vendors and beggars who seem hell-bent on disturbing every moment of a visitor's peace and quiet fail to discourage the sun worshipers.

And I guess the modern visitors are right, since there are few destinations on earth that equal Acapulco's range of vacation options. The trick is knowing what to accept and what to avoid like the plague; that's the reason we have created this specific guide to Mexico's best-known warm-weather retreat.

Obviously, any guidebook to Acapulco must keep pace with and answer the real needs of today's travelers. That's why we've tried to create a guide that's specifically organized, written, and edited for the more demanding modern traveler, one for whom qualitative information is infinitely more desirable than mere quantities of unappraised data. We think that this book, along with all the other guides in our series, represents a new generation of travel guides — one that is especially responsive to modern needs and interests.

For years, dating back as far as Herr Baedeker, travel guides have tended to be encyclopedic, seemingly much more concerned with demonstrating expertise in geography and history than with a real analysis of the sorts of things that actually concern a typical modern tourist. But today, when it is hardly necessary to tell a traveler where Acapulco is (in many cases, the traveler has been there nearly as often as the guidebook editors), it becomes the responsibility of those editors to provide new perspectives and to suggest new directions in order to make the guide genuinely valuable.

That's exactly what we've tried to do in this series. I think you'll notice a different, more contemporary tone to the text, as well as an organization and focus that are distinctive and more functional. And even a random reading of what follows will demonstrate a substantial departure from the standard guidebook orientation, for we've not only attempted to provide information of a more compelling sort, but we also have tried to present the data in a format that makes it particularly accessible.

Needless to say, it's difficult to decide just what to include in a guidebook of this size — and what to omit. Early on, we realized that giving up the encyclopedic approach precluded our listing every single route and restaurant, a realization that helped define our overall editorial focus. Similarly, when we discussed the possibility of presenting certain information in other than strict geographic order, we found that the new format enabled us to arrange data in a way that we feel best answers the questions travelers typically ask.

Large numbers of specific questions have provided the real editorial skeleton for this book. The volume of mail we regularly receive emphasizes that modern travelers want very precise information, so we've tried to organize our material in the most responsive way possible. Readers who want to know the best restaurant in Acapulco or the best beach will have no trouble extracting that data from this guide.

Travel guides are, understandably, reflections of personal taste, and putting one's name on a title page obviously puts one's preferences on the line. But I think I ought to amplify just what "personal" means. Like Steve, I don't believe in the sort of personal guidebook that's a palpable misrepresentation on its face. It is, for example, hardly possible for any single travel writer to visit thousands of restaurants (and nearly as many hotels) in any given year and provide accurate appraisals of each. And even if it were physically possible for one human being to survive such an itinerary, it would of necessity have to be done at a dead sprint, and the perceptions derived therefrom would probably be less valid than those of any other intelligent individual visiting the same establishments. It is, therefore, impossible (especially in a large, annually revised and updated guidebook *series* such as we offer) to have only one person provide all the data on the entire world.

I also happen to think that such individual orientation is of substantially less value to readers. Visiting a single hotel for just one night or eating one hasty meal in a random restaurant hardly equips anyone to provide appraisals that are of more than passing interest. No amount of doggedly alliterative or oppressively onomatopoeic text can camouflage a technique that is essentially specious. We have, therefore, chosen what I like to describe as the "thee and me" approach to restaurant and hotel evaluation and, to a somewhat more limited degree, to the sites and sights we have included in the other sections of our text. What this really reflects is personal sampling tempered by intelligent counsel from informed local sources, and these additional friends-of-the-editors are almost always residents of the area about which they are consulted.

Despite the presence of several editors, writers, researchers, and local contributors, very precise editing and tailoring keep our text fiercely subjective. So what follows is the gospel according to Birnbaum, and represents as much of our own taste and instincts as we can manage. It is probable, therefore, that if you like your beaches largely unpopulated, prefer small hotels with personality to huge high-rise anonymities, and can't tolerate fresh fish that's been relentlessly overcooked, we're likely to have a long and meaningful relationship. Readers with dissimilar tastes may be less enraptured.

I should also point out something about the person to whom this guidebook is directed. Above all, he or she is a "visitor." This means that such elements as restaurants have been specifically picked to provide the visitor with a representative, enlightening, stimulating, and above all pleasant experience. Since so many extraneous considerations can affect the reception and service accorded a regular restaurant patron, our choices can in no way be construed as an exhaustive guide to resident dining. We think we've listed all the best places, in various price ranges, but they were chosen with a visitor's enjoyment in mind.

Other evidence of how we've tried to tailor our text to reflect modern travel habits is most apparent in the section we call DIVERSIONS. Where once it was common for travelers to spend a visit to Mexico's resorts nailed to a single spot, the emphasis today is more likely to be directed toward pursuing some sport or special interest while seeing the surrounding countryside. So we've organized every activity we could reasonably evaluate and arranged the material in a way that is especially accessible to activists of either athletic or cerebral bent. It is no longer necessary, therefore, to wade through a pound or two of superfluous prose just to find the most challenging golf course or nightspot within a reasonable distance of your destination.

Although the sheer beauty of this unique spot along Mexico's Pacific Coast is reason enough to want to visit, there also are a number of added bonuses once you arrive. The entire adjacent coastline offers a veritable cornucopia of activities to challenge the imagination of any visitor. There is lots of undeveloped coastline to explore, as well as day trips (and longer rides) to cities and villages awash in colonial history.

If there is one single thing that best characterizes the revolution in and evolution of current holiday habits, it is that most travelers now consider travel a right rather than a privilege. No longer is a family trip to the far corners of the world necessarily a once-in-a-lifetime thing; nor is the idea of visiting exotic, faraway places in the least worrisome. Travel today translates as the enthusiastic desire to sample all of the world's opportunities, to find that elusive quality of experience that is not only enriching but comfortable. For that reason, we've tried to make what follows not only helpful and enlightening, but the sort of welcome companion of which every traveler dreams.

Finally, I also should point out that every good travel guide is a living enterprise; that is, no part of this text is carved in stone. In our annual revisions, we refine, expand, and further hone all our material to serve your travel needs better. To this end, no contribution is of greater value to us than your personal reaction to what we have written, as well as information reflecting your own experiences while using the book. We earnestly and enthusiastically solicit your comments about this guide *and* your opinions and perceptions about places you have recently visited. In this way, we will be able to provide the most current information — including the actual experiences of recent travelers — and to make those experiences more readily available to others. Please write to us at 10 E. 53rd St., New York, NY 10022.

We sincerely hope to hear from you.

ALEXANDRA MAYES BIRNBAUM

How to Use This Guide

A great deal of care has gone into the special organization of this guidebook, and we believe it represents a real breakthrough in the presentation of travel material. Our aim is to create a new, more modern generation of travel books, and to make this guide the most useful and practical travel tool available today.

Our text is divided into five basic sections in order to present information in the best way on every possible aspect of a vacation to Acapulco. This organization itself should alert you to the vast and varied opportunities available, as well as indicate all the specific data necessary to plan a successful visit. You won't find much of the conventional "swaying palms and shimmering sands" text here; we've chosen instead to deliver more useful and practical information. Prospective itineraries tend to speak for themselves, and with so many diverse travel opportunities, we feel our main job is to highlight what's where and to provide basic information — how, when, where, how much, and what's best — to assist you in making the most intelligent choices possible.

Here is a brief summary of the five sections of this book, and what you can expect to find in each. We believe that you will find both your travel planning and en route enjoyment enhanced by having this book at your side.

GETTING READY TO GO

This mini-encyclopedia of practical travel facts is a sort of know-it-all companion with all the precise information necessary to create a successful trip to Acapulco. There are entries on more than 25 separate topics, including how to get where you're going, what preparations to make before leaving, what to expect, what your trip is likely to cost, and how to avoid prospective problems. The individual entries are specific, realistic, and where appropriate, cost-oriented.

We expect you to use this section most in the course of planning your trip, for its ideas and suggestions are intended to simplify this often confusing period. Entries are intentionally concise, in an effort to get to the meat of the matter with the least extraneous prose. These entries are augmented by extensive lists of specific sources from which to obtain even more specialized data, plus some suggestions for obtaining travel information on your own.

USEFUL WORDS AND PHRASES

Though most resorts in Acapulo have English-speaking staff, at smaller establishments and on most stops along driving routes a little knowledge of Spanish will go a long way. This collection of often-used words and phrases will help you to make a hotel or dinner reservation, order a meal, mail a letter — and even buy toothpaste.

THE CITY

The individual report on Acapulco has been created with the assistance of researchers, contributors, professional journalists, and experts who live in the city. Although useful at the planning stage, THE CITY is really designed to be taken along and used on the spot. The report offers a short-stay guide, including an essay introducing the city as a historic entity and as a contemporary place to visit. *At-a-Glance* material is actually a site-by-site survey of the most important, interesting, and sometimes most eclectic sights to see and things to do. *Sources and Resources* is a concise listing of pertinent tourist information meant to answer myriad potentially pressing questions as they arise — from simple things such as the address of the local tourism office, how to get around, which sightseeing tours to take, and when special events and holidays occur to something more difficult like where to find the best nightspot, which are the shops that have the finest merchandise and/or the most irresistible bargains, and where the best golf, tennis, fishing, and water skiing are to be found. *Best in Town* lists our collection of cost-and-quality choices of the best places to eat and sleep on a variety of budgets.

DIVERSIONS

This section is designed to help travelers find the best places in which to engage in a wide range of physical and cerebral activities, without having to wade through endless pages of unrelated text. This very selective guide lists the broadest possible range of activities, including all the best places to pursue them.

We start with a list of special places to stay and eat, and move to activities that require some perspiration — sports preferences and other rigorous pursuits — and go on to report on a number of more spiritual vacation opportunities. In every case, our suggestions of a particular location — and often our recommendations of a specific hotel — is intended to guide you to that special place where the quality of experience is likely to be highest. Whether you opt for golf or tennis, surfing or sport fishing, bullfights or shopping sprees, each category is the equivalent of a comprehensive checklist of the absolute best in the area.

DIRECTIONS

Here are 2 driving itineraries, from Acapulco's superb beaches to the historic city of Oaxaca, and to Mexico City, the capital. Though they cover a considerable distance, portions of the itineraries can be done as day trips, using Acapulco as a base, while others can be "connected" for longer drives or used individually for short, intensive explorations along the way.

Each entry includes a guide to sightseeing highlights; a cost-and-quality guide to accommodations along the road (small inns, clean and comfortable motels, country hotels, campgrounds, and detours to off-the-main-road discoveries); hints and suggestions for activities; and detailed driving maps of the route, noting points of interest described in the text.

Although each of the book's sections has a distinct format and a special function, they have all been designed to be used together to provide a complete inventory of travel information. To use this book to full advantage, take a few minutes to read the table of contents and random entries in each section to get a firsthand feel for how it all fits together.

Pick and choose needed information. Assume, for example, that your idea of a dream vacation has always been to golf or just bask on a beach in Acapulco, visit the silver capital of Taxco, and explore the major ruins at Monte Albán, but you never really knew how to put such a trip together. Since your vacation will include driving, start by reading the short, informative section on traveling by car in GETTING READY TO GO. This will provide all the factual information needed to organize and prepare a road trip. It will alert you to insurance needs (and direct you to the insurance chapter in the same section of the book) and other equally detailed potential problems and pleasures of a driving vacation in Mexico. But where to go and what to see? Turn to DIVERSIONS: *Scuba and Skin Diving,* for the best dive spots in the waters around Acapulco; *Good Golf,* for information on Acapulco's *Pierre Marqués* course; *Shopping at the Source,* for a primer on how to shop in Mexico — including tips on the art of bargaining — and where the best buys are. Then turn to DIRECTIONS for an explicit guide to our suggested driving routes from Acapulco to the various destinations along the coast and north to Mexico City.

In other words, the sections of this book are building blocks, designed to help you put together the best possible trip. Use them selectively as a tool, a source of ideas, a reference work for accurate facts, and a guidebook to the best buys, the most exciting sights, the most pleasant accommodations, and the tastiest foods — *the best travel experience* that you can possibly have.

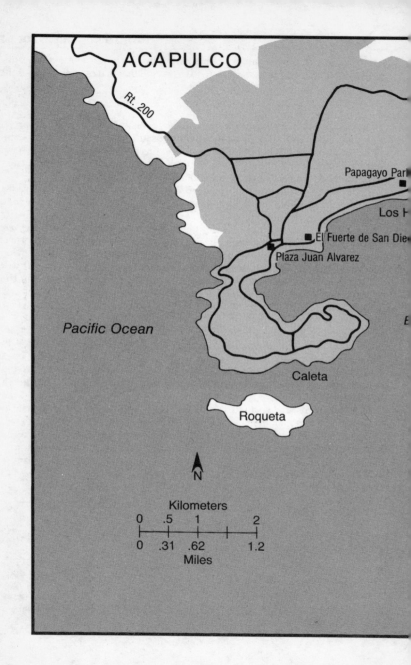

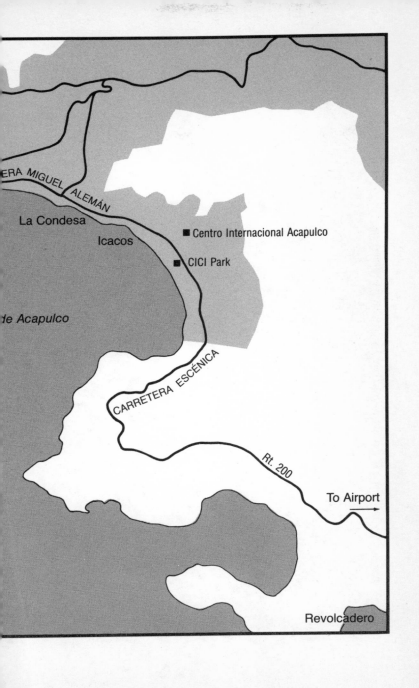

GETTING READY
TO GO

When and How to Go

What's Where

Acapulco, which has an almost legendary reputation as an international beach resort, lies at the foot of the majestic Sierra Madre del Sur on Mexico's Pacific Coast. The hotel-lined gem of a bay lured almost 5 million visitors last year, sharing the pleasures of the sun — and the flesh. Founded in 1530, the city has an interesting Spanish fort and other sights. Unquestionably, however, the chief attraction is its perfect weather. This plush resort area is poised at the edge of the state of Guerrero, which, along with Oaxaca, stretches to the Sierra Madre de Oaxaca. The state of Oaxaca — cool forested mountains, lush tropical valleys, and the humid coastline — is still inhabited by descendants of the ancient Zapotec and Mixtec Indian civilizations, and is famous for its red soil, which yields a variety of agricultural produce, as well as clay for pottery.

East of Acapulco, also on the coast, is the beautiful, unspoiled, and unsophisticated beach resort of Puerto Escondido. Inland from there is the Indian and colonial city of Oaxaca, a center for regional crafts (particularly ceramics and textiles), as well as the base for visits to the nearby magnificent ruins of Monte Albán and Mitla, among others. To the north of Acapulco, a heavily traveled road passes through lands steeped in Aztec culture, including the silver mining center of Taxco and the absolutely ideal climate of Cuernavaca, until it reaches Mexico City, the country's capital and major metropolis.

When to Go

Most people associate Acapulco with winter suntans and beautiful seaside resorts. They aren't wrong. Mexico's Pacific Coast is one of the all-time favorite escapes for North Americans trapped in snow and icy slush. (The winter season begins on December 15, when Mexicans traditionally take their annual 2-week, year-end vacation. It ends around the middle of April, or after *Easter.*)

The destinations covered in this book are blessed with year-round tourism seasons, so there really isn't a "best" time to visit them. But it is important to emphasize that more and more travelers are enjoying the substantial advantages of off-season travel, that is, late spring, summer, and fall at most of the coastal resorts. Getting there and staying there are less expensive during the off-season, as airfares, hotel rooms, and car rental rates go down; and less expensive package tours become available, and the independent traveler can go farther on less, too. What's more, major tourist attractions, beaches, and other facilities tend to be less crowded, and — throughout Mexico — life proceeds at a more leisurely pace.

It should also be noted that what the travel industry refers to as shoulder seasons —

the 1½ to 2 months before and after the peak seasons — often are sought out because they offer fair weather and somewhat smaller crowds. But be aware that very near high-season prices still can prevail during these periods.

CLIMATE AND CLOTHES: Mexico's Pacific Coast is, for good reason, one of the most popular winter vacation areas in North America. In Acapulco, expect beach weather all year, with temperatures generally in the 80s or 90s during the day and in the 70s or 80s at night. Even residents stay out of the strong mid-afternoon sun — whenever you come, bring lots of sunscreen. It may be slightly cooler and windy at times, and the rainy season, which lasts from June through September, drops a couple of hours of refreshing rain in the afternoons. Sailors be warned that the coastal waters have frequent gales and are subject to hurricanes during the summer and fall. In Acapulco, daytime wear is casual and as bare as you dare. Upscale resortwear is worn in most restaurants and nightclubs in the evening.

Travelers can get current readings and extended forecasts through the *Weather Channel Connection,* the worldwide weather report number of the *Weather Channel,* a cable television station. By dialing 900-WEATHER and punching in either the first four letters of the city name or the area code for over 600 cities in the US, an up-to-date recording will provide such information as current temperature, barometric pressure, relative humidity, and wind speed, as well as a general 2-day forecast. Beach, boating, and highway reports are also provided for some locations. Weather information for over 225 international destinations can be obtained by punching in the first four letters of the city. For instance, to hear the weather report for Acapulco, punch in ACAP. (To find out which cities or locations in a given country are covered, enter the first four letters of the *country* name.) Callers also can access information on weather patterns for any time of the year in the area requested, as well as international travel information such as visa requirements, US State Department travel advisories, tipping, and voltage. This 24-hour service can be accessed from any touch-tone phone in the US, and costs 95¢ per minute. The charge will show up on your phone bill. For additional information, write to the *Weather Channel Connection,* 2600 Cumberland Pkwy., Atlanta, GA 30339.

Traveling by Plane

The quickest, most efficient way to get to Acapulco is by air. Despite recent attempts at price simplification by a number of major US carriers, the airlines offering flights to Mexico continue to sell seats at a variety of prices under a vast spectrum of requirements and restrictions. You probably will spend more for your airfare than for any other single item in your travel budget. In order to take advantage of the lowest available fare, you should know what kinds of flights are available, the rules and regulations pertaining to air travel, and all the special package options.

SCHEDULED FLIGHTS: Leading airlines offering regularly scheduled flights to Acapulco from the US, many on a daily basis, include *Aeroméxico, American, Continental, Delta,* and *Mexicana.* As of this writing, direct flights — with no change of plane between the originating and terminating cities — to Acapulco depart from Chicago, Dallas, Houston, Los Angeles, and New York. Connecting flights are available from other US gateways, and some airlines also offer connections through Mexico City.

Tickets – When traveling on one of the many regularly scheduled flights, a full-fare ticket provides maximum travel flexibility (although at considerable expense) because there are no advance booking requirements. A prospective passenger can buy a ticket for a flight right up to the minute of takeoff — if a seat is available. If your ticket is for a round trip, you can make the return reservation whenever you wish — months before you leave or the day before you return. Assuming the foreign immigration requirements are met, you can stay at your destination for as long as you like. (Tickets generally are good for a year and can be renewed if not used.) On some airlines, you may be able to cancel your flight at any time without penalty, on others, cancellation — even of a full-fare ticket — may be subject to a variety of restrictions. It pays to check *before* booking your flight. In addition, while it is true that this category of ticket can be purchased at the last minute, it is advisable to reserve well in advance during popular vacation periods and around holiday times.

Fares – Airfares continue to change so rapidly that even the experts find it difficult to keep up with them. This ever-changing situation is due to a number of factors, including airline deregulation, volatile labor relations, increasing fuel costs, and vastly increased competition.

Perhaps the most common misconception about fares on scheduled airlines is that the cost of the ticket determines how much service will be provided on the flight. This is true only to a certain extent. A far more realistic rule of thumb is that the less you pay for your ticket, the more restrictions and qualifications are likely to come into play *before* you board the plane (as well as after you get off). These qualifying aspects relate to the months (and the days of the week) during which you must travel, how far in advance you must purchase your ticket, the minimum and maximum amount of time you may or must remain away, your willingness to decide on a return date at the time of booking — and your ability to stick to that decision. It is not uncommon for passengers sitting side by side on the same wide-body jet to have paid fares varying by hundreds of dollars, and all too often the traveler paying more would have been equally willing (and able) to accept the terms of the far less expensive ticket.

In general, the great variety of fares to Acapulco can be reduced to four basic categories, including first class, coach (also called economy or tourist class), and excursion or discount fares. A fourth category, called business class, has been added by many airlines in recent years.

A **first class** ticket is your admission to the special section of the aircraft, with larger seats, more legroom, sleeperette seating on some wide-body aircraft, better (or at least more elaborately served) food, free drinks and headsets for movies and music channels, and, above all, personal attention. First class fares are about twice those of full-fare economy, although both first class passengers and those paying full-fare economy fares are entitled to reserve seats and are sold tickets on an open reservation system.

Not too long ago, there were only two classes of air travel, first class and all the rest, usually called economy or tourist. Then **business class** came into being — one of the most successful recent airline innovations. At first, business class passengers were merely curtained off from the other economy passengers. Now a separate cabin or cabins — usually toward the front of the plane — is the norm. While standards of comfort and service are not as high as in first class, they represent a considerable improvement over conditions in the rear of the plane, with roomier seats, more leg and shoulder space between passengers, and fewer seats abreast. Free liquor and headsets, a choice of meal entrées, and a separate counter for speedier check-in are other inducements. As in first class, a business class passenger may travel on any scheduled flight he or she wishes, may buy a one-way or round-trip ticket, and have the ticket remain valid for a year. There are no minimum or maximum stay requirements, no advance booking requirements, and no cancellation penalties, and the fare allows the same free stopover privileges as first class. Airlines often have their own names for their business class services — such as simply Business Class on *American* or Medallion Class on *Delta*.

The terms of the **coach** or **economy** fare may vary slightly from airline to airline, and, in fact, from time to time airlines may be selling more than one type of economy fare. Coach or economy passengers sit more snugly, as many as 10 in a single row on a wide-body jet, behind the first class and business class sections. Normally, alcoholic drinks are not free, nor are the headsets. If there are two economy fares on the books, one (often called "regular economy") still may include free stopovers. The other, less expensive (often called "special economy"), may limit stopovers to one or two, with a charge (typically $25) for each one. Like first class passengers, travelers paying the full coach fare are subject to none of the restrictions that usually are attached to less expensive excursion and discount fares. There are no advance booking requirements, no minimum stay requirements, and (often) no cancellation penalties — but beware, the rules regarding cancellation vary from carrier to carrier. Tickets are sold on an open reservation system: They can be bought for a flight right up to the minute of takeoff (if seats are available), and if the ticket is round-trip, the return reservation can be made any time you wish. Both first class and coach tickets generally are good for a year, after which they can be renewed if not used, and if you ultimately decide not to fly at all, your money may be refunded (again, policies vary). The cost of economy and business class tickets on flights between the US and Mexican coastal resort areas may vary from a basic (low-season) price in effect most of the year to a peak (high-season) price during the winter.

Excursion and other **discount** fares are the airlines' equivalent of a special sale and usually apply to round-trip bookings only. These fares generally differ according to the season and the number of travel days permitted. They are only a bit less flexible than full-fare economy tickets and are, therefore, often useful for both business and holiday travelers. Most round-trip excursion tickets include strict minimum and maximum stay requirements and reservations can be changed only within the specified time limits. So don't count on extending a ticket beyond the prescribed time of return or staying less time than required. Different airlines may have different regulations concerning the number of stopovers permitted, and sometimes excursion fares are less expensive during midweek. The availability of these reduced-rate seats is most limited at busy times, such as holidays. Discount or excursion fare ticket holders sit with the coach passengers and, for all intents and purposes, are indistinguishable from them. They receive all the same basic services, even though they may have paid anywhere between 30% and 55% less for the trip. Obviously, it's wise to make plans early enough to qualify for this less expensive transportation if possible.

These discount or excursion fares may masquerade under a variety of names, they may vary from city to city (from East Coast to the West Coast, especially), but they invariably have strings attached. A common requirement is that the ticket must be purchased a certain number of days — usually between 7 and 21 days — in advance of departure, though it may be booked weeks or months in advance (it has to be "ticketed," or paid for, shortly after booking, however). The return reservation usually has to be made at the time of the original ticketing and often cannot be changed later than a certain number of days (again, usually 7 to 21 days) before the return flight. If events force a change in the return reservation after the date allowed, the passenger may have to pay the difference between the round-trip excursion rate and the round-trip coach rate, although some carriers permit scheduling changes for a nominal fee. In addition, some airlines may allow passengers to use their discounted fares by standing by for an empty seat, even if they don't otherwise have standby fares. Another common condition is a minimum and maximum stay requirement; for example, 1 to 6 days or 6 to 14 days (but including at least a Saturday night). Last, cancellation penalties of up to 50% of the full price of the ticket have been assessed — if a refund is offered at all — so check the specific penalty in effect when you purchase your discount/excursion ticket.

On some airlines, the ticket bearing the lowest price of all the current discount fares is the ticket where no change at all in departure and/or return flights is permitted, and where the ticket price is totally nonrefundable. If you do buy such a nonrefundable ticket, you should be aware of a policy followed by some airlines that may make it easier to change your plans if necessary. For a fee — set by each airline and payable at the airport when checking in — you *may* be able to change the time or date of a return flight on a nonrefundable ticket. However, if the nonrefundable ticket price for the replacement flight is higher than that of the original (as often is the case when trading in a weekday for a weekend flight), you will have to pay the difference. Any such change must be made a certain number of days in advance — in some cases as little as 2 days — of either the original or the replacement flight, whichever is earlier; restrictions are set by the individual carrier. (Travelers holding a nonrefundable or other restricted ticket who must change their plans due to a family emergency should know that some carriers may make special allowances in such situations; for further information, see *Staying Healthy,* in this section.)

■ **Note:** Due to recent changes in many US airlines' policies, nonrefundable tickets are now available that carry none of the above restrictions. Although passengers still may *not* be able to obtain a refund for the price paid, the time or date of a departing or return flight may be changed at any time (assuming seats are available) for a nominal service charge.

Standby fares, at one time the rock-bottom price at which a traveler could fly, recently have become elusive. At the time of this writing, most major scheduled airlines did not regularly offer standby fares on direct flights to Mexico. Because airline fares and their conditions constantly change, however, bargain hunters should not hesitate to ask if such a fare exists at the time they plan to travel.

While the definition of standby varies somewhat from airline to airline, it generally means that you make yourself available to buy a ticket for a flight (usually no sooner than the day of departure), then literally stand by on the chance that a seat will be empty. Once aboard, however, a standby passenger has the same meal service and frills (or lack of them) enjoyed by others in the economy class compartment.

Something else to check is the possibility of qualifying for a **GIT** (Group Inclusive Travel) fare, which requires that a specific dollar amount of ground arrangements be purchased, in advance, along with the ticket. The requirements vary as to the number of travel days and stopovers permitted, and the minimum number of passengers in a group. The actual fares also vary, but the cost will be spelled out in brochures distributed by the tour operators handling the ground arrangements. In the past, GIT fares typically were among the least expensive available from the established carriers, but the prevalence of discount fares has caused group fares to all but disappear from some air routes. Travelers reading brochures on group package tours to Acapulco will find that, in almost all cases, the applicable airfare given as a sample (to be added to the price of the land package to obtain the total tour price) is an APEX fare, the same discount fare available to the independent traveler.

The major airlines serving Acapulco from the US also may offer individual excursion fare rates similar to GIT fares, which are sold in conjunction with ground accommodation packages. Previously called ITX, and sometimes referred to as individual tour-basing fares, these fares generally are offered as part of "air/hotel/car transfer packages," and can reduce the cost of an economy fare by more than a third. The packages are booked for a specific amount of time, with return dates specified; rescheduling and cancellation restrictions and penalties vary from carrier to carrier. These fares most often are offered to popular resort areas — such as Acapulco — and sometimes include a day or more stopover in Mexico City. Airlines offering these packages are *American, Continental,* and *Delta.* (For further information on packages, see *Package Tours,* in this section.)

Travelers looking for the least expensive possible airfares should, finally, scan the pages of their hometown newspapers (especially the Sunday travel section) for announcements of special promotional fares. Most airlines offer their most attractive special fares to encourage travel during slow seasons, and to inaugurate and publicize new routes. Even if none of these factors applies, prospective passengers can be fairly sure that the number of discount seats per flight at the lowest price is strictly limited, or that the fare offering includes a set expiration date — which means it's absolutely necessary to move fast to obtain the lowest possible price.

Among other special airline promotional deals for which you should be on the lookout are discount or upgrade coupons sometimes offered by the major carriers and found in mail-order merchandise catalogues. For instance, airlines sometimes issue coupons that typically cost around $25 each and are good for either a percentage discount or an upgrade on an international airline ticket — including flights to Mexico. The only requirement beyond the fee generally is that a coupon purchaser must buy at least one item from the catalogue. There usually are some minimum airfare restrictions before the coupon is redeemable, but in general these are worthwhile offers. Restrictions often include certain blackout days (when the coupon cannot be used at all), usually imposed during peak travel periods. These coupons are particularly valuable to business travelers who tend to buy full-fare tickets, and while the coupons are issued in the buyer's name, they can be used by others who are traveling on the same itinerary.

It's always wise to ask about discount or promotional fares and about any conditions that might restrict booking, payment, cancellation, or changes in plans. Check the prices from neighboring cities. A special rate may be offered in a nearby city but not in yours, and it may be enough of a bargain to warrant your leaving from that city. Ask if there is a difference in price for midweek versus weekend travel, or if there is a further discount for traveling early in the morning or late at night. Also be sure to investigate package deals, which are offered by virtually every airline. These may include a car rental, accommodations, and dining and/or sightseeing features, in addition to the basic airfare, and the combined cost of packaged elements usually is considerably less than the cost of the exact same elements when purchased separately.

If in the course of your research you come across a deal that seems too good to be true, keep in mind that logic may not be a component of deeply discounted airfares — there's not always any sane relationship between miles to be flown and the price to get there. More often than not, the level of competition on a given route dictates the degree of discount, and don't be dissuaded from accepting an offer that sounds irresistible just because it also sounds illogical. Better to buy that inexpensive fare while it's being offered and worry about the sense — or absence thereof — while you're flying to your desired destination.

When you're satisfied that you've found the lowest possible price for which you can conveniently qualify (you may have to call the airline more than once, because different airline reservation clerks have been known to quote different prices), make your booking. Then, to protect yourself against fare increases, purchase and pay for your ticket as soon as possible after you've received a confirmed reservation. Airlines generally will honor their tickets, even if the operative price at the time of your flight is higher than the price you paid; if fares go up between the time you *reserve* a flight and the time you *pay* for it, you likely will be out of luck. Finally, with excursion or discount fares, it is important to remember that when a reservations clerk says that you must purchase a ticket by a specific date, this is an absolute deadline. Miss the deadline and the airline may automatically cancel your reservation without telling you.

■**Note:** Another wrinkle in the airfare scene is that if the fares go *down* after you purchase your ticket, you *may* be entitled to a refund of the difference. However, this is only possible in certain situations — availability and advance purchase restrictions pertaining to the lower rate are set by the airline. If you suspect that you may be able to qualify for such a refund, check with your travel agent or the airline.

Frequent Flyers – The leading US carriers serving Acapulco — *American, Continental,* and *Delta* — offer a bonus system to frequent travelers. After the first 10,000 miles, for example, a passenger might be eligible for a first class seat for the coach fare; after another 10,000 miles, he or she might receive a discount on his or her next ticket purchase. The value of the bonuses continues to increase as more miles are logged.

Bonus miles also may be earned by patronizing affiliated car rental companies or hotel chains, or by using one of the credit cards that now offers this reward. In deciding whether to accept such a credit card from one of the issuing organizations that tempt you with frequent flyer mileage bonuses on a specific airline, first determine whether the interest rate charged on the unpaid balance is the same as (or less than) possible alternate credit cards, and whether the annual "membership" fee is also equal or lower. If these charges are slightly higher than those of competing cards, weigh the difference against the potential value in airfare savings. Also ask about any bonus miles awarded just for signing up — 1,000 is common, 5,000 generally the maximum.

For the most up-to-date information on frequent flyer bonus options, you may want to subscribe to the monthly newsletter *Frequent.* Issued by Frequent Publications, it provides current information about frequent flyer plans in general, as well as specific data about promotions, awards, and combination deals to help you keep track of the profusion — and confusion — of current and upcoming availabilities. For a year's subscription, send $33 to Frequent Publications, 4715-C Town Center Dr., Colorado Springs, CO 80916 (phone: 800-333-5937).

There also is a monthly magazine called *Frequent Flyer,* but unlike the newsletter mentioned above, its focus is primarily on newsy articles of interest to business travelers and other frequent flyers. Published by Official Airline Guides (PO Box 58543, Boulder, CO 80322-8543; phone: 800-323-3537), *Frequent Flyer* is available for $24 for a 1-year subscription.

Taxes and Other Fees – Travelers who have shopped for the best possible flight at the lowest possible price should be warned that a number of extras will be added to that price and collected by the airline or travel agent who issues the ticket. There also is a $6 International Air Transportation Tax, a departure tax paid by all passengers flying from the US to a foreign destination.

Still another fee is charged by some airlines to cover more stringent security procedures, prompted by recent terrorist incidents. The 10% federal US Transportation Tax applies to travel within the US or US territories. It does not apply to passengers flying between US cities or territories en route to a foreign destination, unless the trip includes a stopover of more than 12 hours at a US point. Someone flying from Boston to Acapulco and stopping in Dallas for more than 12 hours before boarding a flight to Acapulco, for instance, would pay the 10% tax on the domestic portion of the trip. Note that these taxes *usually* (but not always) are included in advertised fares and in the prices quoted by airlines reservations clerks.

Reservations – For those who don't have the time and patience to investigate personally all possible air departures and connections for a proposed trip, a travel agent can be of inestimable help. A good agent should have all the information on which flights go where and when, and which categories of tickets are available on each. Most have computerized reservation links with the major carriers, so that a seat can be reserved and confirmed in minutes. An increasing number of agents also possess fare-comparison computer programs, so they often are very reliable sources of detailed competitive price data. (For more information, see *How to Use a Travel Agent,* in this section.)

When making plane reservations through a travel agent, ask the agent to give the airline your home phone number, as well as your daytime business phone number. All too often the agent uses the agency number as the official contact for changes in flight plans. Especially during the winter — prime time for an escape to Acapulco's sunny shores — weather conditions hundreds or even thousands of miles away can wreak havoc with flight schedules. Aircraft are contantly in use, and a plane delayed in the Orient or on the West Coast can miss its scheduled flight from the East Coast the next morning. The airlines are fairly reliable about getting this sort of information to passengers if they can reach them; diligence does little good at 10 PM if the airline has only the agency's or an office number.

Reconfirmation is strongly recommended for all international flights. Some (though increasingly fewer) reservations to and from international destinations are automatically canceled after a required reconfirmation period (typically 72 hours) has passed — even if you have a confirmed, fully paid ticket in hand. It always is wise to call ahead to make sure that the airline did not slip up in entering your original reservation, or in registering any changes you may have made since, and that it has your seat reservation and/or special meal request in the computer. If you look at the printed information on your ticket, you'll see the airline's reconfirmation policy stated explicitly. Don't be lulled into a false sense of security by the "OK" on your ticket next to the number and time of the flight. This only means that a reservation has been entered; a reconfirmation still may be necessary. If in doubt — call.

If you plan not to take a flight on which you hold a confirmed reservation, by all means inform the airline. Because the problem of "no-shows" is a constant expense for airlines, they are allowed to overbook flights, a practice that often contributes to the threat of denied boarding for a certain number of passengers (see "Getting Bumped," below).

Seating – For most types of tickets, airline seats usually are assigned on a first-come, first-served basis at check-in, although some airlines make it possible to reserve a seat at the time of ticket purchase. Always check in early for your flight, even with advance seat assignments. A good rule of thumb for international flights is to arrive at the airport *at least* 2 hours before the scheduled departure to give yourself plenty of time in case there are long lines.

Most airlines furnish seating charts, which make choosing a seat much easier, but there are a few basics to consider. You must decide whether you prefer a window, aisle, or middle seat. On flights where smoking is permitted, you also should indicate if you prefer the smoking or nonsmoking section.

There is a quarterly publication called the *Airline Seating Guide* that publishes seating charts for most major US airlines and many foreign carriers as well. Your travel agent should have a copy, or you can buy the US edition for $39.95 per year and the international edition for $44.95. Order from Carlson Publishing Co., Box 888, Los Alamitos, CA 90720 (phone: 800-728-4877 or 310-493-4877).

Simply reserving an airline seat in advance, however, actually may guarantee very little. Most airlines require that passengers arrive at the departure gate at least 45 minutes (sometimes more) ahead of time to hold a seat reservation. Some may cancel seat assignments and may not honor reservations of passengers who have not checked in some period of time — usually around 45 minutes, depending on the airline and the airport — before the scheduled departure time, and they *ask* travelers to check in at least 1 hour before all domestic flights and 2 hours before international flights. It pays to read the fine print on your ticket carefully and plan ahead.

A far better strategy is to visit an airline ticket office (or one of a select group of travel agents) to secure an actual boarding pass for your specific flight. Once this has been issued, airline computers show you as checked in, and you effectively own the seat you have selected (although some carriers may not honor boarding passes of passengers arriving at the gate less than 10 minutes before departure). This is also good — but not foolproof — insurance against getting bumped from an overbooked flight and is, therefore, an especially valuable tactic at peak travel times.

Smoking – One decision regarding choosing a seat has been taken out of the hands of many travelers who smoke. Effective February 1990, the US government imposed a ban that prohibits smoking on all flights scheduled for 6 hours or less within the US and its territories. The regulation applies to both domestic and international carriers serving these routes.

In the case of flights to Acapulco, these rules do not apply to nonstop flights directly from the US to Mexico or those with a *continuous* flight time of over 6 hours between stops in the US or its territories. Smoking is not permitted on segments of international flights where the flight time between US landings is under 6 hours — for instance, flights that include a stopover (even with no change of plane) or connecting flights. To further complicate the situation, several individual carriers are banning smoking altogether on certain routes. At the time of this writing, *Northwest* offers only nonsmoking flights to Mexico.

On those flights that do permit smoking, the US Department of Transportation has determined that nonsmoking sections must be enlarged to accommodate all passengers who wish to sit in one. The airline does not, however, have to shift seating to accommodate nonsmokers who arrive late for a flight or travelers flying standby, and in general not all airlines can guarantee a seat in the nonsmoking section on international flights. Cigar and pipe smoking are prohibited on all flights, even in the smoking sections.

For a wallet-size guide that notes in detail the rights of nonsmokers according to these regulations, send a self-addressed, stamped envelope to *ASH (Action on Smoking and Health)*, Airline Card, 2013 H St. NW, Washington, DC 20006 (phone: 202-659-4310).

Meals – If you have specific dietary requirements, be sure to let the airline know well before departure time. The available meals include vegetarian, seafood, kosher, Muslim, Hindu, high-protein, low-calorie, low-cholesterol, low-fat, low-sodium, diabetic, bland, and children's menus (not all of these may be available on every carrier). There is no extra charge for this option. It usually is necessary to request special meals when you make your reservations — check-in time is too late. It's also wise to reconfirm that your request for a special meal has made its way into the airline's computer — the time to do this is 24 hours before departure. (Note that special meals generally are not available on flights within Mexico — particularly on the smaller domestic carriers. If this poses a problem, try to eat before you board, or bring a snack with you.)

Baggage – Travelers from the US face two different kinds of rules. When you fly on a US airline or on a major international carrier, US baggage regulations will be in effect. Though airline baggage allowances vary slightly, in general all passengers are allowed to carry on board, without charge, one piece of luggage that will fit easily under a seat of the plane or in an overhead bin, and whose combined dimensions (length, width, and depth) do not exceed 45 inches. A reasonable amount of reading material, camera equipment, and a handbag also are allowed. In addition, all passengers are allowed to check two bags in the cargo hold: one usually not to exceed 62 inches when length, width, and depth are combined, the other not to exceed 55 inches in combined dimensions. Generally no single bag may weigh more than 70 pounds.

On domestic Mexican flights (aboard such carriers as *Aeroméxico* and *Mexicana*), baggage allowances may be subject to a different weight determination, under which each economy passenger is allowed only a total of 55 pounds (or less) of luggage without additional charge. First class or business class passengers may be allowed a total of 66 pounds. (If you are flying from the US to Mexico and connecting to a domestic flight, you generally will be allowed the same amount of baggage as on the international flight. If you break your trip and then take a domestic flight, the local carrier's weight restrictions apply.)

Charges for additional, oversize, or overweight bags usually are made at a flat rate; the actual dollar amount varies from carrier to carrier. If you plan to travel with any special equipment or sporting gear, be sure to check with the airline beforehand. Most have specific procedures for handling such baggage, and you may have to pay for transport regardless of how much other baggage you have checked. Golf clubs may be checked through as luggage (most airlines are accustomed to handling them), but tennis rackets should be carried onto the plane. Aqualung tanks, depressurized and appropriately packed with padding, and surfboards (minus the fin and padded) also may go as baggage. Snorkeling gear should be packed in a suitcase, duffel, or tote bag. Some airlines require that bicycles be partially dismantled and packaged.

Airline policies regarding baggage allowances for children vary and are usually based on the percentage of full adult fare paid. Although on many US carriers children who are ticket holders are entitled to the same baggage allowance as a full-fare passenger, some carriers allow only one bag per child, which sometimes must be smaller than an adult's bag (around 39 to 45 inches in combined dimensions). Often there is no luggage allowance for a child traveling on an adult's lap or in a bassinet. Particularly for international carriers, it's always wise to check ahead. (For more information, see *Hints for Traveling with Children,* in this section.)

To reduce the chances of your luggage going astray, remove all airline tags from previous trips, label each bag inside and out — with your business address rather than your home address on the outside, to prevent thieves from knowing whose house might be unguarded. Lock everything and double-check the tag that the airline attaches, to make sure that it is coded correctly for your destination: ACA for Acapulco.

If your bags are not in the baggage claim area after your flight, or if they're damaged, report the problem to airline personnel immediately. Keep in mind that policies regarding the specific time limit within which you have to make your claim vary from carrier to carrier. Fill out a report form on your lost or damaged luggage and keep a copy of it and your original baggage claim check. If you must surrender the check to claim a damaged bag, get a receipt for it to prove that you did, indeed, check your baggage on the flight. If luggage is missing, be sure to give the airline your destination and/or a telephone number where you can be reached. Also take the name and number of the person in charge of recovering lost luggage.

Most airlines have emergency funds for passengers stranded away from home without their luggage, but if it turns out that your bags are truly lost and not simply delayed, do not then and there sign any paper indicating you'll accept an offered settlement. Since the airline is responsible for the value of your bags within certain statutory limits ($1,250 per passenger for lost baggage on a US domestic flight; $9.07 per pound or $20 per kilo for checked baggage, and up to $400 per passenger for unchecked baggage, on an international flight), you should take some time to assess the extent of your loss (see *Insurance,* in this section). It's a good idea to keep records indicating the value of the contents of your luggage. A wise alternative is to take a Polaroid picture of the most valuable of your packed items just after putting them in your suitcase.

Be aware that airport security is increasingly an issue worldwide, and in Mexico is taken very seriously. Heavily armed police patrol the airports, and unattended luggage of any description may be confiscated and quickly destroyed. Passengers checking in at a foreign airport may undergo at least two separate inspections of their tickets, passports, and luggage by courteous, but serious, airline personnel — who ask passengers if their baggage has been out of their possession between packing and the airport, or if they have been given gifts or other items to transport — before checked items are accepted.

Airline Clubs – Some US and foreign carriers have clubs for travelers who pay for membership. These clubs are not solely for first class passengers, although a first class ticket *may* entitle a passenger to lounge privileges. Membership entitles the traveler to use the private lounges at airports along their route, to refreshments served in these lounges, and to check-cashing privileges at most of their counters. Extras include special telephone numbers for individual reservations, embossed luggage tags, and a membership card for identification. Airlines serving Mexico that offer membership in such clubs include the following:

American: The *Admiral's Club.* Single yearly membership $225 (plus a onetime $50 initiation fee); spouse an additional $70 per year.

Continental: The *President's Club.* Single yearly membership $150 for the first year; $100 yearly thereafter; spouse an additional $50 per year; 3-year and lifetime membership available.

Delta: The *Crown Club.* Single yearly membership $150; spouse an additional $50 per year.

Note that such companies do not have club facilities in all airports. Other airlines also offer a variety of special services in many airports.

Getting Bumped – A special air travel problem is the possibility that an airline will accept more reservations (and sell more tickets) than there are seats on a given flight. This is entirely legal and is done to make up for "no-shows," passengers who don't show up for a flight for which they have made reservations and bought tickets. If the airline has oversold the flight and everyone does show up, there simply aren't enough seats. When this happens, the airline is subject to stringent rules designed to protect travelers.

In such cases, the airline first seeks ticket holders willing to give up their seats voluntarily in return for a negotiable sum of money or some other inducement, such as an offer of upgraded seating on the next flight or a voucher for a free trip at some other time. If there are not enough volunteers, the airline may bump passengers against their wishes.

Anyone inconvenienced in this way, however, is entitled to an explanation of the criteria used to determine who does or does not get on the flight, as well as compensation if the resulting delay exceeds certain limits. If the airline can put the bumped passengers on an alternate flight that is *scheduled to arrive* at their original destination within 1 hour of their originally scheduled arrival time, no compensation is owed. If the delay is more than 1 hour but less than 2 hours on a domestic US flight, they must be paid denied-boarding compensation equivalent to the one-way fare to their destination (but not more than $200). If the delay is more than 2 hours after the original arrival time on a domestic flight or more than 4 hours on an international flight, the compensation must be doubled (not more than $400). The airline may also offer bumped travelers a voucher for a free flight instead of the denied-boarding compensation. The passenger may be given the choice of either the money or the voucher, the dollar value of which may be no less than the monetary compensation to which the passenger would be entitled. The voucher is not a substitute for the bumped passenger's original ticket; the airline continues to honor that as well.

Keep in mind that the above regulations and policies are only for flights leaving the US, and do *not* apply to charters or to inbound flights from Acapulco, even on US carriers. Airlines carrying passengers between foreign destinations are free to determine what compensation they will pay to passengers who are bumped because of overbooking. They generally spell out their policies on airline tickets. Some foreign airline policies are similar to the US policy; however, don't assume all carriers will be as generous.

To protect yourself as best you can against getting bumped, arrive at the airport extra early, allowing plenty of time to check in and get to the gate. If the flight is oversold, ask immediately for the written statement explaining the airline's policy on denied-boarding compensation and its boarding priorities. If the airline refuses to give you this information, or if you feel they have not handled the situation properly, file a complaint with both the airline and the appropriate government agency (see "Consumer Protection," below).

Delays and Cancellations – The above compensation rules also do not apply if the flight is canceled or delayed, or if a smaller aircraft is substituted due to mechanical problems. Each airline has its own policy for assisting passengers whose flights are delayed or canceled or who must wait for another flight because their original one was overbooked. Most airline personnel will make new travel arrangements if necessary. If the delay is longer than 4 hours, the airline may pay for a phone call or telegram, a meal, and in some cases, a hotel room and transportation to it.

■ **Caution:** If you are bumped or miss a flight, be sure to ask the airline to notify other airlines on which you have reservations or connecting flights. When your name is taken off the passenger list of your initial flight, the computer automatically cancels all of your reservations unless *you* take steps to preserve them.

CHARTER FLIGHTS: By booking a block of seats on a specially arranged flight, charter operators offer travelers air transportation for a substantial reduction over the full coach or economy fare. These operators may offer air-only charters (selling transportation alone) or charter packages (the flight plus a combination of land arrangements such as accommodations, meals, tours, or car rental). Charters are especially attractive to people living in smaller cities or out-of-the-way places, because they frequently leave from nearby airports, saving travelers the inconvenience and expense of getting to a major gateway.

From the consumer's standpoint, charters differ from scheduled airlines in two main respects: You generally need to book and pay in advance, and you can't change the itinerary or the departure and return dates once you've booked the flight. In practice, however, these restrictions don't always apply. Today, most of the charter flights to Mexico have the most popular resort areas, such as Acapulco, as their prime destinations, and although most still require advance reservations, some permit last-minute bookings (when there are unsold seats available), and some even offer seats on a standby basis.

Though charters almost always are round-trip, and it is unlikely that you would be sold a one-way seat on a round-trip flight, on rare occasions one-way tickets on charters are offered. Although it may be possible to book a one-way charter in the US, giving you more flexibility in scheduling your return, note that US regulations pertaining to charters may be more permissive than the charter laws of other countries. For example, if you want to book a one-way charter back to the US, you may find advance booking rules in force.

Some things to keep in mind about the charter game:

1. It cannot be repeated often enough that if you are forced to cancel your trip, you can lose much (and possibly all) of your money unless you have cancellation insurance, which is a *must* (see *Insurance,* in this section). Frequently, if the cancellation occurs far enough in advance (often 6 weeks or more), you may forfeit only a $25 or $50 penalty. If you cancel only 2 or 3 weeks before the flight, there may be no refund at all unless you or the operator can provide a substitute passenger.

2. Charter flights may be canceled by the operator up to 10 days before departure for any reason, usually underbooking. Your money is returned in this event, but there may be too little time for you to make new arrangements.

3. Most charters have little of the flexibility of regularly scheduled flights regarding refunds and the changing of flight dates; if you book a return flight, you must be on it or lose your money.

4. Charter operators are permitted to assess a surcharge, if fuel or other costs warrant it, of up to 10% of the airfare up to 10 days before departure.

5. Because of the economics of charter flights, your plane almost always will be full,

so you will be crowded, though not necessarily uncomfortable. (There is, however, a new movement among charter airlines to provide flight accommodations that are more comfort-oriented, so this situation may change in the near future.)

To avoid problems, *always* choose charter flights with care. When you consider a charter, ask your travel agent who runs it and carefully check the company. The Better Business Bureau in the company's home city can report on how many complaints, if any, have been lodged against it in the past. Protect yourself with trip cancellation and interruption insurance, which can help safeguard your investment if you or a traveling companion is unable to make the trip and must cancel too late to receive a full refund from the company providing your travel services. (This is advisable whether you're buying a charter flight alone or a tour package for which the airfare is provided by charter or scheduled flight.)

Bookings – If you do fly on a charter, read the contract's fine print carefully and pay particular attention to the following:

Instructions concerning payment of the deposit and its balance and to whom the check is to be made payable. Ordinarily, checks are made out to an escrow account, which means the charter company can't spend your money until your flight has safely returned. This provides some protection for you. To ensure the safe handling of your money, make out your check to the escrow account, the number of which must appear by law on the brochure, though all too often it is on the back in fine print. Write the details of the charter, including the destination and dates, on the face of the check; on the back, print "For Deposit Only." Your travel agent may prefer that you make out your check to the agency, saying that it will then pay the tour operator the fee minus commission. It is perfectly legal to write the check as we suggest, however, and if your agent objects too vociferously (he or she should trust the tour operator to send the proper commission), consider taking your business elsewhere. If you don't make your check out to the escrow account, you lose the protection of that escrow should the trip be canceled. Furthermore, recent bankruptcies in the travel industry have served to point out that even the protection of escrow may not be enough to safeguard a traveler's investment. More and more, insurance is becoming a necessity. The charter company should be bonded (usually by an insurance company), and if you want to file a claim against it, the claim should be sent to the bonding agent. The contract will set a time limit within which a claim must be filed.

Specific stipulations and penalties for cancellations. Most charters allow you to cancel up to 45 days in advance without major penalty, but some cancellation dates are 50 to 60 days before departure.

Stipulations regarding cancellation and major changes made by the charterer. US rules say that charter flights may not be canceled within 10 days of departure except when circumstances — such as natural disasters or political upheavals — make it physically impossible to fly. Charterers may make "major changes," however, such as in the date or place of departure or return, but you are entitled to cancel and receive a full refund if you don't wish to accept these changes. A price increase of more than 10% at any time up to 10 days before departure is considered a major change; no price increase at all is allowed during the last 10 days immediately before departure.

At the time of this writing, two companies regularly offered charter flights to Acapulco. As indicated, although these companies are wholesalers and must be contacted through a travel agent, some charter flights sell directly to clients.

Apple Vacations West (25 NW Point Blvd., Elk Grove Village, IL 60007; phone: 800-365-2775). This agency is a wholesaler, so use a travel agent.

Club America Vacations (3379 Peachtree Rd., Suite 625, Atlanta, GA 30326; phone: 800-221-2931). This agency is a wholesaler, so use a travel agent.

For the most current information on charter flight options, the travel newsletter *Jax Fax* regularly features a list of charter companies and packagers offering seats on charter flights. For a year's subscription send a check or money order for $12 to *Jax Fax* (397 Post Rd., Darien, CT 06820; phone: 203-655-8746).

DISCOUNTS ON SCHEDULED FLIGHTS: Promotional fares often are called discount fares because they cost less than what used to be the standard airline fare — full-fare economy. Nevertheless, they cost the traveler the same whether they are bought through a travel agent or directly from the airline. Tickets that cost less if bought from some outlet other than the airline do exist, however. While it is likely that the vast majority of travelers flying to Mexico in the near future will be doing so on a promotional fare or charter rather than on a "discount" air ticket of this sort, it still is a good idea for cost-conscious consumers to be aware of the latest developments in the budget airfare scene. Note that the following discussion makes clear-cut distinctions among the types of discounts available based on how they reach the consumer; in actual practice, the distinctions are not nearly so precise.

Net Fare Sources – The newest notion for reducing the costs of travel services comes from travel agents who offer individual travelers "net" fares. Defined simply, a net fare is the bare minimum amount at which an airline or tour operator will carry a prospective traveler. It doesn't include the amount that normally would be paid to the travel agent as a commission. Traditionally, such commissions amount to about 10% on domestic fares and from 10% to 20% on international fares — not counting significant additions to these commission levels that are paid retroactively when agents sell more than a specific volume of tickets or trips for a single supplier. At press time, at least one travel agency in the US was offering travelers the opportunity to purchase tickets and/or tours for a net price. Instead of earning its income from individual commissions, this agency assesses a fixed fee that may or may not provide a bargain for travelers; it requires a little arithmetic to determine whether to use the services of a net travel agent or those of one who accepts conventional commissions. One of the potential drawbacks of buying from agencies selling travel services at net fares is that some airlines refuse to do business with them, thus possibly limiting your flight options.

Travel Avenue is a fee-based agency that rebates its ordinary agency commission to the customer. For domestic flights, they will find the lowest retail fare, then rebate 7% to 10% (depending on the airline selected) of that fare minus a $10 ticket-writing charge. The rebate percentage for international flights varies from 5% to 16% (again, depending on the airline), and the ticket-writing fee is $25. The ticket-writing charge is imposed per ticket; if the ticket includes more than eight separate flights, an additional $25 fee is charged. Customers using free flight coupons pay the ticket-writing charge, plus an additional $5 coupon-processing fee.

Travel Avenue will rebate its commissions on all tickets, including heavily discounted fares and senior citizen passes. Available 7 days a week, reservations should be made far enough in advance to allow the tickets to be sent by first class mail, since extra charges accrue for special handling. It's possible to economize further by making your own airline reservation, then asking *Travel Avenue* only to write/issue your ticket. For travelers outside the Chicago area, business may be transacted by phone and purchases charged to a credit card. For information, contact *Travel Avenue* at 641 W. Lake St., Suite 201, Chicago, IL 60606-1012 (phone: 312-876-1116 in Illinois; 800-333-3335 elsewhere in the US).

Consolidators and Bucket Shops – Other vendors of travel services can afford to sell tickets to their customers at an even greater discount because the airline has sold the tickets to them at a substantial discount (usually accomplished by sharply increasing commissions to that vendor), a practice in which many airlines indulge, albeit discreetly, preferring that the general public not know they are undercutting their own "list" prices. Airlines anticipating a slow period on a particular route sometimes sell off a certain portion of their capacity at a very great discount to a wholesaler, or consolidator. The wholesaler sometimes is a charter operator who resells the seats to the public as though they were charter seats, which is why prospective travelers perusing the brochures of charter operators with large programs frequently see a number of flights designated as "scheduled service." As often as not, however, the consolidator, in turn, sells the seats to a travel agency specializing in discounting. Airlines also can sell seats directly to such an agency, which thus acts as its own consolidator. The airline offers the seats either at a net wholesale price, but without the volume-purchase requirement that would be difficult for a modest retail travel agency to fulfill, or at the standard price, but with a commission override large enough (as high as 50%) to allow both a profit and a price reduction to the public.

Travel agencies specializing in discounting sometimes are called "bucket shops," a term once fraught with connotations of unreliability in this country. But in today's highly competitive travel marketplace, more and more conventional travel agencies are selling consolidator-supplied tickets, and the old bucket shops' image is becoming respectable. Agencies that specialize in discounted tickets exist in most large cities, and usually can be found by studying the smaller ads in the travel sections of Sunday newspapers.

Before buying a discounted ticket, whether from a bucket shop or a conventional, full-service travel agency, keep the following considerations in mind: To be in a position to judge how much you'll be saving, first find out the "list" prices of tickets to your destination. Then do some comparison shopping among agencies. Also bear in mind that a ticket that may not differ much in price from one available directly from the airline may, however, allow the circumvention of such things as the advance-purchase requirement. If your plans are less than final, be sure to find out about any other restrictions, such as penalties for canceling a flight or changing a reservation. Most discount tickets are non-endorsable, meaning that they can be used only on the airline that issued them, and they usually are marked "nonrefundable" to prevent their being cashed in for a list-price refund.

A great many bucket shops are small businesses operating on a thin margin, so it's a good idea to check the local Better Business Bureau for any complaints registered against the one with which you're dealing — before parting with any money. If you still do not feel reassured, consider buying discounted tickets only through a conventional travel agency, which can be expected to have found its own reliable source of consolidator tickets — some of the largest consolidators, in fact, sell only to travel agencies.

A few bucket shops require payment in cash or by certified check or money order, but if credit cards are accepted, use that option. Note, however, if buying from a charter operator selling both scheduled and charter flights, that the scheduled seats are not protected by the regulations — including the use of escrow accounts — governing the charter seats. Well-established charter operators, nevertheless, may extend the same protections to their scheduled flights, and when this is the case, consumers should be sure that the payment option selected directs their money into the escrow account.

Listed below are several consolidators frequently offering discount fares to Acapulco:

> *International Adventures* (60 E. 42nd St., New York, NY 10165; phone: 212-599-0577).
>
> *25 West Tours* (2490 Coral Way, Miami, FL 33145; phone: 800-423-6954 in Florida; 800-252-5052 elsewhere in the US, or 305-856-0810).

■**Note:** Although rebating and discounting are becoming increasingly common, there is some legal ambiguity concerning them. Strictly speaking, it is legal to discount domestic tickets but not international tickets. On the other hand, the law that prohibits discounting, the Federal Aviation Act of 1958, is consistently ignored these days, in part because consumers benefit from the practice and in part because many illegal arrangements are indistinguishable from legal ones. Since the line separating the two is so fine that even the authorities can't always tell the difference, it is unlikely that most consumers would be able to do so, and in fact it is not illegal to *buy* a discounted ticket. If the issue of legality bothers you, ask the agency whether any ticket you're about to buy would be permissible under the above-mentioned act.

OTHER DISCOUNT TRAVEL SOURCES: An excellent source of information on economical travel opportunities is the *Consumer Reports Travel Letter,* published monthly by Consumers Union. It keeps abreast of the scene on a wide variety of fronts, including package tours, rental cars, insurance, and more, but it is especially helpful for its comprehensive coverage of airfares, offering guidance on all the options from scheduled flights on major or low-fare airlines to charters and discount sources. For a year's subscription, send $37 ($57 for 2 years) to *Consumer Reports Travel Letter* (PO Box 53629, Boulder, CO 80322-3629; phone: 800-234-1970).

Another source is *Travel Smart,* a monthly newsletter with information on a wide variety of trips and additional discount travel services available to subscribers. For a year's subscription, send $37 to Communications House, 40 Beechdale Rd., Dobbs Ferry, NY 10522 (phone: 914-693-8300 in New York; 800-327-3633 elsewhere in the US). For information on other travel newsletters, see *Sources and Resources,* in this section.

Last-Minute Travel Clubs – Still another way to take advantage of bargain airfares is open to those who have a flexible schedule. A number of organizations, usually set up as last-minute travel clubs and functioning on a membership basis, routinely keep in touch with travel suppliers to help them dispose of unsold inventory at discounts of between 15% and 60%. A great deal of the inventory consists of complete package tours and cruises, but some clubs offer air-only charter seats and, occasionally, seats on scheduled flights.

Members pay an annual fee and receive a toll-free hotline telephone number to call for information on imminent trips. In some cases, they also receive periodic mailings with information on bargain travel opportunities for which there is more advance notice. Despite the suggestive names of the clubs providing these services, last-minute travel does not necessarily mean that you cannot make plans until literally the last minute. Trips can be announced as little as a few days or as much as 2 months before departure, but the average is from 1 to 4 weeks' notice.

Among the organizations offering discounted travel opportunities to Acapulco are the following:

> *Discount Travel International* (Ives Building, 114 Forrest Ave., Suite 205, Narberth, PA 19072; phone: 800-334-9294 or 215-668-7184). Annual fee: $45 per household.
>
> *Encore/Short Notice* (4501 Forbes Blvd., Lanham, MD 20706; phone: 301-459-8020; 800-638-0930 for customer service). Annual fee: $36 per family for their Short Notice program only; $48 per family to join the Encore program, which provides additional travel services.
>
> *Last-Minute Travel* (1249 Boylston St., Boston, MA 02215; phone: 800-LAST-MIN or 617-267-9800). No fee.
>
> *Moment's Notice* (425 Madison Ave., New York, NY 10017; phone: 212-980-9550). Annual fee: $45 per family.

Spur-of-the-Moment Tours and Cruises (10780 Jefferson Blvd., Culver City, CA 90230; phone: 310-839-2418 in southern California; 800-343-1991 elsewhere in the US). No fee.

Traveler's Advantage (3033 S. Parker Rd., Suite 1000, Aurora, CO 80014; phone: 800-548-1116). Annual fee: $49 per family.

Vacations to Go (2411 Fountain View, Suite 201, Houston, TX 77057; phone: 800-338-4962). Annual fee: $19.95 per family.

Worldwide Discount Travel Club (1674 Meridian Ave., Miami Beach, FL 33139; phone: 305-534-2082). Annual fee: $40 per person; $50 per family.

Generic Air Travel – Organizations that apply the same flexible-schedule idea to air travel only and arrange for flights at literally the last minute also exist. The service they provide sometimes is known as "generic" air travel, and it operates somewhat like an ordinary airline standby service except that the organizations running it do not guarantee flights to a specific destination, but only to a general region, and offer seats on not one but several scheduled and charter airlines.

One pioneer of generic flights is *Airhitch* (2790 Broadway, Suite 100, New York, NY 10025; phone: 212-864-2000), which arranges flights to Acapulco from various US cities at relatively low prices. Prospective travelers stipulate a range of acceptable departure dates and their desired destination, along with alternate choices, and pay the fare in advance. They are then sent a voucher good for travel *on a space-available basis* on flights to their destination *region* (i.e., not necessarily the specific destination requested) during this time period. The week before this range of departure begins, travelers must contact *Airhitch* for specific information about flights that probably will be available and instructions on how to proceed for check-in. Once passengers have actually boarded an outbound flight, they are guaranteed a return flight 1 week later by the same carrier or tour operator through whom the flight was booked. If the client does not accept any of the suggested flights or cancels his or her travel plans after selecting a flight, the amount paid may be applied toward a future fare or the flight arrangements can be transferred to another individual (although, in both cases, an additional fee may be charged). No refunds are offered unless the prospective passenger does not ultimately get on any flight in the specified date-range; in such a case, the full fare is refunded. (Note that *Airhitch*'s slightly more expensive "Target" program, which provides confirmed reservations on specific dates to specific destination, offers passengers greater — but not guaranteed — certainty regarding flight arrangements). The company's Sunhitch program is available for week-long stays in Acapulco from December through April.

Bartered Travel Sources – Suppose a hotel buys advertising space in a newspaper. As payment, the hotel gives the publishing company the use of a number of hotel rooms in lieu of cash. This is barter, a common means of exchange among hotels, airlines, car rental companies, cruise lines, tour operators, restaurants, and other travel service companies. When a bartering company finds itself with empty airline seats (or excess hotel rooms, or cruise ship cabin space, and so on) and offers them to the public, considerable savings can be enjoyed.

Bartered travel clubs often offer discounts of up to 50% to members who pay an annual fee (approximately $50 at press time) which entitles them to select the flights, cruises, hotel rooms, or other travel services that the club obtained by barter. Members usually present a voucher, club credit card, or scrip (a dollar-denomination voucher negotiable only for the bartered product) to the hotel, which in turn subtracts the dollar amount from the bartering company's account.

Selling bartered travel is a perfectly legitimate means of retailing. One advantage to club members is that they don't have to wait until the last minute to obtain flight or room reservations.

Among the companies specializing in bartered service, those that frequently offer members travel services to Acapulco include the following:

> *The Travel Guild* (18210 Redmond Way, Redmond, WA 98052; phone: 206-861-1900). Annual fee: $48 per family.
>
> *Travel World Leisure Club* (225 W. 34th St., Suite 2203, New York, NY 10122; phone: 800-444-TWLC or 212-239-4855). Annual fee: $50 per person; $20 for each additional member of a family.

Although another company, *IGT (In Good Taste) Services* (1111 Lincoln Road, 4th Floor, Miami Beach, FL 33139; phone: 800-444-8872 or 305-534-7900), offers discounts on a variety of travel services and occasionally sells bartered travel arrangements as well; at press time, they were offering only dining discounts in Acapulco. Their annual membership fee is $48 per family.

CONSUMER PROTECTION: Consumers who feel that they have not been dealt with fairly by an airline should make their complaints known. Begin with the customer service representative at the airport where the problem occurs. If he or she cannot resolve your complaint to your satisfaction, write to the airline's consumer office. In a businesslike, typed letter, explain what reservations you held, what happened, the names of the employees involved, and what you expect the airline to do to remedy the situation. Send copies (never the originals) of the tickets, receipts, and other documents that back your claims. Ideally, all correspondence should be sent via certified mail, return receipt requested. This provides proof that your complaint was received.

Passengers with consumer complaints — lost baggage, compensation for getting bumped, violations of smoking and nonsmoking rules, deceptive practices by an airline, charter regulations — who are not satisfied with the airline's response should contact the US Department of Transportation (DOT), Consumer Affairs Division (400 Seventh St., SW, Room 10405, Washington, DC 20590; phone: 202-366-2220). DOT personnel stress, however, that consumers should initially direct their complaints to the airline that provoked them.

Travelers with an unresolved complaint involving a foreign carrier also can contact the US Department of Transportation. DOT personnel will do what they can to help resolve all such complaints, although their influence may be limited. Consumers with complaints against specific Mexican airlines or other travel-related services should try to contact either the local tourist authority in the area where the problem occurred or a US representative of the Mexican Ministry of Tourism (see *Mexican Consulates and Tourist Offices in the US,* in this section, for addresses). The agency usually will try to resolve the complaint or, if it is out of their jurisdiction, will refer the matter to the proper authorities.

Remember, too, that the federal Fair Credit Billing Act permits purchasers to refuse to pay for credit card charges for services that have not been delivered, so the onus of dealing with the receiver for a bankrupt airline falls on the credit card company. Do not rely on another airline to honor the ticket you're holding, since the days when virtually all major carriers subscribed to a default protection program that bound them to do so are long gone. Some airlines may voluntarily step forward to accommodate the stranded passengers of a fellow carrier, but this is now an entirely altruistic act.

The deregulation of US airlines has meant that travelers must find out for themselves what they are entitled to receive. The US Department of Transportation's informative consumer booklet *Fly Rights,* is a good place to start. To receive a copy, send $1 to the Superintendent of Documents, US Government Printing Office (Washington, DC

20402-9325; phone: 202-783-3238). Specify its stock number, 050-000-00513-5, and allow 3 to 4 weeks for delivery.

■ **Note:** Those who tend to experience discomfort due to the change in air pressure while flying may be interested in the free pamphlet *Ears, Altitude and Airplane Travel;* for a copy send a self-addressed, stamped, business-size envelope to the *American Academy of Otolaryngology* (One Prince St., Alexandria, VA 22314; phone: 703-836-4444). And for when you land, *Overcoming Jet Lag* offers some helpful tips on minimizing post-flight stress; it is available from Berkeley Publishing Group (PO Box 506, Mail Order Dept., East Rutherford, NJ 07073; phone: 800-631-8571) for $6.95, plus shipping and handling.

Traveling by Ship

 There was a time when traveling by ship was extraordinarily expensive, time-consuming, utterly elegant, and utilized almost exclusively for getting from one point to another. No longer primarily pure transportation, cruising currently is riding a wave of popularity as a leisure activity in its own right, and the host of new ships (and dozens of rebuilt old ones) testifies dramatically to the attraction of vacationing on the high seas. Cruise lines are flocking to Acapulco, as repeat passengers seek new, more unusual itineraries, and first-time visitors choose seaborne transportation to explore south of the border.

Among the destinations favored by cruise ship passengers, Mexico, with stops at Acapulco, ranks extremely high. Cruise travel today also is the most leisurely way to get to Acapulco. From eastern US ports, cruise ships sail through the Panama Canal and call at popular resorts along Mexico's Pacific Coast. Sailings from California docks reverse the transcanal route, but by far the best-known cruise course to Mexico runs from Los Angeles down the west coast of Mexico to such legendary ports of call as Acapulco, Puerto Vallarta, and Mazatlán — a real cruise itinerary, but one that was made famous on TV by that oceanic icon, the "Love Boat."

Many modern-day cruise ships seem much more like motels-at-sea than the classic liners of a couple of generations ago, but they are consistently comfortable and passengers are often pampered. Cruise prices can be quite reasonable, and since the single cruise price covers all the major items in a typical vacation — transportation, accommodations, all meals, entertainment, a full range of social activities, sports, and recreation — a traveler need not fear any unexpected assaults on the family travel budget.

Generally, people take a cruise ship to Mexico for the sheer pleasure of being at sea, because it's part of a far broader itinerary, or because of a special interest in a particular area that is best visited by ship. Cruise lines promote sailings to Mexico as "get away from it all" vacations. But prospective cruise ship passengers will find that the variety of cruises is tremendous, and the quality, while generally high, varies depending on shipboard services, the tone of shipboard life, the cost of the cruise, and operative itineraries. Although there are less expensive ways to see Mexico, the romance and enjoyment of a sea voyage remain irresistible for some. Such sojourners should find out as much as possible before signing on for a seagoing vacation (after all, it's hard to get off in mid-ocean).

CRUISES TO MEXICO: There are a number of cruise lines that include Acapulco as part of their Mexican itineraries. These lines either sail directly to Mexico or offer passengers the option of joining a leg of longer cruises — such as cruises through the Panama Canal to or from the Caribbean — that stop over in Acapulco. Other cruises, sailing to or from Acapulco, can be added on to the beginning or end of your stay. Prices vary greatly in the cruise ship category, depending on the level of luxury, accommodations, and length of the journey.

Below is a list of cruise lines and ships sailing to Mexico from the US with a stop in Acapulco:

Commodore Cruise Line (800 Douglas Rd., Suite 700, Coral Gables, FL 33134; phone: 800-237-5361). The *Enchanted Isle* makes 21-day transcanal sailings between New York and San Diego that stop in Acapulco.

Crystal Cruises (2121 Ave. of the Stars, Los Angeles, CA 90067; phone: 800-446-6645). The *Crystal Harmony* makes several transcanal itineraries that either stop in Acapulco or have Acapulco as an embarking/disembarking point. Ranging from 10 to 17 days, these cruises sail along the Mexican Riviera and some of them stop at Caribbean islands.

Cunard (555 Fifth Ave., New York, NY 10017; phone: 800-5-CUNARD in the US or 800-268-3705 in Canada). The *Queen Elizabeth 2,* one of the largest and most comfortable vessels afloat, includes Acapulco among the ports of call on its transcanal cruises between New York or Ft. Lauderdale and Los Angeles or Honolulu. These transcanal cruises are available as segments of the *QE II*'s World Cruise. *Cunard*'s *Sagafjord, Sea Goddess I,* and *Vistafjord* all also make several transcanal cruises stopping in Acapulco. The transcanal cruises range from 14 to 16 days. The *Sea Goddess I* also offers a 7-day Mexican Riviera cruise which includes Acapulco as a port of call.

Holland America Line (300 Elliott Ave. W., Seattle, WA 98119; phone: 800-426-0327). It offers 11- to 21-day transcanal sailings that include Acapulco as a port of call. These itineraries sail between Ft. Lauderdale/Tampa/New York/New Orleans on the East Coast and Los Angeles/San Francisco/Vancouver on the West Coast.

P & O Cruises (c/o Express Travel Services, Empire State Building, Suite 7718, 350 Fifth Ave., New York, NY 10118; phone: 212-629-3630 in New York State; 800-223-5799 elsewhere in the US). Both of its world cruise itineraries on board the *Sea Princess* and *Canberra* include Acapulco as a port of call. Passengers can take segments of it or the entire 92-day sailing.

Princess Cruises (10100 Santa Monica Blvd., Santa Monica, CA 90067; phone: 800-421-0522). This is it, folks, the "Love Boat" — or perhaps we should say the Love Boats — in person. The *Dawn Princess* sails round trip from Los Angeles along the Mexican Riviera on a 10-day cruise, stopping in Acapulco and other well-known west coast resort areas. A shorter version of this cruise is on board the *Regal Princess,* which sails between Acapulco and Los Angeles. A variety of transcanal itineraries, ranging from 10 to 16 days, is available on board the *Royal Princess, Sky Princess, Regal Princess,* and *Pacific Princess.* Most include Acapulco as a port of call, others either embark or disembark at Acapulco.

Royal Cruise Line (One Maritime Plaza, San Francisco, CA 94111; phone: 800-227-5628 or 415-956-7200). The *Crown Odyssey* and the *Royal Odyssey* offer 9- to 12-day Mexican Riviera cruises round trip from Los Angeles or San Francisco and include Acapulco as a port of call. A shorter version also is available between Acapulco and Los Angeles or San Francisco. The *Royal Odyssey* and the *Golden Odyssey* offer 9- to 11-day transcanal cruises between Acapulco and San Juan or Aruba. Those who wish to combine transcanal cruising with Caribbean destinations can choose between 14- to 16-day itineraries, with stops at many Mexican Riviera ports as well as Caribbean islands including Jamaica, Aruba, Barbados, Grenada, US Virgin Islands, and Antigua.

Royal Caribbean Cruise Line (1050 Caribbean Way, Miami, FL 33132; phone: 800-432-6559 in Florida; 800-327-6700 elsewhere in US and Canada). Seven-day sailings between Los Angeles and Acapulco are offered on *Sun Viking* and the *Song of America*. Pre- and post-cruise land packages in Acapulco are available.

Royal Viking Lines (95 Merrick Way, Coral Gables, FL 33134; phone: 800-422-8000). The *Royal Viking Sun* and the *Royal Viking Queen* make 16- to 21-day transcanal cruises from San Francisco to Ft. Lauderdale that stop in Acapulco and other resort areas. The *Royal Viking Queen* also makes 13-day sailings between San Francisco and Bridgetown that include Acapulco as a port of call.

Seabourn Cruise Line (55 Francisco St., San Francisco, CA 94133; phone: 800-351-9595). The *Seabourn Spirit* offers 12- to 24-day transcanal sailings with Acapulco as either an embarking or disembarking port. Many of the itineraries include several Caribbean ports of call.

In addition to the standard vacation-on-the-high-seas cruises, specialty packages aboard ships sailing to Mexico are increasingly popular. For instance, several cruise lines offer special programs or facilities for handicapped, single, or older travelers.

A monthly newsletter that may be of interest to those planning to cruise Mexican waters is *Ocean and Cruise News,* which offers comprehensive coverage of the latest on the cruise ship scene. A year's subscription costs $24. Contact *Ocean and Cruise News,* PO Box 92, Stamford, CT 06904 (phone: 203-329-2787).

■**A final note on picking a cruise:** A "cruise-only" travel agency can best help you choose a cruise ship and itinerary. Cruise-only agents are best equipped to tell you about a particular ship's "personality," the kind of person with whom you'll likely be traveling on a particular ship, what dress is appropriate (it varies from ship to ship), and much more. Travel agencies that specialize in booking cruises usually are members of the *National Association of Cruise Only Agencies (NACOA).* For a listing of the agencies in your area (requests are limited to three states), send a self-addressed, stamped envelope to *NACOA,* PO Box 7209, Freeport, NY 11520, or call 516-378-8006.

Traveling by Car

Driving is the best way to explore out-of-the-way regions of Mexico on the way to or from your visit in Acapulco. The privacy, comfort, and convenience of touring by car can't be matched by any other form of transportation. A car provides maximum flexibility, allowing visitors to cover large amounts of territory, to visit major cities and sites, or to move from one small town to the next while exploring the countryside. You go where you want when you want, and can stop along the way as often as you like for a meal, a nap, or a spectacular view.

Mexico's highways and roads are renowned for their scenery. Sudden, unexpected glimpses of tropical flowers, desert plants, pine trees, mountains, and aquamarine waters form the moving backdrop of the road as you drive. The distances between cities and towns are usually reasonable, and a visitor can use a car's flexibility to maximum advantage. When planning your driving route, however, be *very* conservative in estimating driving time — *driving or stopping by the roadside after dark can be very dangerous.* Drivers should be aware of latter-day bandits who have been known to stop, assault, and rob tourists. In DIRECTIONS, you will find our choices of the most interesting driving itineraries, as well as approximate distances to help in your calculations.

Most roads are well surfaced, but you will find few of the multi-lane highways found in the US, except around the larger cities. In general, secondary and lesser roads also are kept in reasonably good condition, although this may not always be the case, particularly during the rainy season. If you are planning to explore off the beaten track, consider renting a four-wheel-drive vehicle. Either way, there is plenty to see en route.

As the only road often goes through the middle of the town or resort area, be prepared to slow down as you pass through busy, populated centers. The speed limit on the best highways is 110 kilometers per hour (approximately 69 miles per hour). Speeds always are given in kilometers per hour and distances in kilometers (a kilometer is equal to approximately .62 miles); major highway signs use international symbols, which are quite easy to understand.

License – A valid US driver's license from his or her state of residence enables a US citizen to drive in Mexico. (You do not need an International Driving Permit.) Your US license also will be required for renting a car, and in most cases, you will need to present a major credit card. If you are driving across the border from the US, however, remember that a driver's license cannot be used as proof of citizenship. For information on valid proof of citizenship, see *Entry Requirements and Documents,* in this section.

Car Permits – You must have a car permit to drive in Mexico, but getting it is a routine matter at the border. The guards at the border will provide a free permit and a tourist card entitling you to either a specific amount of time in Mexico (30 days to 6 months) or for multiple exits and entries. (A 6-month car permit also may be acquired at one of the Mexican consulates in the US.) It is essential that you show the guards at the border the car's registration and proof of ownership. If you are driving into Mexico in a car rented in the US or in a vehicle belonging to someone else, carry a notarized affidavit stating that you have the right to drive the car in Mexico (in the case of rental firms, the appropriate paperwork will be provided on request). The same applies for a trailer.

■**Note:** Regulations recently instituted by the Mexican government now require that US drivers entering Mexico with their own cars present proof that the vehicle they are driving carries full insurance coverage in the US (comprehensive coverage including theft and third-party liability) or post a bond, which can be as high as 50% of the value of the car. This ruling applies to visitors who are traveling beyond the so-called "free zone," which extends 20 miles from the US–Mexican border, and who intend to stay in Mexico less than 3 months. Contact the Mexican Embassy in Washington (phone: 202-728-1630) or the nearest Mexican Consulate for additional information (see *Mexican Consulates and Tourist Offices in the US,* in this section, for addresses).

Maps – Consult road maps. A number of the automobile clubs listed below offer their members (and members of affiliated clubs) free or inexpensive maps. Maps also are available at service stations on both sides of the border.

A company with more than half a century of experience in maps of Mexico is *Guía Roji* (31 J. Moran, México, DF 11850; phone: 5-277-2307 or 5-702-0931). They publish road maps of all Mexican states and wall maps of several Mexican cities (as of this writing, there are no wall maps for Acapulco). Their road atlas, called *Atlas de Carreteras,* costs about $22 and is extremely useful for the motorist. Other *Guía Roji* maps are available from *Sanborn's Mexican Insurance Service* US offices (at 2009 S. 10th St., McAllen, TX 78502; phone: 512-686-0711; and 2212 Santa Ursula, Laredo, TX 78040-3122; phone: 512-722-0931).

The *Rand McNally Cosmopolitan Map of Mexico* ($2.95) is a wall map that indicates each Mexican state in a different color. While its size and scale are not practical for touring use, it can be helpful before leaving for Mexico. All major highways are indicated, and there is no problem figuring out what is near what. For use on the road, the *Rand McNally Road Atlas: US, Canada and Mexico* ($7.95 paperback) is excellent. Both of these publications may be found in bookstores or can be ordered directly from *Rand McNally* (150 E. 52nd St., New York, NY 10022; phone: 212-758-7488); call for information on charges for postage and handling.

Perhaps the most detailed series of maps available are those published by the *Dirección General de Geografía*. A broad selection of maps of Mexico is available, with the emphasis ranging from topography to tourism. Numerous bookstores in Mexican cities carry these maps. A variety of Mexican maps also is available by writing to the *Servicio Meteorológico Nacional* (192 Av. Observatorio, Tacubaya, México, DF 11860).

A good source for most of the maps listed above, and just about any other kind of map of just about anywhere in the world, including Mexico, is *Map Link* (25 E. Mason St., Suite 201, Santa Barbara, CA 93101; phone: 805-965-4402). They carry the particularly useful *Pemex Mexican Road Atlas* ($11.95), which includes a city plan of Acapulco, as well maps of the broader *International Travel Maps (ITM)* series, which covers much of Mexico. If they don't stock a map of the area in which you are interested, they will do their best to get it for you.

Automobile Clubs – Most Mexican automobile clubs offer emergency service to any breakdown victim, whether a club member or not; however, only members of these clubs or affiliated clubs may have access to certain information services and receive discounted or free towing and repair services.

Members of the *American Automobile Association (AAA)* often are entitled automatically to a number of services from foreign clubs. With almost 33 million members in chapters throughout the US and Canada, the *AAA* is the largest automobile club in North America. *AAA* affiliates throughout the US provide a variety of travel services to members, including a travel agency, trip planning, fee-free traveler's checks, and roadside assistance. They will help plan an itinerary, send a map with clear routing directions, and even make hotel reservations. Most of these services apply to traveling in both the US and Mexico. (Note that the *AAA* no longer reimburses members for on-the-road expenses — such as towing or repairs — incurred while in Mexico.) Although *AAA* members receive maps and other brochures for no charge or at a discount (depending on the publication and branch), non-members also can order from an extensive selection of highway and topographical maps. You can join the *AAA* through local chapters (listed in the telephone book under *AAA*) or contact the national office, 1000 AAA Dr., Heathrow, FL 32746-5063 (phone: 407-444-8544).

The *American Automobile Association* also is affiliated with a Mexican automobile association, the *Asociación Mexicana Automovilística (AMA;* Mexican Automobile Association), with branches in the metropolitan Mexico City area, Cuernavaca, and Puebla. *AMA*'s main office is at 7 Calle Orizaba, México, DF 06700 (phone: 5-208-8329 or 5-511-6285). The association provides a variety of maps in English at no charge. And, in some parts of Mexico, *AAA* members can call the *AMA* for emergency service.

The *Automóvil Club de Mexico,* perhaps the most widely based in Mexico, also can be helpful to *AAA* members, as well as members of other automobile associations belonging to the *International Federation of Automobile Associations* (ask if a club is a member before joining). The association also provides a number of useful road maps — free. The main office is at 140 Calle Miguel E. Schultz, México, DF 06470 (phone: 5-705-0258).

Breakdowns – If you break down on the road, immediate emergency procedure is to get the car off the road. If the road has a narrow shoulder, try to get all the way off, even if you have to hang off the shoulder a bit. Better yet, try to make it to an area where the shoulder is wider — if you are crawling along well below the speed limit, use your emergency flasher to warn other drivers. To signal for help, raise the hood, and tie a white handerkerchief or rag to the door handle or radio antenna. Don't leave the car unattended, and don't try any major repairs on the road.

The major Mexican highways are patrolled by Mexico's **Green Angel** fleet of emergency service trucks. They are manned by English-speaking crews and carry equipment for a modest range of on-the-road repairs. (Don't expect miracles, just an adequate, average repair job for a common emergency.) The Green Angels (called *Angeles Verdes*) know how to change tires, give first aid, and take care of minor problems. They also carry gasoline and oil and provide information on road conditions. Except for parts and fuel, the service is free. That's why they're called "angels" — they literally cruise the main highways looking for motorists to rescue. Sooner or later, if you break down on a main road, one of the Green Angels will get to you, as crews patrol every day (from 8 AM to 8 PM). Supplementing their efforts are the following hotline emergency numbers for tourists needing guidance or help: 915-250-0123, 915-250-8601, 915-250-8419, 915-250-8221, or 915-250-8555. (When calling within the Mexico City area, do *not* dial 915.)

Gasoline – *Pemex* (an acronym for *Petróleos Mexicanos*) is the only brand of gasoline and oil sold in Mexico since the petroleum industry was nationalized. Gasoline is sold in liters (approximately 3.8 liters equal 1 gallon), and two grades of gas are available: Nova (or regular) from the blue pump, and higher-priced Extra (or premium) from the silver pump (though Extra often is difficult if not impossible to find). There also is "*magna plus*" (unleaded) in the green pump. Both grades, premium and regular, come in leaded and unleaded varieties; ask the gas station attendant for "*con plomo*" if you want *leaded* gas or "*magna sin*" or "*sin plomo*" (they're synoymous) for *unleaded.*

Gas prices everywhere rise and fall depending upon the world supply of oil. US visitors generally will find gasoline to be slightly less expensive than they are accustomed to paying in the US. Be prepared to pay for gas in cash (American oil company credit cards aren't accepted by *Pemex*). And if you request the attendants to check your oil and water or coolant in your radiator, or wipe your windshield, be sure to tip them between 500 and 1,000 pesos. We recommend tipping gas station attendants even if you are only filling up. They usually are hard working and underpaid, and you'd be amazed at how many pesos it takes to make up the differences between their wages and those of gas station attendants in the US.

Particularly when traveling in rural areas, fill up whenever you come to a gas station. It may be a long way to the next station. You *don't* want to get stranded on an isolated stretch — so it is a good idea to bring along an extra few gallons in a steel container. Also note that in rural areas, gasoline may be diluted with water or kerosene. So if the car stops after you have just filled up, it could be due to impure gasoline.

RENTING A CAR: Most visitors who want to drive in Mexico rent a car through a travel agent or international rental firm before leaving home, or from a local company once in Mexico. Another possibility, also arranged before departure, is to rent the car as part of a larger travel package.

Renting is not inexpensive, but it is possible to economize by determining your own needs and then shopping around among the car rental companies until you find the best deal. As you comparison shop, keep in mind that rates vary considerably, not only from city to city, but also from location to location within the same city. For instance, it might be less expensive to rent a car from an office in the center of a city rather than at the airport. Ask about special rates or promotional deals, such as weekend or weekly rates, bonus coupons for airline tickets, or 24-hour rates that include gas and unlimited mileage.

Rental car companies operating in Mexico can be divided into three basic categories: large national or international companies, regional companies, and local companies. Because of aggressive local competition, the cost of renting a car can be less expensive once a traveler arrives in Mexico, compared to the prices quoted in advance in the US. Local companies usually are less expensive than the international giants (although travelers who do not speak fluent Spanish may have to rule out smaller local companies that rent primarily to natives).

Given this situation, it's tempting to wait until arriving to scout out the lowest-priced rental from the company located the farthest from the airport high-rent district and offering no pick-up services. But if your arrival coincides with a holiday or a peak travel period, you may be disappointed to find that even the most expensive car in town was spoken for months ago. Whenever possible, it is best to reserve in advance, anywhere from a few days in slack periods to a month or more during the busier seasons.

If you can read and speak Spanish, and decide to wait until after you arrive in Mexico and let your fingers do the walking through the local phone books, you'll often find a surprising number of small companies listed. Often the best guide to sorting through the options is the local tourist board, which usually can provide recommendations and a list of reputable firms.

Even if you do rent in advance, be aware that many Mexican car rental experiences bear little resemblance to the normally efficient process found almost everywhere in the US. It is not all uncommon, for example, to arrive at an airport rental counter — even that of a giant international company — and have your confirmed reservation greeted with a shrug: No cars available. (If you use a car rental firm's toll-free number to reserve a vehicle, it *may* make a difference if you arrive with written confirmation of your reservations in hand — leaving enough time for the rental company to mail it to you before you leave home. Also be sure you get a receipt for any deposit.) It is similarly common that the class and make of car you ordered will be notable by its absence. More shrugs. And even when you do get a car, and even when it is precisely the brand and type you want, chances are that its physical appearance and mechanical condition will be substantially inferior to similar rental cars you are used to driving in the US. Caveat renter.

Travel agents can arrange rentals for clients, but it is just as easy to call and rent a car yourself. Listed below are several national Mexican rental companies, as well as the major international rental companies represented in Acapulco that have information and reservations numbers that can be dialed toll-free from the US (note that these numbers are all for the companies' international divisions, which handle Mexican rentals):

Auto Europe (phone: 800-223-5555). Has 2 locations in Acapulco, and 1 at the airport.

Avis (phone: 800-331-1212). Has 3 locations in Acapulco, and 1 at the airport.

Budget Rent-A-Car (phone: 800-472-3325). Has 1 location at the airport.

Dollar Rent A Car (phone: 800-800-4000). Has 4 locations in Acapulco, and 1 at the airport.

Economovil Rent (phone: 5-604-5960 or 5-604-2118 for the main office in Mexico City). Has 2 locations in Acapulco.

Hertz (phone: 800-654-3001). Has 2 locations in Acapulco, and 1 at the airport.

National Car Rental (phone: 800-328-4567). Has 2 locations in Acapulco.

For further information on local car rental companies, see *Sources and Resources,* THE CITY.

Requirements – Whether you decide to rent a car in advance from a large international rental company with Mexican branches or wait to rent from a local company, you should know that renting a car is rarely as simple as signing on the dotted line and roaring off into the night. If you are renting for personal use, you must have a valid driver's license and will have to convince the renting agency that (1) you are personally creditworthy, and (2) you will bring the car back at the stated time. This will be easy if you have a major credit card; most rental companies accept credit cards in lieu of a cash deposit, as well as for payment of your final bill. If you prefer to pay in cash, leave your credit card imprint as a "deposit," then pay your bill in cash when you return the car.

If you are planning to rent a car once in Mexico, *Avis, Budget, Hertz,* and other US rental companies usually *will* rent to travelers paying in cash and leaving either a credit card imprint or a substantial amount of cash as a deposit. This is not necessarily standard policy, however, as some of the other international chains, and a number of regional and local Mexican companies, will *not* rent to an individual who doesn't have a valid credit card. In this case, you may have to call around to find a company that accepts cash.

Also keep in mind that although the minimum age to drive a car in Mexico is 18 years, the minimum age to rent a car is set by the rental company. (Restrictions vary from company to company, as well as at different locations of the same firm.) Many firms have a minimum age requirement of 21 years, some raise that to 23 or 25 years, and for some models of cars it rises to 30 years. The upper age limit at many companies is between 69 and 75; others have no upper limit or may make drivers above a certain age subject to special conditions.

Costs – Finding the most economical car rental will require some telephone shopping on your part. As a *general* rule, expect to hear lower prices quoted by the smaller, strictly local companies than by the well-known international names, with those of the national Mexican companies falling somewhere between the two.

If driving short distances for only a day or two, the best deal may be a per-day, per-mile (or per-kilometer) rate: You pay a flat fee for each day you keep the car, plus a per-mile (or per-kilometer) charge. An increasingly common alternative is to be granted a certain number of free miles or kilometers each day and then be charged on a per-mile or per-kilometer basis over that number.

A better alternative for Mexican touring is a flat per-day rate with unlimited free mileage; this certainly is the most economical rate if you plan to drive over 100 miles. (*Note:* When renting a car in Mexico, the term "mileage" may refer to either miles or kilometers.) Make sure that the low, flat daily rate that catches your eye, however, is indeed a per-day rate: Often the lowest price advertised by a company turns out to be available only with a minimum 3-day rental — fine if you want the car that long, but not the bargain it appears if you really intend to use it no more than 24 hours for in-city driving. Flat weekly rates also are available, and some flat monthly rates that represent a further saving over the daily rate.

Another factor influencing cost is the type of car you rent. Rentals generally are based on a tiered price system, with different sizes of cars — variations of budget, economy, regular, and luxury often listed as A (the smallest and least expensive) through F, G, or H, and sometimes even higher. Charges may increase by only a few dollars a day through several categories of subcompact and compact cars — where most of the competition is — then increase by great leaps through the remaining classes of full-size and luxury cars and passenger vans. The larger the car, the more it costs to rent and the more gas it consumes, but for some people the greater comfort and extra luggage space of a larger car (in which bags and sporting gear can be safely locked out of sight) may make it worth the additional expense. In some areas, models with standard stick shifts are more common and those with automatic transmissions are, therefore, more expensive.

Electing to pay for collision damage waiver (CDW) protection will add considerably to the cost of renting a car. You may be responsible for the *full value* of the vehicle being rented, but you can dispense with the possible obligation by buying the offered waiver at a cost of around $9 to $13 a day for rentals in Mexico. Before making any decisions about optional collision damage waivers, check with your own insurance agent and determine whether your personal automobile insurance policy covers rented vehicles; if it does, you probably won't need to pay for the waiver. Be aware, too, that increasing numbers of credit card companies automatically provide CDW coverage if the car rental is charged to the appropriate credit card. However, the specific terms of such coverage differ sharply among individual credit card companies, so check with the credit card company for information on the nature and amount of coverage provided. Business travelers also should be aware that, at the time of this writing, *American Express* had withdrawn its automatic CDW coverage from some corporate *Green* card accounts — watch for similar cutbacks by other credit card companies.

When inquiring about CDW coverage and costs, you should be aware that a number of the major international car rental companies now are automatically including the cost of this waiver in their quoted prices. This does not mean that they are absorbing this cost and you are receiving free coverage — total rental prices have increased to include the former CDW charge. The disadvantage of this inclusion is that you probably will not have the option to refuse this coverage, and will end up paying the added charge — even if you already are adequately covered by your own insurance policy or through a credit card company.

Additional costs to be added to the price tag include drop-off charges or one-way service fees. The lowest price quoted by any given company may apply only to a car that is returned to the same location from which it was rented. A slightly higher rate may be charged if the car is to be returned to a different location (even within the same city).

Also, don't forget to factor in the price of gas. Rental cars usually are delivered with a full tank of gas. (This is not always the case, however, so check the gas gauge when picking up the car, and have the amount of gas noted on your rental agreement if the tank is not full.) Remember to fill the tank before you return the car or you will have to pay to refill it, and gasoline at the car rental company's pump always is much more expensive than at a service station. This policy may vary for smaller local and regional companies; ask when picking up the vehicle. Before leaving the lot, also check that the rental car has a spare tire and jack in the trunk.

Fly/Drive Packages – Airlines, charter companies, car rental companies, and tour operators have been offering fly/drive packages for years, and even though the basic components of the package have changed somewhat — return airfare, a car waiting at the airport, and perhaps a night's lodging all for one inclusive price used to be the rule — the idea remains the same. You rent a car *here* for use *there* by booking it along with other arrangements for the trip. These days, the very minimum arrangement possible is the result of a tie-in between a car rental company and an airline, which entitles customers to a rental car for less than the company's usual rates, provided they show proof of having booked a flight on that airline. For information on available packages, check with the airline or your travel agent.

■ **Note:** When reserving and picking up your rental car, always ask for any available maps and information on the areas in which you will be driving; some companies also may offer brochures outlining scenic driving routes.

Package Tours

If the mere thought of buying a package for travel to Mexico conjures up visions of a trip spent marching in lockstep with a horde of frazzled fellow travelers, remember that packages have come a long way. For one thing, not all packages necessarily are escorted tours, and the one you buy does not have to include any organized touring at all — nor will it necessarily include traveling companions. If it does, however, you'll find that people of all sorts — many just like yourself — are taking advantage of packages today because they are economical and convenient, save you an immense amount of planning time, and exist in such variety that it's virtually impossible not to find one that fits at least the majority of your travel preferences. Given the high cost of travel these days, packages have emerged as a particularly wise buy.

In essence, a package is just an amalgam of travel services that can be purchased in a single transaction. A package (tour or otherwise) to or around Mexico may include any or all of the following: round-trip transportation from your home to Mexico, local transportation (and/or car rentals), accommodations, some or all meals, sightseeing, entertainment, transfers to and from the hotel at each destination, taxes, tips, escort service, and a variety of incidental features that might be offered as options at additional cost. In other words, a package can be any combination of travel elements, from a fully escorted tour offered at an all-inclusive price to a simple fly/drive booking allowing you to move about totally on your own. Its principal advantage is that it saves money: The cost of the combined arrangements invariably is well below the price of all the same elements if bought separately, and particularly if transportation is provided by charter or discount flight, the whole package could cost less than just a round-trip economy airline ticket on a regularly scheduled flight. A package provides more than economy and convenience: It releases the traveler from having to make individual arrangements for each separate element of a trip.

Tour programs generally can be divided into two categories — "escorted" (or locally hosted) and "independent." An escorted tour means that a guide will accompany the group from the beginning of the tour through to the return flight; a locally hosted tour means that the group will be met upon arrival by a local host. On independent tours, there generally is a choice of hotels, meal plans, and sightseeing trips, as well as a variety of special excursions. The independent plan is for travelers who do not want a totally set itinerary, but who do prefer confirmed hotel reservations. Whether choosing an escorted or independent tour, always bring along complete contact information for your tour operator in case a problem arises, although US tour operators often have local affiliates who can give additional assistance or make other arrangements on the spot.

To determine whether a package — or, more specifically, *which* package — fits your travel plans, start by evaluating your interests and needs, deciding how much and what you want to spend, see, and do. Gather whatever package tour information is available for your schedule. Be sure that you take the time to read the brochure *carefully* to determine precisely what is included. Keep in mind that travel brochures are written to entice you into signing up for a package tour. Often the language is deceptive and devious. For example, a brochure may quote the lowest prices for a package tour based on facilities that are unavailable during the off-season, undesirable at any season, or just plain nonexistent. Information such as "breakfast included" or "plus tax" (which can add up) should be taken into account. Note, too, that the prices quoted in brochures almost always are based on double occupancy: The rate listed is for each of two people sharing a double room, and if you travel alone, the supplement for single accommodations can raise the price considerably (see *Hints for Single Travelers,* in this section).

In this age of erratic airfares, the brochure most often will *not* include the price of an airline ticket in the price of the package, though sample fares from various gateway cities usually will be listed separately as extras to be added to the price of the ground arrangements. Before figuring your actual cost, check the latest fares with the airlines, because the samples invariably are out of date by the time you read them. If the brochure gives more than one category of sample fares per gateway city — such as an individual tour-basing fare, a group fare, an excursion, or other discount ticket — your travel agent or airline tour desk will be able to tell you which one applies to the package you choose, depending on when you travel, how far in advance you book, and other factors. When the brochure does include round-trip transportation in the package price, don't forget to add the cost of round-trip transportation from your home to the departure city to come up with the total cost of the package.

Finally, read the general information regarding terms and conditions and the responsibility clause (usually in fine print at the end of the descriptive literature) to determine the precise elements for which the tour operator is — and is not — liable. Here the tour operator frequently expresses the right to change services or schedules as long as equivalent arrangements are offered. This clause also absolves the operator of responsibility for circumstances beyond human control, such as hurricanes or floods, or injury to you or your property. While reading, ask the following questions:

1. Does the tour include airfare or other transportation, sightseeing, meals, transfers, taxes, baggage handling, tips, or any other services? Do you want all these services?
2. If the brochure indicates that "some meals" are included, does this mean a welcoming and farewell dinner, two breakfasts, or every evening meal?
3. What classes of hotels are offered? If you will be traveling alone, what is the single supplement?
4. Does the tour itinerary or price vary according to the season?
5. Are the prices guaranteed; that is, if costs increase between the time you book and the time you depart, can surcharges unilaterally be added?
6. Do you get a full refund if you cancel? If not, be sure to obtain cancellation insurance.
7. Can the operator cancel if too few people join? At what point?

One of the consumer's biggest problems is finding enough information to judge the reliability of a tour packager, since individual travelers seldom have direct contact with the firm putting the package together. Usually, a retail travel agent is interposed between customer and tour operator, and much depends on his or her candor and cooperation. So ask a number of questions about the tour you are considering. For example:

- Has the agent ever used a package provided by this tour operator?
- How long has the tour operator been in business? Check the Better Business Bureau in the area where the tour operator is based to see if any complaints have been filed against it.
- Is the tour operator a member of the *United States Tour Operators Association* (*USTOA*, 211 E. 51st St., Suite 12B, New York, NY 10022; phone: 212-944-5727)? The *USTOA* will provide a list of its members on request; it also offers a useful brochure, *How to Select a Package Tour.*
- How many and which companies are involved in the package?
- If air travel is by charter flight, is there an escrow account in which deposits will be held; if so, what is the name of the bank?

This last question is very important. US law requires that tour operators place every charter passenger's deposit and subsequent payment in a proper escrow account. Money paid into such an account cannot legally be used except to pay for the costs of a particular package or as a refund if the trip is canceled. To protect your investment, you should either make your check payable to the escrow account or use a credit card. (As this procedure follows the same guidelines as payments for charter flights, see our discussion in *Traveling by Plane.*)

■**A word of advice:** Purchasers of vacation packages who feel they're not getting their money's worth are more likely to get a refund if they complain in writing to the operator — and bail out of the whole package immediately. Alert the tour operator or resort manager to the fact that you are dissatisfied, that you will be leaving for home as soon as transportation can be arranged, and that you expect a refund. They may have forms to fill out detailing your complaint; otherwise, state your case in a letter. Even if difficulty in arranging immediate transportation home detains you, your dated, written complaint should help in procuring a refund from the operator.

The following is a list of many of the major US operators who provide escorted or independent packages to Acapulco. Some offer AP ("American Plan" — including all meals), others MAP ("Modified American Plan" — breakfast and one main meal included daily), a few include only breakfast, and others leave you to make your own arrangements for meals. Most tour operators offer several departure dates, depending on the length of the tour and areas visited. As indicated, some operators are wholesalers only, and will deal only with a travel agent.

American Airlines FlyAAway Vacations (Southern Reservation Center, Mail Drop 1000, Box 619619, Dallas/Ft. Worth Airport, TX 75261-9619; phone: 800-321-2121). Offers 4-day packages in Acapulco.

American Express Travel Related Services (300 Pinnacle Way, Norcross, GA 30071; phone: 800-327-7737 or 404-368-5100). Offers Acapulco packages, for 4 days or longer. It also offers 8- and 15-day escorted tours of Mexico that include Acapulco.

Asti Tours (21 E. 40th St., New York, NY 10016; phone: 800-535-3711 in New York; 800-223-7728 elsewhere in the US). Offers air/hotel packages.

Cavalcade Tours (450 Harmon Meadow Blvd., Secaucus, NJ 07096-1568; phone: 800-521-2319 or 201-617-7100). Offers minimum 3-day air/hotel packages.

Continental's Grand Destinations (PO Box 1460, Milwaukee, WI 53201-1460; phone: 800-634-5555). Offers air/hotel packages to Acapulco.

Fishing International (4010 Montecito Ave., Santa Rosa, CA 95405; phone: 800-950-4242 or 707-542-4242). Books fishing packages that include hotel, fishing boat, tackle, bait, and crew in Acapulco.

Fling Vacations (999 Postal Rd., Allentown, PA 18103; phone: 800-523-9624). Offers 3- to 21-day air/hotel packages. The tour operator is a wholesaler, so use a travel agent.

Four Winds Travel (PO Box 693, Old Greenwich, CT 06870; phone: 203-698-0944). Offers 11-day escorted tours in Mexico from Guadalajara to Acapulco, and visits small villages along the way.

Funway Holidays Funjet (8907 N. Port Washington Rd., Milwaukee, WI 53217; phone: 414-351-3553). Offers hotel packages to Acapulco. The tour operator is a wholesaler, so use a travel agent.

Globus Gateway/Cosmos Tours (95-25 Queens Blvd., Rego Park, NY 11374; phone: 718-268-1700 or 718-268-7000 in New York State; 800-221-0090 elsewhere in the US). Offers a 9-day escorted tour from Mexico City to Acapulco. This operator is a wholesaler, so use a travel agent.

GoGo Tours (contact the central office for the nearest location: 69 Spring St.,

Ramsey, NJ 07446-0507; phone: 201-934-3820). Offers city and honeymoon packages. This operator is a wholesaler, so use a travel agent.

Ibero Travel (PO Box 758, Forest Hills, NY 11375; phone: 800-882-6678 or 718-263-0200 in New York State, 800-654-2376 elsewhere in the US). Offers a minimum 3-night Acapulco package.

Liberty Travel (contact the central office for the nearest location: 69 Spring St., Ramsey, NJ 07446; phone: 201-934-3500). Offers customized, independent packages including a variety of features.

Saga Holidays (120 Boylston St., Boston, MA 02116; phone: 800-343-0273 or 617-451-6808). Offers a 14-day Highlights of Mexico escorted tour. It includes a 2-day stay in Acapulco and visits Cuernavaca, Mexico City, San Miguel de Allende, Taxco, Guadalajara, and Morelia.

Sanborn Tours (1007 Main St., Bastrop, TX 78602; phone: 800-531-5440 or 512-321-1131). Offers 8-day escorted tours of Mexico that include Acapulco, Cuernavaca, Mexico City, and Taxco. There's also a 5-day hosted tour of Acapulco that includes hotel, half-day sightseeing, and airport transfers.

Sunmakers (15375 SE 30th Place, Suite 350, Bellevue, WA 98007; phone: 800-841-4321). Offers air/hotel packages for a minimum of 3 days. This operator is a wholesaler, so use a travel agent.

Travel Impressions (465 Smith St., Farmingdale, NY 11735; phone: 800-284-0077 in the Southeast, Midwest, and western US; 800-284-0044 or 800-284-0055 in the Northeast and elsewhere in the US). Offers minimum 3-day air/hotel packages. This company also offers 6- or 7-night charter packages (with hotel) to Acapulco.

Trek America (PO Box 1338, Gardena, CA 90249; phone: 800-221-0596 or 213-323-5775). Offers a 21- or 25-day trekking tour between Los Angeles and Mexico City with 2 days spent in Acapulco. It explores many coastal villages en route.

Preparing

Calculating Costs

 DETERMINING A BUDGET: A realistic appraisal of travel expenses is the most crucial bit of planning you will undertake before any trip. It is also, unfortunately, one for which it is most difficult to give precise, practical advice.

In Mexico, estimating travel expenses depends on the mode of transportation you choose, how long you will stay, and, in some cases, what time of year you plan to travel. In addition to the basics of transportation, hotels, meals, and sightseeing, you have to take into account seasonal price changes that apply on certain air routings.

When calculating costs, start with the basics, the major expenses being transportation, accommodations, and food. However, don't forget such extras as local transportation, shopping, and such miscellaneous items as laundry and tips. Package programs can reduce the price of a vacation in Mexico, because the rates obtained by the tour packager are usually lower than the tariffs for someone traveling on a free-lance basis, that is, paying for each element — airfare, meals, car rental — separately.

Other expenses, such as the cost of local sightseeing tours and other excursions, will vary depending on the tour and the guide you select. The tourist information office and most of the better hotels will have someone at the front desk to provide a rundown on the cost of local tours and full-day excursions in and out of the city. Travel agents also can provide this information.

In planning any travel budget, it also is wise to allow a realistic amount for both entertainment and recreation. Are you planning to spend time sightseeing and visiting local tourist attractions? Do you intend to rent a catamaran or take parasailing lessons? Is daily golf or tennis a part of your plan? Finally, don't forget that if haunting discotheques or other nightspots is an essential part of your vacation, or you feel that one dinner show may not be enough, allow for the extra cost of nightlife.

If at any point in the planning process it appears impossible to estimate expenses, consider this suggestion: The easiest way to put a ceiling on the price of all these elements is to buy a package tour. A totally planned and escorted one, with almost all transportation, rooms, meals, sightseeing, local travel, tips, and a dinner show or two included and prepaid, provides a pretty exact total of what the trip will cost beforehand, and the only surprise will be the one you spring on yourself by succumbing to some irresistible, expensive souvenir. And keep in mind, particularly when calculating the major expenses, that costs vary according to fluctuations in the exchange rate — that is, how many pesos a dollar will buy.

■ **Note:** The combination of rapid peso devaluation and Mexico's inflation rate has led the government to authorize increases in hotel rates of as much as 35% from time to time. Between the time you originally make your hotel reservations and the day you arrive, the price in US dollars may vary substantially from the price originally quoted. To avoid paying more than you expected, it's wise to confirm rates by writing directly to hotels or by calling their representatives in the US.

Planning a Trip

123 Travelers fall into two categories: those who make lists and those who do not. Some people prefer to plot the course of their trip to the finest detail, with contingency plans and alternatives at the ready. For others, the joy of a voyage is its spontaneity; exhaustive planning only lessens the thrill of anticipation and the sense of freedom.

For most travelers, however, any week-plus trip to Acapulco can be too expensive for an "I'll take my chances" type of attitude. Even perennial gypsies and anarchistic wanderers have to take into account the time-consuming logistics of getting around, and even with minimal baggage, they need to think about packing. Hence, at least some planning is crucial.

This is not to suggest that you work out your itinerary in minute detail before you go; but it's still wise to decide certain basics at the very start: where to go, what to do, and how much to spend. These decisions require a certain amount of consideration. So before rigorously planning specific details, you might want to establish your general travel objectives:

1. How much time will you have for the entire trip, and how much of it are you willing to spend getting where you're going?
2. What interests and/or activities do you want to pursue while on vacation? Do you want to visit one, a few, or several different places?
3. At what time of year do you want to go?
4. Do you want peace and privacy or lots of activity and company?
5. How much money can you afford to spend for the entire vacation?

There is an abundance of travel information on Mexico, including Acapulco. You can seek the assistance of travel agents, turn to travel clubs such as *AAA* and other motoring organizations, or use general travel sources such as guidebooks, brochures, and maps. Mexican tourist offices in ths US and Mexico have brochures and extensive material on all parts of Mexico, and there's a 24-hour information hotline in Mexico City (phone: 5-250-0123, 5-250-0493, 5-250-0151, or 5-250-0589). The US Government Printing Office's brochure *Tips for Travel* is another source of general information to the country. It can be obtained by sending $1 to the Superintendent of Documents (US Government Printing Office, Washington, DC 20402; phone: 202-783-3238).

You now can make almost all of your own travel arrangements if you have time to follow through with hotels, airlines, tour operators, and so on. But you'll probably save considerable time and energy if you have a travel agent make arrangements for you. The agent also should be able to advise you of alternative arrangements of which you may not be aware. Only rarely will a travel agent's services cost a traveler any money, and they may even save you some (see *How to Use a Travel Agent,* below).

If you are traveling by plane and want to benefit from savings offered by a charter flight to Acapulco (see *Traveling by Plane,* in this section), you may need reservations as much as 3 months in advance. In the high season, hotel reservations also are required months in advance. Many hotels in Acapulco require deposits before they will guarantee reservations, and this most often is the case during peak travel periods. (Be sure to request a receipt for any deposit.) Travel during *Easter Week,* the *Christmas/New Year* period, and local festival and national holiday times also requires reservations well in advance.

Make a list of any valuable items you are carrying with you, including credit card numbers and the serial numbers of your traveler's checks. Put copies in your purse or pocket and leave other copies at home. Put a label with your name and home address on the inside of your luggage for identification in case of loss. Put your name and business address — *never your home address* — on a label on the outside of your luggage. (Those who run businesses from home should use the office address of a friend or relative.)

Review your travel documents. If you are traveling by air, check that your ticket has been filled in correctly. The left side of the ticket should have a list of each stop you will make (even if you are only stopping to change planes), beginning with your departure point. Be sure that the list is correct, and count the number of copies to see that you have one for each plane you will take. If you have confirmed reservations, be sure that the column marked "status" says "OK" beside each flight. Have in hand vouchers or proof of payment for any reservation for which you've paid in advance; this includes hotels, transfers to and from the airport, sightseeing tours, car rentals, and special events. Although policies vary from carrier to carrier, it's still smart to reconfirm your flight 48 to 72 hours before departure, both going and returning.

Finally, you always should bear in mind that despite the most careful plans, things do not always occur on schedule — especially in Mexico, where *ahora* ("now") means anytime between today and tomorrow, and *ahorita* ("right now") means anytime within the next few hours. If you maintain a flexible attitude and try to accept minor disruptions as less than cataclysmic, you will enjoy yourself a lot more.

How to Use a Travel Agent

 A reliable travel agent remains your best source of service and information for planning a trip abroad, whether you have a specific itinerary and require an agent only to make reservations or you need extensive help in sorting through the maze of airfares, tour offerings, hotel packages, and the scores of other arrangements that may be involved in a trip to Acapulco.

Know what you want from a travel agent so that you can evaluate what you are getting. It is perfectly reasonable to expect your agent to be a thoroughly knowledgeable travel specialist, with information about your destination and, even more crucial, a command of current airfares, ground arrangements, and other wrinkles in the travel scene.

Most travel agents work through computer reservations systems (CRS). These are used to assess the availability and cost of flights, hotels, and car rentals, and through them they can book reservations. Despite reports of "computer bias," in which a computer may favor one airline over another, the CRS should provide agents with the entire spectrum of flights available to a given destination and the complete range of fares, in considerably less time than it takes to telephone the airlines individually — and at no extra cost to the client.

Make the most intelligent use of a travel agent's time and expertise; understand the economics of the industry. As a client, traditionally you pay nothing for the agent's services; with few exceptions, it's all free, from hotel bookings to advice on package tours. Any money the travel agent makes on the time spent arranging your itinerary — booking hotels, resorts, or flights, or suggesting activities — comes from commissions paid by the suppliers of these services — the airlines, hotels, and so on. These commissions generally run from 10% to 15% of the total cost of the service, although suppliers often reward agencies that sell their services in volume with an increased commission, called an override. In most instances, you'll find that travel agents make their time and experience available to you at no charge, and you do not pay more for an airline ticket, package tour, or other product bought from a travel agent than you would for the same one bought directly from the supplier.

Exceptions to the general rule of free service by a travel agency are the agencies beginning to practice net pricing. In essence, such agencies return their commissions and overrides to their customers and make their income by charging a flat fee per transaction instead (thus adding a charge after a reduction for the commission has been made). Net fares and fees are a growing practice, though hardly widespread.

Even a conventional travel agent sometimes may charge a fee for special services. These chargeable items may include long-distance telephone or cable costs incurred in making a booking, for reserving a room in a place that does not pay a commission (such as a small, out-of-the-way hotel), or for a special attention such as planning a highly personalized itinerary. A fee also may be assessed in instances of deeply discounted airfares.

Choose a travel agent with the same care with which you would choose a doctor or lawyer. You will be spending a good deal of money on the basis of the agent's judgment, so you have a right to expect that judgment to be mature, informed, and interested. At the moment, unfortunately, there aren't many standards within the travel agent industry to help you gauge competence, and the quality of individual agents varies enormously.

At present, only nine states have registration, licensing, or other forms of travel agent–related legislation on their books. Rhode Island licenses travel agents; Florida, Hawaii, Iowa, and Ohio register them; and California, Illinois, Oregon, and Washington have laws governing the sale of transportation or related services. While state licensing of agents cannot absolutely guarantee competence, it can at least ensure that an agent has met some minimum requirements.

Perhaps the best-prepared agents are those who have completed the CTC Travel Management program offered by the *Institute of Certified Travel Agents (ICTA)* and carry the initials CTC (Certified Travel Counselor) after their names. This indicates a relatively high level of expertise. For a free list of CTCs in your area, send a self-addressed, stamped, #10 envelope to *ICTA,* 148 Linden St., Box 56, Wellesley, MA 02181 (phone: 617-237-0280 in Massachusetts; 800-542-4282 elsewhere in the US).

An agent's membership in the *American Society of Travel Agents (ASTA)* can be a useful guideline in making a selection. But keep in mind that *ASTA* is an industry organization, requiring only that its members be licensed in those states where required; be accredited to represent the suppliers whose products they sell, including airline and cruise tickets; and adhere to its Principles of Professional Conduct and Ethics code. *ASTA* does not guarantee the competence, ethics, or financial soundness of its members, but it does offer some recourse if you feel you have been dealt with unfairly. Complaints may be registered with *ASTA* (Consumer Affairs Dept., 1101 King St., Alexandria, VA 22314; phone: 703-739-2782). First try to resolve the complaint directly with the supplier. For a list of *ASTA* members in your area, send a self-addressed, stamped, #10 envelope to *ASTA,* Public Relations Dept., at the address above.

There also is the *Association of Retail Travel Agents (ARTA),* a smaller but highly respected trade organization similar to *ASTA.* Its member agencies and agents similarly agree to abide by a code of ethics, and complaints about a member can be made to *ARTA*'s Grievance Committee, 1745 Jeff Davis Hwy., Arlington, VA 22202-3402 (phone: 800-969-6069 or 703-553-7777).

Perhaps the best way to find a travel agent is by word of mouth. If the agent (or agency) has done a good job for your friends over a period of time, it probably indicates a certain level of commitment and competence. Always ask not only for the name of the company, but also for the name of the specific agent with whom your friends dealt, for it is that individual who will serve you, and quality can vary widely within a single agency. There are some superb travel agents in the business, and they can facilitate vacation or business arrangements.

You may decide to use a travel agent within Mexico to set up tours for the duration or for portions of your stay. Among the leading travel agencies that have offices in Acapulco are the following:

American Express Travel Related Services: 709-1 Costera Miguel Alemán (phone: 74-845550).

Aviamex Tours de México: Centro Comercial, 224/225 Placa Condesa (phone: 74-844755 or 74-843715).

Turismo Caleta: 4 Andrea Doria (phone: 74-846570; fax: 74-846571).

Wagons-lits Mexicana: In the lobby of *Las Brisas Hotel* (phone: 74-841650, ext. 394).

Entry Requirements and Documents

Regardless of the transportation you use, you will need a tourist card to enter Mexico. The only exception to this rule is that if you intend to visit border towns (those within approximately 12½ miles/20 km of the Mexican border) and not to travel any farther into Mexico, you can do so without a tourist card for a stay of up to 24 hours.

In order to obtain a tourist card, you must have proof of your US citizenship. This proof may consist of an original or certified copy of a birth certificate, a voter's registration certificate, or a valid passport. Those forms of identification without a photograph also must be accompanied by some form of official photo ID. A driver's license alone will not suffice, however, nor will a credit card or military papers. A naturalized citizen must present at least one of the following documents: naturalization papers, a US passport, or an affidavit of citizenship.

A tourist card can be obtained from a number of sources, including any Mexican Ministry of Tourism office or Mexican consulate in the US; the Mexican government border offices at any port of entry; and some travel agencies. Regardless of where you obtain the card, when you cross the border you must sign it in the presence of the Mexican immigration official, who also may ask to see proof of your citizenship. For those arriving by plane, the card can be obtained from any airline ticket office and it must be presented along with proof of citizenship when you land in Mexico. The tourist card allows you to stay in Mexico for a specified number of days; if you request one for 90 days — the maximum is 6 months — you don't have to stay that long but you are covered for that period of time.

To obtain a tourist card, minors under 18 who are traveling alone must have a passport and a copy of a letter (indicating permission) signed by both parents or legal guardians. If the minor is traveling with only one parent or guardian, a passport and a letter signed by the other (or proof that this person is the sole legal guardian) is needed. Note that the letter must be notarized and be accompanied by a detailed itinerary of the minor's travel plans.

During your stay in Mexico, you always should carry your tourist card with you, although you aren't likely to be asked for it after the border crossing. If you happen to lose your card, you should report it immediately to the nearest office of the Secretaría de Gobernación. They should be able to replace it for you.

US citizens will not need any vaccination certificates in order to enter Mexico for a short period of time. There are, however, a number of vaccinations that travelers to Mexico would be well advised to have before leaving and medicines that should be brought along. (See *Staying Healthy,* in this section, for our recommendations and other information on health concerns and precautions.)

A valid passport is the best proof of US citizenship to carry when traveling through

Mexico. You should keep your passport with you at all times, and if you lose it while abroad, immediately report the loss to the nearest US consulate or embassy (for locations in Mexico, see *Legal Aid and Consular Services,* in this section). It's likely to speed up the replacement process if you have a record of your passport number and the place and date of its issue (a photocopy of the first page of your passport is perfect). Keep this information separate from your passport — you might want to give it to a traveling companion to hold or put it in the bottom of your suitcase.

DUTY AND CUSTOMS: As a general rule, the requirements for bringing the majority of items into Mexico is that they must be quantities small enough not to imply commercial import.

If you are accustomed to certain American brands of bourbon or whiskey (although imported brands are increasingly available in Mexico, they are very costly), you are allowed to bring 2 liters of liquor into Mexico duty-free — any amount over this will be taxed. And if you prefer American cigarettes, be advised that the limit is 1 carton (20 packs). Each person also may bring in one still and one video camera, plus a total of 12 rolls of film and/or video cartridge tapes. For further information on Mexican customs regulations, contact the Mexican Ministry of Tourism offices or Mexican consulates in the US (see *Sources and Resources,* in this section, for addresses).

If you are bringing along a computer, camera, or other electronic equipment for your own use that you will be taking back to the US, you should register the item with the US Customs Service in order to avoid paying duty both entering and returning from Mexico. (Also see *Customs and Returning to the US,* in this section.) For information on this procedure, as well as for a variety of pamphlets on US Customs regulations, contact the local office of the US Customs Service or the central office, PO Box 7407, Washington, DC 20044 (phone: 202-566-8195).

■ **One rule to follow:** When passing through customs, it is illegal not to declare dutiable items; penalties range from stiff fines and seizure of the goods to prison terms. So don't try to sneak anything through — it just isn't worth it.

Insurance

It is unfortunate that most decisions to buy travel insurance are impulsive and usually are made without any real consideration of the traveler's existing policies. Therefore, the first person with whom you should discuss travel insurance is your own insurance broker, not a travel agent or the clerk behind the airport insurance counter. You may discover that the insurance you already carry protects you adequately while you travel or that you need no more than excess value insurance for baggage, or trip cancellation insurance.

TYPES OF INSURANCE: To make insurance decisions intelligently, however, you first should understand the basic categories of travel insurance and what they cover. Then you can decide what you should have in the broader context of your personal insurance needs, and you can choose the most economical way of getting the desired protection: through riders on existing policies; with onetime short-term policies; through a special program put together for the frequent traveler; through coverage that's part of a travel club's benefits; or with a combination policy sold by insurance companies through brokers, automobile clubs, tour operators, and travel agents.

There are seven basic categories of travel insurance:

1. Baggage and personal effects insurance
2. Personal accident and sickness insurance
3. Trip cancellation and interruption insurance

4. Default and/or bankruptcy insurance
5. Flight insurance (to cover injury or death)
6. Automobile insurance (for driving your own or a rented car)
7. Combination policies

Baggage and Personal Effects Insurance – Ask your insurance agent if baggage and personal effects are included in your current homeowner's policy, or if you will need a special floater to cover you for the duration of a trip. The object is to protect your bags and their contents in case of damage or theft anytime during your travels, not just while you're in flight and covered by the airline's policy. Furthermore, only limited protection is provided by the airline (see *Traveling by Plane,* in this section).

If you are carrying goods worth more than the maximum protection offered by the airline, consider excess value insurance. Additional coverage is available from the airlines at an average, currently, of $1 to $2 per $100 worth of coverage, up to a maximum of $5,000. This insurance can be purchased at the airline counter when you check in, though you should arrive early to fill out the necessary forms and to avoid holding up other passengers.

Major credit card companies also provide coverage for lost or delayed baggage — and this coverage often also is over and above what the airline will pay. The basic coverage is automatic for all cardholders who use the credit card to purchase tickets, but to qualify for additional coverage, cardholders generally must enroll.

American Express: Provides $500 coverage for checked baggage; $1,250 for carry-on baggage; and $250 for valuables, such as cameras and jewelry.

Carte Blanche and Diners Club: Each provides $1,250 worth of free insurance for checked or carry-on baggage that's lost or damaged.

Discover Card: Offers $500 insurance for checked baggage and $1,250 for carry-on baggage — but to qualify for this coverage, cardholders first must purchase additional flight insurance (see "Flight Insurance," below).

MasterCard and Visa: Baggage insurance coverage is set by the issuing institution.

Additional baggage and personal effects insurance also is included in certain of the combination travel insurance policies discussed below.

■**A note of warning:** Be sure to read the fine print of any excess value insurance policy; there often are specific exclusions, such as cash, tickets, furs, gold and silver objects, art, and antiques. And remember that insurance companies ordinarily will pay only the depreciated value of the goods rather than their replacement value. The best way to protect the items you're carrying in your luggage is to take photos of your valuables and keep a record of the serial numbers of such items as cameras, laptops, radios, and so on. This will establish that you do, indeed, own the objects. If your luggage disappears en route or is damaged, deal with the situation immediately.

Personal Accident and Sickness Insurance – This covers you in case of illness during your trip or death in an accident. Most policies insure you for hospital and doctor's expenses, lost income, and so on. In most cases, it is a standard part of existing health insurance policies, though you should check with your insurance broker to be sure that your policy will pay for any medical expenses incurred abroad. If not, take out a separate vacation accident policy or an entire vacation insurance policy that includes health and life coverage.

One company offering such comprehensive health and life insurance policies is *Wallach & Co.* Both their HealthCare Global and HealthCare Abroad programs may be bought in combination with trip cancellation and baggage insurance at extra cost.

For information, write to *Wallach & Co.,* 107 W. Federal St., Box 480, Middleburg, VA 22117-0480 (phone: 703-687-3166 in Virginia; 800-237-6615 elsewhere in the US).

Trip Cancellation and Interruption Insurance – Most charter and package tour passengers pay for their travel well before departure. The disappointment of having to miss a vacation because of illness or any other reason pales before the awful prospect that not all (and sometimes none) of the money paid in advance might be returned. So cancellation insurance for any package tour is a must.

Although cancellation penalties vary (they are listed in the fine print of every tour brochure, and before you purchase a package tour you should know exactly what they are), rarely will a passenger get more than 50% of this money back if forced to cancel within a few weeks of scheduled departure. Therefore, if you book a package tour or charter flight, you should have trip cancellation insurance to guarantee full reimbursement or refund should you, a traveling companion, or a member of your immediate family get sick, forcing you to cancel your trip or *return home early.*

The key here is *not* to buy just enough insurance to guarantee full reimbursement for the cost of the package or charter in case of cancellation. The proper amount of coverage should be sufficient to reimburse you for the cost of having to catch up with a tour after its departure or having to travel home at the full economy airfare (from the farthest destination on your itinerary) if you have to forgo your return flight of your charter. There is usually quite a discrepancy between a charter fare and the amount necessary to travel the same distance on a regularly scheduled flight at full economy fare.

Trip cancellation insurance is available from travel agents and tour operators in two forms: as part of a short-term, all-purpose travel insurance package (sold by the travel agent); or as specific cancellation insurance designed by the tour operator for a specific charter tour. Generally, tour operators' policies are less expensive, but also less inclusive. Cancellation insurance also is available directly from insurance companies or their agents as part of a short-term, all-inclusive travel insurance policy.

Before you decide on a policy, read each one carefully. (Either type can be purchased from a travel agent when you book the charter or package tour.) Be certain that your policy includes enough coverage to pay your fare from the farthest destination on your itinerary should you have to miss the charter flight. Also, be sure to check the fine print for stipulations concerning "family members" and "pre-existing medical conditions," as well as allowances for living expenses if you must delay your return due to bodily injury or illness.

Default and/or Bankruptcy Insurance – Although trip cancellation insurance usually protects you if *you* are unable to complete — or begin — your trip, a fairly recent innovation is coverage in the event of default and/or bankruptcy on the part of the tour operator, airline, or other travel supplier. In some travel insurance packages, this contingency is included in the trip cancellation portion of the coverage; in others, it is a separate feature. Either way, it is becoming increasingly important. Although sophisticated travelers have long known to beware of the possibility of default or bankruptcy when buying a charter flight ticket or a tour package, in recent years more than a few respected airlines have unexpectedly revealed their shaky financial condition, sometimes leaving hordes of stranded ticket holders in their wake. Moreover, the value of escrow protection of a charter passenger's funds lately has been unreliable. While default/bankruptcy insurance will not ordinarily result in reimbursement in time to pay for new arrangements, it can ensure that you will get your money back, and even independent travelers buying no more than an airplane ticket may want to consider it.

Flight Insurance – Airlines have carefully established limits of liability for injury to or the death of passengers on international flights. For international flights to, from, or with a stopover in the US, all carriers are liable for up to $75,000 per passenger.

For all other international flights, the liability is based on where you purchase the ticket: If booked in advance in the US, the maximum liability is $75,000; if arrangements are made abroad, the liability is $10,000. But remember, these liabilities are not the same thing as insurance policies; every penny that an airline eventually pays in the case of injury or death will likely be subject to a legal battle.

But before you buy last-minute flight insurance from an airport vending machine, consider the purchase in light of your total existing insurance coverage. A careful review of your current policies may reveal that you already are amply covered for accidental death, sometimes up to three times the amount provided for by the flight insurance you're buying at the airport.

Be aware that airport insurance, the kind typically bought at a counter or from a vending machine, is among the most expensive forms of life insurance coverage, and that even within a single airport, rates for approximately the same coverage vary widely. Often policies sold in vending machines are more expensive than those sold over the counter, even when they are with the same national company.

If you buy your plane ticket with a major credit card, you generally receive automatic insurance coverage at no extra cost. Additional coverage usually can be obtained at extremely reasonable prices, but a cardholder must sign up for it in advance. (Note that rates vary slightly for residents of some states.) As we went to press, the travel accident and life insurance policies of these major credit cards were as follows:

American Express: Automatically provides $100,000 in insurance to its *Green, Gold,* and *Optima* cardholders, and $500,000 to *Platinum* cardholders. With *American Express,* $4.50 per ticket buys an additional $250,000 worth of flight insurance; $7.50 buys $500,000 worth; and $14 provides an added $1 million worth of coverage.

Carte Blanche: Automatically provides $125,000 flight insurance.

Diners Club: Provides $350,000 free flight insurance. An additional $250,000 worth of insurance is available for $4; $500,000 costs $6.50.

Discover Card: Provides $500,000 free flight insurance. An additional $250,000 worth of insurance is available for $4.50; $500,000 costs $6.50.

MasterCard and Visa: Insurance coverage for each is set by the issuing institution.

Automobile Insurance – When you rent a car, the rental company is required to offer you insurance. In your car rental contract, you'll see that for about $9 to $13 a day, you may buy optional collision damage waiver (CDW) protection. (If partial coverage with a deductible is included in the rental contract, the CDW will cover the deductible in the event of an accident, and can cost as much as $25 per day.)

If you do not accept the CDW coverage, you may be liable for as much as the full retail value of the rental car; by paying for the CDW you are relieved of all responsibility for any damage to the car. Before agreeing to this coverage, however, check with your own broker about your existing personal automobile insurance policy. It very well may cover your entire liability exposure without any additional cost, or you automatically may be covered by the credit card company to which you are charging the cost of your rental. To find out the amount of rental car insurance provided by major credit cards, contact the issuing institutions.

You also should know that an increasing number of the major international car rental companies are automatically including the cost of the CDW in their basic rates. Car rental prices have increased to include this coverage, although rental company ad campaigns may promote this as a new, improved rental package "benefit." The disadvantage of this inclusion is that you may not have the option to turn down the CDW — even if you already are adequately covered by your own insurance policy or through a credit card company.

Combination Policies – Short-term insurance policies, which may include a combination of any or all of the types of insurance discussed above, are available through retail insurance agencies, automobile clubs, and many travel agents. These combination policies are designed to cover you for the duration of a single trip.

Companies offering policies of this type include the following:

Access America (PO Box 90310, Richmond, VA 23230; phone: 800-284-8300).

Carefree Travel Insurance (Arm Coverage, PO Box 310, Mineola, NY 11501; phone: 800-645-2424 or 516-294-0220).

NEAR Services (450 Prairie Ave., Suite 101, Calumet City, IL 60409; phone: 800-654-6700, or 708-868-6700 in the Chicago area).

Tele-Trip (3201 Farnam St., Omaha, NE 68131; phone: 402-345-2400 in Nebraska; 800-228-9792 elsewhere in the US).

Travel Assistance International (1133 15th St. NW, Suite 400, Washington, DC 20005; phone: 202-331-1609 in Washington, DC; 800-821-2828 elsewhere in the US).

The Travelers Company (Ticket and Travel Plans, One Tower Sq., Hartford, CT 06183-5040; phone: 203-277-2319 in Connecticut; 800-243-3174 elsewhere in the US).

Travel Guard International (1145 Clark St., Stevens Point, WI 54481; phone: 715-345-0505 in Wisconsin; 800-826-1300 elsewhere in the US).

Hints for Handicapped Travelers

From 40 to 50 million people in the US alone have some sort of disability, and over half this number are physically handicapped. Like everyone else today, they — and the uncounted disabled millions around the world — are on the move. More than ever before, they are demanding facilities they can use comfortably, and they are being heard.

Those who have chosen to visit Mexico are in luck, because more and more disabled travelers are returning from this most luscious of destinations bearing tales of ramped sidewalks, a style of warm-weather architecture that erects fewer barriers between the indoors and the outdoors, and sightseeing tours designed especially for them. Also, in recent years, a series of imaginative, pan-American programs aimed at improving facilities and services for the handicapped in Mexico and Latin America have been initiated. Chief among these is *Partners of the Americas,* with chapters based in 45 states, which coordinates joint projects with these states in various Mexican and Latin American areas. *Partners of the Americas* also maintains a library with information on programs for the handicapped throughout Mexico, as well as Central and South America, and they often can put disabled travelers in touch with self-help organizations of disabled persons in these locations. For more information, contact the central office of *Partners of the Americas,* 1424 K St. NW, Suite 700, Washington, DC 20005 (phone: 800-322-7844 or 202-628-3300).

Despite this effort to develop special facilities for the disabled, however, handicapped travelers face pretty much the same problems in Mexico as in most other parts of the world. Rural areas have no facilities. Cities have some, but there is no consistency.

PLANNING: Collect as much information as you can about your specific disability and facilities for the disabled in Mexico. Make your travel arrangements well in advance and specify to all services involved the exact nature of your condition or restricted mobility to ensure accommodations and facilities to suit your needs. The best way to find out if your intended destination can accommodate a handicapped traveler is to write or call the local tourist authority or hotel and ask specific questions. If you require a corridor of a certain width to maneuver a wheelchair or if you need rails on the bathroom walls for support, ask the hotel manager. A travel agent or an organization that deals with your particular disability — for example, the *American Foundation for the Blind* — will supply the most up-to-date information on the subject. The following organizations offer general information on access:

ACCENT on Living (PO Box 700, Bloomington, IL 61702; phone: 309-378-2961). This information service for persons with disabilities provides a free list of travel agencies specializing in trips for the disabled; for a copy send a self-addressed, stamped envelope. Also offers a wide range of publications, including a quarterly magazine ($10 per year; $17.50 for 2 years) for travelers with disabilities.

Information Center for Individuals with Disabilities (Fort Point Pl., 1st Floor, 27-43 Wormwood St., Boston, MA 02210; phone: 800-462-5015 in Massachusetts; 617-727-5540/1 elsewhere in the US; both numbers provide voice and TDD — telecommunications device for the deaf). The center offers information and referral services on disability-related issues, publishes fact sheets on travel resources, and can help you research your trip.

Mobility International USA (*MIUSA;* PO Box 3551, Eugene, OR 97403; phone: 503-343-1284; both voice and TDD). This US branch of *Mobility International* (the main office is at 228 Borough High St., London SE1 1JX, England; phone: 44-71-403-5688), a nonprofit British organization with affiliates worldwide, offers members advice and assistance — -including information on accommodations and other travel services, and publications applicable to the traveler's disability. *Mobility International* also offers a quarterly newsletter and a comprehensive sourcebook, *A World of Options for the 90s: A Guide to International Education Exchange, Community Service and Travel for Persons with Disabilities* ($14 for members; $16 for non-members). Membership includes the newsletter and is $20 a year; subscription to the newsletter alone is $10 annually.

National Rehabilitation Information Center (8455 Colesville Rd., Suite 935, Silver Spring, MD 20910; phone: 301-588-9284). A general information, resource, research, and referral service.

Paralyzed Veterans of America (*PVA;* PVA/ATTS Program, 801 18th St. NW, Washington, DC 20006; phone: 202-416-7708 in Washington, DC; 800-424-8200 elsewhere in the US). The members of this national service organization all are veterans who have suffered spinal cord injuries, but it offers advocacy services and information to all disabled persons. *PVA* also sponsors *Access to the Skies (ATTS),* a program that coordinates the efforts of the air travel industry to increase accessibility. Members receive several helpful publications and notification of conferences of interest to disabled travelers.

Royal Association for Disability and Rehabilitation (*RADAR;* 25 Mortimer St., London W1N 8AB, England; phone: 44-71-637-5400). Offers a number of useful publications, including a comprehensive guide to international travel, *Holidays and Travel Abroad 1992/1993 — A Guide for Disabled People* (just over £3 as we went to press; payment must be sent in British pounds).

Society for the Advancement of Travel for the Handicapped (*SATH;* 347 Fifth Ave., Suite 610, New York, NY 10016; phone: 212-447-7284). Members of this nonprofit organization include consumers and travel service professionals. For an annual fee of $45 ($25 for students and travelers 65 and older), members receive a quarterly newsletter and have access to information and referral services. Also offers two useful publications: *Travel Tips for the Handicapped* (a series of informative fact sheets) and *The United States Welcomes Handicapped Visitors* (a 48-page guide covering domestic transportation and accommodations that includes useful hints for disabled travelers abroad); to order, send a self-addressed, #10 envelope and $1 per title for postage.

Travel Information Service (Moss Rehabilitation Hospital, 1200 W. Tabor Rd., Philadelphia, PA 19141-3099; phone: 215-456-9600 for voice; 215-456-9602 for TDD). This service assists physically handicapped people in planning trips and supplies detailed information on accessibility for a nominal fee.

Blind travelers should contact the *American Foundation for the Blind* (15 W. 16th St., New York, NY 10011; phone: 800-829-0500 or 212-620-2147) and *The Seeing Eye* (Box 375, Morristown, NJ 07963-0375; phone: 201-539-4425); both provide useful information on resources for the visually impaired. *Note:* Seeing Eye dogs arriving in Mexico must be accompanied by a certificate of inoculation against rabies, hepatitis, and distemper, as well as a certificate of health, issued within the previous 3 months and certified by the US Department of Agriculture. These certificates must be authorized by a Mexican consul (for a fee of $20 at press time). *The American Society for the Prevention of Cruelty to Animals* (*ASPCA*, Education Dept., 441 E. 92nd St., New York, NY 10128; phone: 212-876-7700) offers a useful booklet, *Traveling With Your Pet* ($5, postpaid), which lists inoculation and other requirements by country.

In addition, there are a number of publications — from travel guides to magazines — of interest to handicapped travelers. Among these are the following:

Access to the World, by Louise Weiss, offers sound tips for the disabled traveler ($16.95; Facts on File, 460 Park Ave. S., New York, NY 10016; phone: 212-683-2244 in New York State; 800-322-8755 elsewhere in the US; 800-443-8323 in Canada).

The Diabetic Traveler is a useful quarterly newsletter. Each issue highlights a single destination or type of travel and includes information on general resources and hints for diabetics. A 1-year subscription costs $15. When subscribing, ask for the free fact sheet including an index of special articles; back issues are available for $4 each (PO Box 8223 RW, Stamford, CT 06905; phone: 203-327-5832).

Guide to Traveling with Arthritis, a free brochure available by writing to the Upjohn Company (PO Box 307-B, Coventry, CT 06238), provides common-sense tips on trip planning and comfort while traveling.

Handicapped Travel Newsletter is a bimonthly publication edited by wheelchair-bound Vietnam veteran and world traveler Michael Quigley. To subscribe, send $10 to PO Box 269, Athens, TX 75751 (phone: 903-677-1260).

Handi-Travel: A Resource Book for Disabled and Elderly Travellers, by Cinnie Noble, is full of practical tips for those with disabilities affecting mobility, hearing, or sight. To order, send $12.95, plus postage, to the *Canadian Rehabilitation Council for the Disabled,* 45 Sheppard Ave. E., Suite 801, Toronto, Ontario M2N 5W9, Canada (phone: 416-250-7490; both voice and TDD).

The Itinerary, a bimonthly travel magazine for people with disabilities, includes information on accessibility, tours, adaptive devices and aids, special services, and travel hints. To subscribe, send $10 to PO Box 2012, Bayonne, NJ 07002-2012 (phone: 201-858-3400).

The Physically Disabled Traveler's Guide, by Rod W. Durgin and Norene Lindsay, rates accessibility and includes a list of organizations specializing in travel for the disabled. It is available for $9.95, plus shipping and handling, from *Resource Directories,* 3361 Executive Pkwy., Suite 302, Toledo, OH 43606 (phone: 419-536-5353 in the Toledo area; 800-274-8515 elsewhere in the US).

Ticket to Safe Travel offers useful information for diabetic travelers. This reprint of an article is available from the *American Diabetes Association;* for the nearest local chapter, contact the central office at 505 Eighth Ave., 21st Floor, New York, NY 10018 (phone: 212-947-9707 in New York State; 800-232-3472 elsewhere in the US).

Travel for the Patient with Chronic Obstructive Pulmonary Disease, a publication of the George Washington University Medical Center, provides practical suggestions for those with asthma, bronchitis, or other lung ailments. To order, send $2 to Dr. Harold Silver, 1601 18th St. NW, Washington, DC 20009 (phone: 202-667-0134).

Traveling Like Everybody Else: A Practical Guide for Disabled Travelers, by Jacqueline Freedman and Susan Gersten, offers travel tips and resources, including lists of accessible accommodations and tour operators specializing in tours for disabled travelers. To order, send $11.95, plus postage, to Modan Publishing, PO Box 1202, Bellmore, NY 11710 (phone: 516-679-1380).

Travel Tips for Hearing Impaired People, a free pamphlet for deaf and hearing-impaired travelers, is available by sending a self-addressed, stamped, business-size envelope to the *American Academy of Otolaryngology,* One Prince St., Alexandria, VA 22314 (phone: 703-836-4444).

Travel Tips for People with Arthritis, a 31-page booklet, provides helpful information regarding transportation, trip planning, medical considerations, and conserving your energy while traveling. It also includes listings of helpful resources for disabled travelers. For a copy, contact your local *Arthritis Foundation* chapter, or send $1 to the national office, PO Box 19000, Atlanta, GA 30326 (phone: 404-872-7100).

The Wheelchair Traveler lists accessible accommodations in Mexico, including Acapulco. To order a copy, and for current pricing, contact the author, Douglass R. Annand, 123 Ball Hill Rd., Milford, NH 03055 (phone: 603-673-4539).

A few more basic resources to look for are *Travel for the Disabled* ($19.95) and *Directory of Travel Agencies for the Disabled* ($19.95), both by Helen Hecker, and *Wheelchair Vagabond* (hardcover, $14.95; paperback, $9.95), by John G. Nelson. All three titles are published by Twin Peaks Press, PO Box 129, Vancouver, WA 98666 (phone: 800-637-CALM or 206-694-2462). The publisher offers a catalogue of 26 other books on travel for the disabled for $2.

PLANE: Disabled passengers should always make reservations well in advance, and should provide the airline with all relevant details of their condition. These details include information on mobility and equipment that you will need the airline to supply — such as a wheelchair for boarding or portable oxygen for in-flight use. Be sure that the person to whom you speak fully understands the degree of your disability — the more details provided, the more effective help the airline can give you.

On the day before your flight, call back to make sure that all arrangements have been prepared, and arrive early on the day of the flight so that you can board before the rest of the passengers. It's a good idea to bring a medical certificate with you, stating your specific disability or the need to carry particular medicine.

Because most airports have jetways (corridors connecting the terminal with the door of the plane), a disabled passenger usually can be taken as far as the plane, and sometimes right onto it, in a wheelchair. If not, a narrow boarding chair may be used to take you to your seat. Your own wheelchair, which will be folded and put in the baggage compartment, should be tagged as escort luggage to assure that it's available at planeside upon landing rather than in the baggage claim area. Travel is not quite as simple if your wheelchair is battery-operated: Unless it has non-spillable batteries, it might not be accepted on board, and you will have to check with the airline ahead of time to find out how the batteries and the chair should be packaged for the flight. Usually people in wheelchairs are asked to wait until other passengers have disembarked. If you are making a tight connection, be sure to tell the attendant.

Passengers who use oxygen may not use their personal supply in the cabin, though it may be carried on the plane as cargo (the tank must be emptied) when properly packed and labeled. If you will need oxygen during the flight, the airline will supply it to you (there is a charge) provided you have given advance notice — 24 hours to a few days, depending on the carrier.

Among the airlines flying to Acapulco, TDD toll-free lines for the hearing-impaired are provided by *American* (phone: 800-582-1573 in Ohio; 800-543-1586 elsewhere in the US), *Continental* (phone: 800-343-9195), and *Delta* (phone: 800-831-4488).

The free booklet *Air Transportation of Handicapped Persons* explains the general guidelines that govern air carrier policies. For a copy, write to the US Department of Transportation (Distribution Unit, Publications Section, M-443-2, Washington, DC 20590) and ask for "Free Advisory Circular #AC-120-32." *Access Travel: A Guide to the Accessibility of Airport Terminals,* a free publication of the *Airport Operators Council International,* provides information on more than 500 airports worldwide — including major Mexican airports — and offers ratings of 70 features, such as wheelchair-accessible bathrooms, corridor width, and parking spaces. For a copy, contact the Consumer Information Center (Dept. 563W, Pueblo, CO 81009; phone: 719-948-3334). Useful information on every stage of air travel, from planning to arrival, is provided in the booklet *Incapacitated Passengers Air Travel Guide.* To receive a free copy, write to the International Air Transport Association (Publications Sales Department, 2000 Peel St., Montreal, Quebec H3A 2R4, Canada; phone: 514-844-6311).

SHIP: Check with your travel agent or cruise line when making reservations, as some cruise ships cannot accommodate handicapped travelers because of their many sets of narrow steps, which are less convenient than wide ramps. Handicapped travelers are advised to book their trip at least 90 days in advance to reserve specialized cabins. *Cunard, Holland America,* and *Royal Cruise Line* offer sailings to Acapulco for the physically challenged.

For those in wheelchairs or with limited mobility, one of the best sources for evaluating a ship's accessibility is the free chart issued by the *Cruise Lines International Association* (500 Fifth Ave., Suite 1407, New York, NY 10110; phone: 212-921-0066). The chart lists accessible ships and indicates whether they accommodate standard-size or only narrow wheelchairs, have ramps, wide doors, low or no doorsills, handrails in the rooms, and so on. (For further information on ships cruising Mexican waters, see *Traveling by Ship,* in this section.)

GROUND TRANSPORTATION: Perhaps the simplest solution to getting around is to travel with an able-bodied companion who can drive. Another alternative in Mexico is to hire a driver/translator with a car — be sure to get a recommendation from a reputable source. The organizations listed above may be able to help you make arrangements — another source is your hotel concierge.

If you are accustomed to driving your own hand-controlled car and determined to rent one in Mexico, you may have to do some extensive research. If agencies do provide hand-controlled cars, they are apt to be offered only on a limited basis and usually are in high demand. The best course is to contact the major car rental companies listed in *Traveling by Car,* in this section, well before your departure, but be forewarned: You still may be out of luck. Other sources for information on vehicles adapted for the handicapped are the organizations discussed above.

The *American Automobile Association (AAA)* publishes a helpful book, *The Handicapped Driver's Mobility Guide.* Contact the central office of your local *AAA* club for availability and pricing, which may vary in different branch offices.

TOURS: Programs designed for the physically impaired are run by specialists who have researched hotels, restaurants, and sites to be sure they present no insurmountable obstacles. The following travel agencies or tour operators specialize in making group or individual arrangements for travelers with physical or other disabilities:

Access: The Foundation for Accessibility by the Disabled (PO Box 356, Malverne, NY 11565; phone: 516-887-5798). A travelers' referral service that acts as an intermediary with tour operators and agents worldwide, and provides information on accessibility.

Accessible Journeys (412 S. 45th St., Philadelphia, PA 19104; phone: 215-747-0171). Arranges for traveling companions who are medical professionals — registered or licensed practical nurses, therapists, or doctors (all are experienced travelers). Several prospective companions' profiles and photos are sent to the client for perusal, and if one is acceptable, the "match" is made. The client usually pays all travel expenses for the companion, plus a set fee to compensate for wages the companion would be making at his or her usual job. This company also offers tours and cruises for people with special needs, although you don't have to take one of their tours to hire a companion through them.

Accessible Tours/Directions Unlimited (720 N. Bedford Rd., Bedford Hills, NY 10507; phone: 914-241-1700 in New York State; 800-533-5343 elsewhere in the continental US). Arranges group or individual tours for disabled persons traveling in the company of able-bodied friends or family members. Accepts the unaccompanied traveler if completely self-sufficient.

Dialysis at Sea Cruises (611 Barry Place, Indian Rocks Beach, FL 34635; phone: 800-544-7604 or 813-596-7604). Offers cruises that include full medical services, including a nephrologist (a specialist in kidney disease) and dialysis nurses. Although family and companions are welcome, the number of patients usually is limited to roughly ten travelers per trip.

Evergreen Travel Service (4114 198th St. SW, Suite 13, Lynnwood, WA 98036-6742; phone: 800-435-2288 or 206-776-1184). Offers worldwide tours and cruises for the disabled (Wings on Wheels Tours), sight impaired/blind (White Cane Tours), and hearing impaired/deaf (Flying Fingers Tours). Most programs are first class or deluxe, and include a trained escort.

Flying Wheels Travel (143 W. Bridge St., Box 382, Owatonna, MN 55060; phone: 800-535-6790 or 507-451-5005). Handles both tours and individual arrangements.

The Guided Tour (613 W. Cheltenham Ave., Suite 200, Melrose Park, PA 19126; phone: 215-782-1370). Arranges tours for people with developmental or learning disabilities and sponsors separate tours for members of the same population who also are physically disabled or who simply need a slower pace.

Sprout (893 Amsterdam Ave., New York, NY 10025; phone: 212-222-9575). Arranges travel programs for mildly and moderately disabled teens and adults.

USTS Travel Horizons (11 E. 44th St., New York, NY 10017; phone: 800-487-8787 or 212-687-5121). Travel agent and registered nurse Mary Ann Hamm makes all arrangements for travelers requiring kidney dialysis.

Whole Person Tours (PO Box 1084, Bayonne, NJ 07002-1084; phone: 201-858-3400). Owner Bob Zywicki travels the world with his wheelchair and offers a lineup of escorted tours (many conducted by him) for the disabled. *Whole Person Tours* also publishes *The Itinerary* (see above).

Travelers who would benefit from being accompanied by a nurse or physical therapist also can hire a companion through *Traveling Nurses' Network,* a service provided by Twin Peaks Press (PO Box 129, Vancouver, WA 98666; phone: 800-637-CALM or

206-694-2462). For a $10 fee, clients receive the names of three nurses, whom they can then contact directly; for $125, the agency will make all the hiring arrangements for the client. Travel arrangements also may be made in some cases — the fee for this further service is determined on an individual basis.

A similar service is offered by *MedEscort International* (ABE International Airport, PO Box 8766, Allentown, PA 18105; phone: 800-255-7182 in the continental US; elsewhere call 215-791-3111). Clients can arrange to be accompanied by a nurse, paramedic, respiratory therapist, or physician through *MedEscort.* The fees are based on the disabled traveler's needs. This service also can assist in making travel arrangements.

Hints for Single Travelers

Just about the last trip in human history on which the participants were neatly paired was the voyage of Noah's Ark. Ever since, passenger lists and tour groups have reflected the same kind of asymmetry that occurs in real life, as countless individuals set forth to see the world unaccompanied (or unencumbered, depending on your outlook) by spouse, lover, friend, or relative. Unfortunately, traveling alone can turn a traveler into a second class citizen.

The truth is that the travel industry is not very fair to people who vacation by themselves. People traveling alone almost invariably end up paying more than individuals traveling in pairs. Most travel bargains, including package tours, accommodations, resort packages, and cruises, are based on *double occupancy* rates. This means that the per-person price is offered on the basis of two people traveling together and sharing a double room (which means they each will spend a good deal more on meals and extras). The single traveler will have to pay a surcharge, called a single supplement, for exactly the same package. In extreme cases, this can add as much as 35% — and sometimes more — to to the basic per-person rate.

Don't despair, however. Throughout Mexico, there are scores of smaller hotels and other hostelries where, in addition to a cozier atmosphere, prices still are quite reasonable for the single traveler. And some ship lines have begun to offer special cruises for singles.

The obvious, most effective alternative is to find a traveling companion. Even special "singles' tours" that promise no supplements are usually based on people sharing double rooms. Perhaps the most recent innovation along these lines is the creation of organizations that "introduce" the single traveler to other single travelers, somewhat like a dating service. Some charge fees, others are free, but the basic service offered is the same: to match an unattached person with a compatible travel mate, often as part of the company's own package tours. Among such organizations are the following:

Partners-in-Travel (PO Box 491145, Los Angeles, CA 90049; phone: 213-476-4869). Members receive a list of singles seeking traveling companions; prospective companions make contact through the agency. The membership fee is $40 per year and includes a chatty newsletter (6 issues per year).

Singleworld (401 Theodore Fremd Ave., Rye, NY 10580; phone: 914-967-3334 or 800-223-6490 in the continental US). For a yearly fee of $25, this club books members on tours and cruises, and arranges shared accommodations, allowing individual travelers to avoid the single supplement charge; members also receive a quarterly newsletter. *Singleworld* also offers its own package tours for singles, with departures categorized by age group: 35 or younger, or tours for all ages.

Travel Companion Exchange (PO Box 833, Amityville, NY 11701; phone: 516-454-0880). This group publishes a newsletter for singles and a directory of individuals looking for travel companions. On joining, members fill out a lengthy questionnaire and write a small listing (much like an ad in a personal column). Based on these listings, members can request copies of profiles and contact prospective traveling companions. It is wise to join well in advance of your planned vacation so that there's enough time to determine compatibility and plan a joint trip. Membership fees, including the newsletter, are $36 for 6 months or $60 a year for a single-sex listing; $66 and $120, respectively, for a complete listing. Subscription to the newsletter alone costs $24 for 6 months or $36 per year.

Also note that certain cruise lines offer guaranteed shared rates for single travelers, whereby cabin mates are selected on request. Two cruise lines that provide such rates are *Cunard* (phone: 800-221-4770) and *Royal Cruise Line* (phone: 800-622-0538 or 415-956-7200 in California; 800-227-4534 elsewhere in the US).

In addition, a number of tour packagers cater to single travelers. These companies offer packages designed for individuals interested in vacationing with a group of single travelers or in being matched with a traveling companion. Among the better established of these agencies are the following:

Gallivanting (515 E. 79th St., Suite 20F, New York, NY 10021; phone: 800-933-9699 or 212-988-0617). Offers 1- to 2-week tours for singles ages 25 through 55, including cruises and outdoor activities such as hiking, rafting, hot air ballooning, snorkeling, and sailing. *Gallivanting* also matches singles of the same sex willing to share accommodations in order to avoid paying single supplement charges, and the agency guarantees this arrangement if bookings are paid for at least 75 days in advance.

Grand Circle Travel (347 Congress St., Boston, MA 02210; phone: 800-221-2610 or 617-350-7500). Arranges extended vacations, escorted tours and cruises for the over-50 traveler, including singles. Membership, which is automatic when you book a trip through *Grand Circle,* includes travel discounts and other extras, such as a Pen Pals service for singles seeking traveling companions.

Marion Smith Singles (611 Prescott Pl., North Woodmere, NY 11581; phone: 516-791-4852, 516-791-4865, or 212-944-2112). Specializes in tours for singles ages 20 to 50, who can choose to share accommodations to avoid paying single supplement charges.

Saga International Holidays (120 Boylston St., Boston MA 02116; phone: 800-343-0273 or 617-451-6808). A subsidiary of a British company specializing in older travelers, many of them single, *Saga* offers a broad selection of packages for people age 60 and over, or those 50 to 59 traveling with someone 60 or older. Although anyone can book a *Saga* trip, a $15 club membership includes a subscription to their newsletter, as well as other publications and travel services — such as a matching service for single travelers.

Singles in Motion (545 W. 236th St., Suite 1D, Riverdale, NY 10463; phone: 718-884-4464). Offers a number of packages for single travelers, including tours, cruises, and excursions focusing on outdoor activities such as hiking and biking.

Solo Flights (127 S. Compo Rd., Westport, CT 06880; phone: 203-226-9993). Represents a number of packagers and cruise lines and books singles on individual and group tours.

STI (8619 Reseda Blvd., Suite 103, Northridge, CA 91324; phone: 800-525-0525 throughout the US). Specializes in travel for 18- to 30-year-olds. Offers escorted tours ranging from 2 weeks to 2 months.

Travel in Two's (239 N. Broadway, Suite 3, N. Tarrytown, NY 10591; phone: 914-631-8409). This company books solo travelers on packages offered by a number of companies (at no extra cost to clients), offers its own tours, and matches singles with traveling companions. Many offerings are listed in their quarterly *Singles Vacation Newsletter,* which costs $5 per issue or $15 per year.

A good book for single travelers is *Traveling On Your Own,* by Eleanor Berman, which offers tips on traveling solo and includes information on trips for singles, ranging from outdoor adventures to educational programs. Available in bookstores, it also can be ordered by sending $12.95, plus postage and handling, to Random House, Order Dept., 400 Hahn Rd., Westminster, MD 21157 (phone: 800-733-3000).

Single travelers also may want to subscribe to *Going Solo,* a newsletter that offers helpful information on going on your own. Issued 6 times a year, a subscription costs $29. Contact Doerfer Communications, PO Box 1035, Cambridge, MA 02238 (phone: 617-876-2764).

Hints for Older Travelers

Special discounts and more free time are just two factors that have given Americans over age 65 a chance to see the world at affordable prices. Senior citizens make up an ever-growing segment of the travel population, and the trend among them is to travel more frequently and for longer periods of time.

PLANNING: When planning a vacation, prepare your itinerary with one eye on your own physical condition and the other on a topographical map. Keep in mind variations in climate, terrain, and altitudes, which may pose some danger for anyone with heart or breathing problems.

Older travelers may find the following publications of interest:

The Discount Guide for Travelers Over 55, by Caroline and Walter Weintz, is an excellent book for budget-conscious older travelers. Published by Penguin USA, it is currently out of print; check your local library.

Going Abroad: 101 Tips for Mature Travelers offers tips on preparing your trip and commonsense precautions en route. This concise, free booklet is available from *Grand Circle Travel,* 347 Congress St., Boston, MA 02210 (phone: 800-221-2610 or 617-350-7500).

The International Health Guide for Senior Citizen Travelers, by Dr. W. Robert Lange, covers a variety of topics. It also includes a list of resource organizations that provide medical assistance for travelers. It is available for $4.95 postpaid from Pilot Books, 103 Cooper St., Babylon, NY 11702 (phone: 516-422-2225).

The Mature Traveler is a monthly newsletter that provides information on travel discounts, places of interest, and useful tips for travelers 49 and up. To subscribe, send $24.50 to GEM Publishing Group, PO Box 50820, Reno, NV 89513 (phone: 702-786-7419).

Take a Camel to Lunch and Other Adventures for Mature Travelers, by Nancy O'Connell, offers offbeat and unusual adventures for travelers over 50. Available at bookstores or directly from Bristol Publishing Enterprises (PO Box 1737, San Leandro, CA 94577; phone: 800-346-4889 or 510-895-4461) for $8.95, plus shipping and handling.

Travel Tips for Older Americans is a useful booklet that provides good, basic advice. This US State Department publication (stock number 044-000-02270-2) can be ordered by sending a check or money order for $1 to the Superintendent of Documents (US Government Printing Office, Washington, DC 20402) or by calling 202-783-3238 and charging the order to a credit card.

Unbelievably Good Deals & Great Adventures That You Absolutely Can't Get Unless You're Over 50, by Joan Rattner Heilman, offers travel tips for older travelers, including discounts on accommodations and transportation, as well as a list of organizations for seniors. It is available for $7.95, plus shipping and handling, from Contemporary Books, 180 N. Michigan Ave., Chicago, IL 60601 (phone: 312-782-9181).

HEALTH: Health facilities in Mexico generally are good; however, an inability to speak the language can pose a problem. A number of organizations exist to help travelers avoid or deal with medical emergencies while traveling.

Pre-trip medical and dental checkups are strongly recommended. Prepare a personal medical kit to take abroad, which should include vital medical information, enough of any medication you need to last for the duration of your trip, and some basic first-aid ingredients (for further information, see *Staying Healthy,* in this section).

DISCOUNTS AND PACKAGES: Because guidelines change from place to place, it is a good idea for older travelers to inquire in advance about discounts on transportation, hotels, concerts, movies, museums, and other activities. Some hotel chains, airlines, bus companies, cruise lines, car rental companies, and other travel suppliers offer discounts to older travelers.

Some discounts, however, are extended only to bona fide members of certain senior citizens organizations. For instance, *Sheraton* offers a 25% discount to any senior citizen and participating *Holiday Inns* offer 10% discounts for *AARP* members — in both cases, these discounts may not apply during certain "blackout" periods. (See listings below for more information on *AARP* benefits.) Because the same organizations frequently offer package tours, the benefits of membership are twofold: Those who join can take advantage of discounts as individual travelers and also reap the savings that group travel affords. In addition, because the age requirements for some of these organizations are quite low (or nonexistent), the benefits can begin to accrue early.

In order to take advantage of these discounts, you should carry proof of your age (or eligibility). A driver's license, membership card in a recognized senior citizens' organization, or a Medicare card should be adequate. Among the organizations dedicated to helping older travelers see the world are the following:

American Association of Retired Persons (AARP; 601 E St. NW, Washington, DC 20049; phone: 202-434-2277). The largest and best-known of these organizations. Membership is open to anyone 50 or over, whether retired or not; dues are $8 a year, $20 for 3 years, or $45 for 10 years, and include spouse. The *AARP* Travel Experience Worldwide program, available through *American Express Travel Related Services,* offers members tours, cruises, and other travel programs designed exclusively for older travelers that cover the globe. Members can book these services by calling *American Express* at 800-927-0111 for land and air travel, or 800-745-4567 for cruises.

Mature Outlook (Customer Service Center, 6001 N. Clark St., Chicago, IL 60660; phone: 800-336-6330). Through its *TravelAlert,* tours, cruises, and other vacation packages are available to members at special savings. Hotel and car rental discounts and travel accident insurance also are available. Membership is open to anyone 50 years of age or older, costs $9.95 a year, and includes a bimonthly newsletter and magazine.

National Council of Senior Citizens (1331 F St. NW, Washington, DC 20004; phone: 202-347-8800). Here, too, the emphasis is on keeping costs low. This nonprofit organization offers members a different roster of package tours each year, as well as individual arrangements through its affiliated travel service, *Vantage Travel Service.* Although most members are over 50, membership is open to anyone (regardless of age) for an annual fee of $12 per person or couple. Lifetime membership costs $150.

Certain travel agencies and tour operators offer special trips geared to older travelers. Among them are the following:

Evergreen Travel Service (4114 198th St. SW, Suite 13, Lynnwood, WA 98036-6742; phone: 800-435-2288 or 206-776-1184). This specialist in trips for persons with disabilities recently introduced Lazybones Tours, a program offering leisurely tours for older travelers.

Grand Circle Travel (347 Congress St., Boston, MA 02210; phone: 800-221-2610 or 617-350-7500). Caters exclusively to the over-50 traveler and packages a large variety of escorted tours, cruises, and extended vacations. Membership, which is automatic when you book a trip through *Grand Circle,* includes discount certificates on future trips and other extras, including a helpful free booklet, *Going Abroad: 101 Tips for Mature Travelers.*

Saga International Holidays (120 Boylston St., Boston MA 02116; phone: 800-343-0273 or 617-451-6808). Offers a broad selection of packages for people age 60 and over or those 50 to 59 traveling with someone 60 or older. Although anyone can book a *Saga* trip, a $15 club membership includes a subscription to their newsletter, as well as other publications and travel services.

Many travel agencies, particularly the larger ones, are delighted to make presentations to help a group of senior citizens select destinations. A local chamber of commerce should be able to provide the names of such agencies. Once a time and place are determined, an organization member or travel agent can obtain group quotations for transportation, accommodations, meal plans, and sightseeing. Larger groups usually get the best breaks.

Hints for Traveling with Children

 What better way to encounter the world's variety than in the company of the young, wide-eyed members of your family? Their presence does not have to be a burden or an excessive expense. The current generation of discounts for children and family package deals can make a trip together quite reasonable.

A family trip will be an investment in your children's future, making geography and history come alive to them, and leaving a sure memory that will be among the fondest you will share with them someday. Their insights will be refreshing to you; their impulses may take you to unexpected places with unexpected dividends.

PLANNING: Here are several hints for making a trip with children easy and fun.

1. Children, like everyone else, will derive more pleasure from a trip if they know something about their destination before they arrive. Begin their education about a month before you leave. Using maps, travel magazines, and books, give children a clear idea of where you are going and how far away it is.
2. Children should help to plan the itinerary, and where you go and what you do should reflect some of their ideas. If they already know something about the sites they'll visit, they will have the excitement of recognition when they arrive.

3. Children also will enjoy learning some Spanish phrases — a few basics like *"hola!"* (hello), *"adiós"* (good-bye), and *"gracias"* (thanks).
4. Familiarize the children with *pesos*. Give them an allowance for the trip, and be sure they understand just how far it will or won't go.
5. Give children specific responsibilities: The job of carrying their own flight bags and looking after their personal things, along with some other light chores, will give them a stake in the journey.
6. Give each child a travel diary or scrapbook to take along.

One useful resource to which you may want to refer is the *Berlitz Jr. Spanish* instructional series for children. The series combines an illustrated storybook with a lively 60-minute audiocassette; the set is available for $19.95, plus shipping and handling, from Macmillan Publishing Company, Front and Brown Sts., Riverside, NJ 08075 (phone: 800-257-5755).

For parents, *Travel With Your Children* (*TWYCH;* 80 Eighth Ave., New York, NY 10011; phone: 212-206-0688) publishes a newsletter, *Family Travel Times,* that focuses on families with young travelers and offers helpful hints. An annual subscription (10 issues) is $35 and includes a copy of the "Airline Guide" issue (updated every other year), which focuses on the subject of flying with children. This special issue is available separately for $10.

Another newsletter devoted to family travel is *Getaways.* This quarterly publication provides reviews of family-oriented literature, activities, and useful travel tips. To subscribe, send $25 to *Getaways,* att. Ms. Brooke Kane, PO Box 8282, McClean, VA 22107 (phone: 703-534-8747).

Also of interest to parents traveling with their children is *How to Take Great Trips With Your Kids,* by psychologist Sanford Portnoy and his wife, Joan Flynn Portnoy. The book includes helpful tips from fellow family travelers, tips on economical accommodations and touring by car, as well as over 50 games to play with your children en route. It is available for $8.95, plus shipping and handling, from Harvard Common Press, 535 Albany St., Boston, MA 02118 (phone: 617-423-5803).

Another book on family travel, *Travel with Children* by Maureen Wheeler, offers a wide range of practical tips on traveling with children. It is available for $10.95, plus shipping and handling, from Lonely Planet Publications, Embarcadero West, 112 Linden St., Oakland, CA 94607 (phone: 510-893-8555). Another title worth looking for is *Great Vacations with Your Kids,* by Dorothy Jordan (Dutton: $12.95).

Finally, parents arranging a trip with their children may want to deal with an agency specializing in family travel, such as *Let's Take the Kids* (1268 Devon Ave., Los Angeles, CA 90064; phone: 800-726-4349 or 213-274-7088). In addition to arranging and booking trips for individual families, this group occasionally organizes trips for single-parent families traveling together. They also offer a parent travel network, whereby parents who have been to a particular destination can evaluate it for others.

GETTING THERE AND GETTING AROUND: Begin early to investigate all available discount and charter flights, as well as any package deals and special rates offered by the major airlines. Booking is sometimes required up to 2 months in advance. You may well find that charter plans offer no reductions for children, or not enough to offset the risk of last-minute delays or other inconveniences to which charters are subject. The major scheduled airlines, on the other hand, almost invariably provide hefty discounts for children. If traveling by ship, note that children under 12 usually travel at a considerably reduced fare on cruise lines.

Plane – When you make your reservations, tell the airline that you are traveling with a child. Children ages 2 through 12 generally travel at about half to two-thirds of the regular full-fare adult ticket price on most international flights. This children's fare, however, usually is much higher than an excursion fare (which also may be even further reduced for children.) On many international flights, children under 2 travel at about 10% of the adult fare if they sit on an adult's lap. A second infant without a second adult would pay the fare applicable to children ages 2 through 11.

Although some airlines will, on request, supply bassinets for infants, most carriers encourage parents to bring their own safety seat on board, which then is strapped into the airline seat with a regular seat belt. This is much safer — and certainly more comfortable — than holding the child in your lap. If you do not purchase a seat for your baby, you have the option of bringing the infant restraint along on the off-chance that there might be an empty seat next to yours — in which case some airlines will let you use that seat at no charge for your baby and infant seat. However, if there is no empty seat available, the infant seat no doubt will have to be checked as baggage (and you may have to pay an additional charge), since it generally does not fit under the airplane seats or in the overhead racks. The safest bet is to pay for a seat.

Be forewarned: Some safety seats designed primarily for use in cars do not fit into plane seats properly. Although nearly all seats manufactured since 1985 carry labels indicating whether they meet federal standards for use aboard planes, actual seat sizes may vary from carrier to carrier. At the time of this writing, the FAA was in the process of reviewing and revising the federal regulations regarding infant travel and safety devices — it was still to be determined if children should be *required* to sit in safety seats and whether the airlines will have to provide them.

If using one of these infant restraints, you should try to get bulkhead seats which will provide extra room to care for your child during the flight. You also should request a bulkhead seat when using a bassinet — again, this is not as safe as strapping the child in. On some planes bassinets hook into a bulkhead wall; on others they are placed on the floor in front of you. (Note that bulkhead seats often are reserved for families traveling with children.) As a general rule, babies should be held during takeoff and landing.

Request seats on the aisle if you have a toddler or if you think you will need to use the bathroom frequently. Carry onto the plane all you will need to care for and occupy your children during the flight — formula, diapers, a sweater, books, favorite stuffed animals, and so on. Dress your baby simply, with a minimum of buttons and snaps, because the only place you may have to change a diaper is at your seat or in a small lavatory. The flight attendant can warm a bottle for you.

On most US carriers, you also can ask for a hot dog or hamburger instead of the airline's regular dinner if you give at least 24 hours' notice. Some, but not all, airlines have baby food aboard. While you should bring along toys from home, also ask about children's diversions. Some carriers have terrific free packages of games, coloring books, and puzzles.

When the plane takes off and lands, make sure your baby is nursing or has a bottle, pacifier, or thumb in its mouth. This sucking will make the child swallow and help to clear stopped ears. A piece of hard candy will do the same thing for an older child.

Parents traveling by plane with toddlers, children, or young teenagers may want to consult *When Kids Fly*, a free booklet published by Massport (Public Affairs Dept., 10 Park Plaza, Boston, MA 02116-3971; phone: 617-973-5600), which includes helpful information on airfares for children, infant seats, what to do in the event of overbooked or canceled flights, and so on.

■**Note:** Newborn babies, whose lungs may not be able to adjust to the altitude, should not be taken aboard an airplane. And some airlines may refuse to allow a pregnant woman in her 8th or 9th month to fly. Check with the airline ahead of time and carry a letter from your doctor stating that you are fit to travel — and indicating the estimated date of birth.

Ship – Some shipping lines offer cruises that feature special activities for children, particularly during periods that coincide with major school holidays like *Christmas, Easter,* and the summer months. On such cruises, children may be charged special cut-rate fares and there are youth counselors to organize activities. Occasionally, a shipping line even offers free passage during the summer months for children under the age of 16 occupying a stateroom with two (full-fare) adult passengers. Your travel agent should know which cruise lines offer such programs.

Car – Touring by car allows greater flexibility for traveling and packing. Games and simple toys, such as magnetic checkerboards or drawing pencils and pads, also provide a welcome diversion. And frequent stops so that children can run around make car travel much easier. You may want to stock the car with a variety of favorite snacks, and if you pack an ice chest and a grill, you can stop for picnics. You may want to bring dry ice, since ice isn't so easy to come by in rural areas. Near the larger cities, ice cubes are sold at gasoline service stations and ice blocks are available from the local beer distributors. However, use this ice *only* for keeping food chilled in coolers — *never* put it in drinks, as you can't count on the quality of the water from which it was made.

ACCOMMODATIONS AND MEALS: Often a cot for a child will be placed in a hotel room at little or no extra charge. If you wish to sleep in separate rooms, special rates sometimes are available for families; some places do not charge for children under a certain age. In many of the larger chain hotels, the staff is more used to children. These hotels also are likely to have swimming pools or gamerooms — both popular with most youngsters. Many large resorts also have recreation centers for children. Cabins, bungalows, condominiums, and other rental options offer families privacy, flexibility, some kitchen facilities, and often lower costs.

Although it is difficult to find adequate baby-sitting services in most Mexican cities, most better hotels will try to arrange for a sitter. Whether the sitter is hired directly or through an agency, ask for and check references and keep in mind that the candidates may not speak much, if any, English.

At mealtime, don't deny yourself or your children the delights of a new style of cooking. Children like to know what kind of food to expect, so it will be interesting to look up Mexican dishes before leaving. Encourage your children to try new things; however, even though simple tacos, burritos, and cheese-filled tortillas are similar to hamburgers and grilled cheese sandwiches, they may not fill the bill for some children. In resort areas such as Acapulco, you will be able to find American-style food.

Things to Remember

1. If you are spending your vacation touring, pace the days with children in mind. Break the trip into half-day segments, with running around or "doing" time built in.
2. Don't forget that a child's attention span is far shorter than an adult's. Children don't have to see every sight or all of any sight to learn something from their trip; watching, playing with, and talking to other children can be equally enlightening.
3. Let your children lead the way sometimes; their perspective is different from yours, and they may lead you to things you would never have noticed on your own.
4. Remember the places that children love to visit: aquariums, zoos, beaches, nature trails, and so on. Among the activities that may pique their interest are bicycling, snorkeling, boat trips, exploring ruins, and viewing natural habitat exhibits.

On the Road

Credit and Currency

 It may seem hard to believe, but one of the greatest (and least understood) costs of travel is money itself. If that sounds simplistic, consider the fact that you can lose as much as 30% of your dollar's value simply by changing money at the wrong place or in the wrong form. Your one single objective in relation to the care and retention of your travel funds is to make them stretch as far as possible. This requires more than merely ferreting out the best airfare or the most charming budget hotel. It means being canny about the management of money itself. Herewith, a primer on making money go as far as possible while traveling.

CURRENCY: The basic unit of Mexican currency is the **peso**, which, like the dollar, is based on a decimal system and subdivides into 100 units, called centavos. Used only as a basis for translating dollars into pesos, the centavo has been taken out of circulation. Paper bills *(billetes)* are found in denominations of 1,000, 2,000, 5,000, 10,000, 20,000, 50,000, and 100,000 pesos (note that the 1,000-peso bill is no longer printed, although it is still accepted). Coins *(monedas)* are found in 1-peso, 5-peso, 10-peso, 20-peso, 50-peso, 100-peso, 200-peso, 500-peso, 1,000-peso, and 5,000-peso denominations.

Although US dollars may be accepted in Mexico (particularly at points of entry), you certainly will lose a percentage of your dollars' buying power if you do not take the time to convert them into pesos. By paying for goods and services in the local currency, you save money by not negotiating invariably unfavorable exchange rates for every small purchase, and avoid difficulty where US currency is not readily — or happily — accepted. *Throughout this book, unless specifically stated otherwise, prices are given in US dollars.*

There is no limit to the amount of US currency that can be brought into Mexico. To avoid problems anywhere along the line, it's advisable to fill out any customs forms provided when leaving the US on which you can declare all money you are taking with you — cash, traveler's checks, and so on. US law requires that anyone taking more than $10,000 into or out of the US must report this fact on customs form No. 4790, which is available at all international airports or from any office of US Customs. If taking over $10,000 out of the US, you must report this *before* leaving the US; if returning with such an amount, you should include this information on your customs declaration. Although travelers usually are not questioned by customs officials about currency when entering or leaving, the sensible course is to observe all regulations just to be on the safe side.

FOREIGN EXCHANGE: Because of the volatility of exchange rates, be sure to check the current value of the peso before finalizing any travel budget. And before you actually depart on your trip, be aware of the most advantageous exchange rate offered by various financial institutions — US banks, currency exchange firms (at home or abroad), or foreign banks.

For the best sense of current trends, follow the rates posted in the financial section of your local newspaper or in such international newspapers as the *International Herald Tribune.* You can check with your own bank or with *Thomas Cook Foreign Exchange* (for the nearest location, call 800-972-2192 in Illinois; 800-621-0666 elsewhere in the US). *Harold Reuter and Company,* a currency exchange service in New York City (200 Park Ave., Suite 332 E., New York, NY 10166; phone: 212-661-0826), also is particularly helpful in determining current trends in exchange rates. *Ruesch International* offers up-to-date foreign-currency information and currency-related services (such as converting foreign-currency checks into US dollars). *Ruesch* also offers a pocket-size *Foreign Currency Guide* (good for estimating general equivalents while planning) and a helpful brochure, *6 Foreign Exchange Tips for the Traveler.* Contact *Ruesch International* at one of the following addresses: 3 First National Plaza, Suite 2020, Chicago, IL 60602 (phone: 312-332-5900); 1925 Century Park E., Suite 240, Los Angeles, CA 90067 (phone: 213-277-7800); 608 Fifth Ave., "Swiss Center," New York, NY 10020 (phone: 212-977-2700); or 1350 Eye St. NW, 10th Floor and street level, Washington, DC 20005 (phone: 800-424-2923 or 202-408-1200).

In Mexico, you will find the official rate of exchange posted in banks, airports, money exchange houses, hotels, and some shops. As a general rule, expect to get more pesos for your US dollar at banks than at any other commercial establishment. Exchange rates do change from day to day, and most banks offer the same (or very similar) exchange rates. (In a pinch, the convenience of cashing money in your hotel — sometimes on a 24-hour basis — *may* make up for the difference in the exchange rate.) Don't try to bargain in banks or hotels — no one will alter the rates for you.

If banks are closed, you may want to try the money exchange houses *(casas de cambio)* located throughout Mexico, including Acapulco. Money exchange houses are financial institutions that charge a fee for the service of exchanging dollars for local currency. When considering alternatives, be aware that although the rate varies among these establishments, the rates of exchange offered are bound to be slightly less favorable than the terms offered at nearby banks — again, don't be surprised if you get fewer pesos for your dollar than the rate published in the papers.

That said, however, the following rules of thumb are worth remembering:

Rule number one: Never (repeat: *never*) exchange more than $10 for foreign currency at hotels, restaurants, or retail shops. If you do, you are sure to lose a significant amount of your dollar's buying power. If you do come across a storefront exchange counter offering what appears to be an incredible bargain, there's too much counterfeit specie in circulation to take the chance (see Rule number three, below).

Rule number two: Estimate your needs carefully; if you overbuy, you lose twice — buying and selling back. Every time you exchange money, someone is making a profit, and rest assured it isn't you. Use up foreign notes before leaving, saving just enough for airport departure taxes (which often must be paid in local currency), other last-minute incidentals, and tips.

Rule number three: Don't buy money on the black market. The exchange rate may be better, but it is a common practice to pass off counterfeit bills to unsuspecting foreigners who aren't familiar with the local currency. It's usually a sucker's game, and you almost always are the sucker; it also can land you in jail.

Rule number four: Learn the local currency quickly and keep abreast of daily fluctuations in the exchange rate. Rates change to some degree every day. For rough calculations, it is quick and safe to use round figures, but for purchases and actual currency exchanges, carry a small pocket calculator to help you compute the exact rate. Inexpensive calculators specifically designed to convert currency amounts for travelers are widely available.

When changing money, don't be afraid to ask how much commission you're being charged, and the exact amount of the prevailing exchange rate. In fact, in any exchange of money for goods or services, you should work out the rate before making any payment.

TIP PACKS: It's not a bad idea to buy a *small* amount of foreign coins and banknotes before your departure. The advantages of tip packs are threefold:

1. You become familiar with the currency (really the only way to guard against making mistakes or being cheated during your first few hours in a new country).
2. You are guaranteed some money should you arrive when a bank or exchange counter isn't open or available.
3. You don't have to depend on hotel desks, porters, or taxi drivers to change your money.

TRAVELER'S CHECKS: It's wise to carry traveler's checks while on the road instead of (or in addition to) cash, since it's possible to replace them if they are stolen or lost; you usually can receive partial or full replacement funds the same day if you have your purchase receipt and proper identification. With adequate proof of identification (credit cards, driver's license, passport), traveler's checks are as good as cash in most hotels, restaurants, stores, and banks.

You will be able to cash traveler's checks fairly easily in major resort areas like Acapulco, but don't expect to meander into a one-burro town and be able to get instant cash. Also note that more and more establishments are beginning to restrict the amount of traveler's checks they will accept or cash, so it is wise to purchase at least some of your checks in small denominations — say, $10 and $20.

Although some traveler's checks are available in foreign currencies — at press time, only *Visa* traveler's checks were available in pesos — the exchange rates offered by the issuing institutions in the US generally are far less favorable than those available from banks both in the US and abroad. Therefore, it usually is better to carry the bulk of your travel funds abroad in US dollar denomination traveler's checks.

Every type of traveler's check is legal tender in banks around the world, and each company guarantees full replacement if checks are lost or stolen. After that the similarity ends. Some charge a fee for purchase, others are free; you can buy traveler's checks at almost any bank, and some are available by mail. Most important, each traveler's check issuer differs slightly in its refund policy — the amount refunded immediately, the accessibility of refund locations, the availability of a 24-hour toll-free emergency hotline and refund service, and the time it will take for you to receive replacement checks. For instance, *American Express* guarantees replacement of lost or stolen traveler's checks in under 3 hours at any *American Express* office — other companies may not be as prompt. (Note that *American Express*'s 3-hour policy is based on a traveler's being able to provide the serial numbers of the lost checks. Without these numbers, refunds can take much longer.)

We cannot overemphasize the importance of knowing how to replace lost or stolen checks. Be sure to make a photocopy of the refund instructions that will be given to you by the issuing institution at the time of purchase. To avoid complications should you need to redeem lost checks (and to speed up the replacement process), keep the purchase receipt and an accurate list, by serial number, of the checks that have been spent or cashed. You may want to incorporate this information in an "emergency packet," also including your passport number and date of issue, the numbers of the credit cards you are carrying, and any other bits of information you shouldn't be without. Always keep these records separate from the checks and the original records themselves (you may want to give them to a traveling companion to hold).

Although most people understand the desirability of carrying funds in the form of traveler's checks as protection against loss or theft, an equally good reason is that US dollar traveler's checks invariably get a better rate of exchange than cash does — usually by at least 1% (although the discrepancy has been known to be substantially higher). The reasons for this are technical, and less prevalent in Mexico than elsewhere — the official rate of exchange posted by Mexican banks usually is the rate used to exchange *any* form of US currency — but potential savings still exist and it is a fact of travel life that should not be ignored.

That 1% won't do you much good, however, if you have already have spent it *buying* your traveler's checks. Several of the major traveler's check companies charge 1% for the acquisition of their checks. To receive fee-free traveler's checks you may have to meet certain qualifications — for instance, *Thomas Cook*'s checks issued in US currency are free if you make your travel arrangements through its travel agency. *American Express* traveler's checks are available without charge to members of the *American Automobile Association (AAA)*. Holders of some credit cards (such as the *American Express Platinum* card) also may be entitled to free traveler's checks. The issuing institution (e.g., the particular bank at which you purchase them) may itself charge a fee. If you purchase traveler's checks at a bank in which you or your company maintains significant accounts (especially commercial accounts of some size), the bank may absorb the 1% fee as a courtesy.

■**Note:** *American Express* cardholders now can order traveler's checks by phone through a new service called *Cheques on Call.* By dialing 800-55-FOR-TC, *Green* cardholders can order up to $1,000, *Gold* cardholders $2,500, and *Platinum* cardholders $10,000 of *American Express* traveler's checks during any 7-day period. In addition, the usual 1% acquisition fee is waived for *Gold* and *Platinum* cardholders. There is no postage charge if the checks are sent by first class mail; *Federal Express* delivery is available for a fee.

American Express, Bank of America, Citicorp, MasterCard, Thomas Cook, and *Visa* all offer traveler's checks. Here is a list of the major companies issuing traveler's checks and the numbers to call in the event that loss or theft makes replacement necessary:

American Express: To report lost or stolen checks in the US and Canada, call 800-221-7282; in Mexico, call the nearest *American Express* office, or the Mexican regional center at 635-326-2525 during business hours; 635-326-2666, collect, after 5 PM (central standard time).

Bank of America: To report lost or stolen checks in the US, call 800-227-3460. In Mexico, call 415-622-3800 or 415-624-5400, collect.

Citicorp: To report lost or stolen checks in the US, call 800-645-6556 or 800-541-8882 in the continental US. In Mexico and elsewhere worldwide, call 813-623-1709 or 813-626-4444, collect.

MasterCard: Note that *Thomas Cook MasterCard* (below) is now handling all *MasterCard* traveler's check inquiries and refunds.

Thomas Cook MasterCard: To report lost or stolen checks in the US, call 800-223-7373. In Mexico, call 212-974-5696 or 609-987-7300, collect, and they will direct you to the nearest branch of *Thomas Cook.*

Visa: To report lost or stolen checks in the continental US, call 800-227-6811. In Mexico, call 415-574-7111, collect.

CREDIT CARDS: Some establishments you may encounter during the course of your travels may not honor any credit cards and some may not honor all cards, so there is a practical reason to carry more than one. The following is a list of credit cards that enjoy wide domestic and international acceptance:

American Express: Cardholders can cash personal checks for traveler's checks and cash at *American Express* or its representatives' offices in the US up to the following limits (within any 21-day period): $1,000 for *Green* and *Optima* cardholders; $5,000 for *Gold* cardholders; and $10,000 for *Platinum* cardholders. Check cashing also is available to cardholders who are guests at participating hotels (up to $250), and for holders of airline tickets, at participating airlines (up to $50). Free travel accident, baggage, and car rental insurance if ticket or rental is charged to card; additional insurance also is available for additional cost. For further information or to report a lost or stolen *American Express* card, call 800-528-4800 throughout the continental US; elsewhere in the US and in Mexico, contact a local *American Express* representative or call 212-477-5700, collect.

Carte Blanche: Free travel accident, baggage, and car rental insurance if ticket or rental is charged to card; additional insurance also is available at additional cost. For medical, legal, and travel assistance worldwide, call 800-356-3448 throughout the US; in Mexico, call 214-680-6480, collect. For further information or to report a lost or stolen *Carte Blanche* card, call 800-525-9135 throughout the US; in Mexico, call 303-790-2433, collect.

Diners Club: Emergency personal check cashing for cardholders staying at participating hotels and motels (up to $250 per stay). Free travel accident, baggage, and car rental insurance if ticket or rental is charged to card; additional insurance also is available for an additional fee. For medical, legal, and travel assistance available worldwide, call 800-356-3448 throughout the US; elsewhere, call 214-680-6480, collect. For further information or to report a lost or stolen *Diners Club* card, call 800-525-9135 throughout the US; in Mexico, call 303-790-2433, collect.

Discover Card: Offered by a subsidiary of Sears, Roebuck & Co., it provides cardholders with cash advances at numerous automatic teller machines and *Sears* stores throughout the US. For further information or to report a lost or stolen *Discover* card, call 800-DISCOVER throughout the US; in Mexico, call 302-323-7841, collect. Note that at press time, the *Discover* card was not yet accepted in Mexico; call for current information when planning your trip.

MasterCard: Cash advances are available at participating banks worldwide. Check with your issuing bank for information. *MasterCard* also offers a 24-hour emergency lost card service; call 800-826-2181 throughout the US; in Mexico; call 314-275-6690, collect.

Visa: Cash advances are available at participating banks worldwide. Check with your issuing bank for information. *Visa* also offers a 24-hour emergency lost card service; call 800-336-8472 throughout the US. In Mexico, call 415-574-7700, collect.

One of the thorniest problems relating to the use of credit cards abroad concerns the rate of exchange at which a purchase is charged. Be aware that the exchange rate in effect on the date that you make a foreign purchase or pay for a foreign service has nothing at all to do with the rate of exchange at which your purchase is billed to you when you get the invoice (sometimes months later) in the US. The amount that the credit card company charges is either a function of the exchange rate at which the establishment's bank processed it or the rate in effect on the day your charge is received at the credit card center. (There is 1-year limit on the time a business or hotel can take to forward its charge slips.)

The principle at work in this credit-card exchange rate roulette is simple, but very hard to predict. You make a purchase at a particular dollar versus local currency exchange rate. If the dollar gets stronger in the time between purchase and billing, your purchase actually costs you less than you anticipated. If the dollar drops in value during the interim, you pay more than you thought you would. There isn't much you can do about these vagaries except to follow one very broad, very clumsy rule of thumb: If the dollar is doing well at the time of purchase, its value increasing against the local currency, use your credit card on the assumption that it still will be doing well when billing takes place. If the dollar is doing badly, assume it will continue to do badly and pay with traveler's checks or cash. If you get too badly stuck, the best recourse is to complain, loudly. Be aware, too, that most credit card companies charge an unannounced, un-itemized 1% fee for converting foreign currency charges to US dollars.

SENDING MONEY TO MEXICO: If you have used up your traveler's checks, cashed as many emergency personal checks as your credit card allows, drawn on your cash advance line to the fullest, and still need money, it is possible to have it sent to you via the following services:

American Express (phone: 800-926-9400 or 800-955-7777 for Spanish). Offers a service called "MoneyGram," completing money transfers in anywhere from 10 minutes to 5 days. The sender can go to any *American Express* office in the US and transfer money by presenting cash, a personal check, money order, or credit card — *Discover* (even though it is not accepted in Mexico, the *Discover* card *can* be used to send funds via the "MoneyGram" service), *MasterCard, Visa,* or *American Express Optima* card. (No other *American Express* or other credit cards are accepted.) *American Express Optima* cardholders also can arrange for this transfer over the phone. The minimum transfer charge is $25, which rises with the amount of the transaction. Up to $10,000 can be transferred in each transaction (additional funds can be sent in separate transactions), but credit card users are limited to the amount of pre-established credit line. To collect at the other end, the receiver must go to a branch office of *American Express* or an affiliated Mexican bank and show identification (passport, driver's license, or other picture ID).

Western Union Telegraph Company (phone: 800-325-4176). To send money to Mexico, a friend or relative can go, cash in hand, to any *Western Union* office in the US, where, for a *minimum* charge of $13 (it rises with the amount of the transaction), the funds will be wired to one of the offices of *Telecom,* Mexico's telegraph network. When the money arrives in Mexico — in the case of Acapulco, from 24 to 36 hours (although transfers can take as long as 3 days) — you will not be notified; you must go to the local *Western Union* branch office or agent to inquire. The funds will be turned over in pesos, based on the rate of exchange in effect on the day of receipt. For a higher fee, the US party to this transaction may call *Western Union* with a *MasterCard* or *Visa* number to send up to $2,000, although larger transfers will be sent to a predesignated location.

If you are literally down to your last cent and have no other way to obtain cash, the US consular agent in Acapulco (phone: 74-857207) or the nearest US consulate (see *Legal Aid and Consular Services,* in this section) will let you call home to set these matters in motion.

CASH MACHINES: Automatic teller machines (ATMs) are increasingly common worldwide. Some banks provide ATM service only for their own customers at bank branches. If, however, your bank participates in one of the international ATM networks (most do), you can use the "cash card" and your personal identification code or number (also called a PIC or PIN) provided by the bank at any ATM in the same electronic network for financial transactions, including withdrawing cash. Network ATMS generally are located in banks, commercial and transportation centers, and near major tourist attractions.

Both *Cirrus* (phone: 800-4-CIRRUS) and *Plus System* (800-THE-PLUS) networks maintain thousands of ATM locations worldwide, including hundreds of locations throughout Mexico. *MasterCard* and *Visa* holders may use their cards to draw cash against their credit lines on either system.

As we went to press, both *Cirrus* and *PLUS System* machines were available at the following locations in Acapulco (most are at *Banamex* branches):

- Av. Costera Miguel Alemán, Esq. S. Vizcaino
- 2085 Av. Costera Miguel Alemán
- 739 Cuauhtémoc (Sucursal Progreso)

In addition, there were two other *Cirrus* machines located in Acapulco, at 78-1 Av. Costera Miguel Alemán, Col. Centro, and at 212 Av. Costera Miguel Alemán, Col. Centro.

Information about the *Cirrus* and *Plus* systems also is available at member bank branches, where you can obtain free booklets listing the locations of machines worldwide. Note that a recent change in banking regulations permits financial institutions in the US to subscribe to *both* the *Cirrus* and *Plus* systems, allowing users of either network to withdraw funds from ATMs at participating banks. This change does not, however, apply to banks in Mexico, and remember, regulations there may vary.

Accommodations

 The best Mexican hotels combine the modern, standardized style of American chains with the continental elegance of European service and a lush, tropical charm unique to Mexico. The enormous growth of tourism in Mexico in recent years has been marked by a corresponding growth in accommodations of all kinds and styles. The popular beach resort areas, such as Acapulco, offer some of the world's most luxurious hotels and resorts in splendid settings.

A number of properties in Acapulco are part of well-known international hotel chains. The most elegant of these offer a broad range of facilities and amenities, as well as competent, attentive service. These hotels are modern and comfortable, often include fine restaurants, and the prices, as you would expect, are relatively high. Comparable independent establishments in this area often are even more elegant than the chains. Medium-size hotels can be equally modern, or at least modernized, but are more likely to offer local ambience and charm; in general, they're also more reasonably priced. Some establishments offer the added allure of stunning views, snow white beaches, various sports facilities, and spas. In many hotels, you can splurge and enjoy a life of luxury and leisure, sipping exotic drinks beneath a bougainvillea on your own terrace, at a relatively low cost compared to that of the equivalent degree of decadence in the US.

At the other end of the spectrum are hotels that offer moderate to inexpensive accommodations. These include numerous clean and inexpensive hostelries of every type — modern or colonial, secluded, centrally located, or on the road — that offer basic amenities, which may or may not include a private bath, air conditioning, TV sets, in-room telephones, bar and/or meal service, and swimming pools. Here the charm consists of a genuine welcome, personal hospitality, often striking scenery, and privacy.

Since room prices in all Mexican hotels are controlled and regulated by the Mexican Ministry of Tourism, they remain stable within basic categories — reflected in this book in the categories expensive, moderate, and inexpensive. For information on specific properties, see THE CITY, DIRECTIONS, and DIVERSIONS.

RENTAL OPTIONS: An attractive accommodations alternative for the visitor content to stay in one spot for a week or more is to rent one of the numerous properties available in Acapulco. These offer a wide range of luxury and convenience, depending on the price you want to pay. One of the charms of staying in a house, apartment, condominium, cottage, villa or other rented vacation home is that you will feel much more like a visitor than a tourist.

A vacation in a furnished rental has both the advantages and disadvantages of living "at home" abroad. It can be less expensive than staying in a first class hotel, although very luxurious and expensive rentals are available, too. It has the comforts of home, including a kitchen, which can mean potential savings on food. On the other hand, a certain amount of housework is involved because if you don't eat out, you have to cook, and though some rentals (especially the luxury ones) include a cleaning person, most don't. (If the rental doesn't include domestic help, arrangements often can be made with a nearby service for far less than in the US.)

For a family, two or more couples, or a group of friends, the per-person cost — even for a more luxurious rental — can be quite reasonable. Weekly and monthly rates are available to reduce costs still more. But best of all is the amount of space, which no conventional hotel room can equal. As with hotels, the rates for properties in some areas are seasonal, rising during the peak travel season, while for others they remain the same year-round. To have your pick of the properties available, you should begin to make arrangements for a rental at least 6 months in advance.

Rental Property Agents and Discounts – There are several ways of finding a suitable rental property. They may be listed along with other accommodations in publications of local tourist boards. Many tour wholesalers regularly include rental packages among their offerings; these generally are available through a travel agent. Their plans typically include rental of the property (or several properties, but usually for a minimum stay per location), a rental car, and airfare.

A number of companies rent properties throughout Mexico. They handle the booking and confirmation paperwork, and can be expected to provide more information about the properties they handle than that which might ordinarily be gleaned from a listing in an accommodations guide. Following is a list of such agencies and their offerings in Acapulco:

At Home Abroad (405 E. 56th St., Suite 6H, New York, NY 10022-2412; phone: 212-421-9165). Rents modest to luxurious villas, usually by the week.

Creative Leisure (951 Transport Way, Petaluma, CA 94954; phone: 800-4-CON-DOS in the US and Canada). Rents elegant suites and private villas.

La Cure Villas (11661 San Vicente Blvd., Suite 1010, Los Angeles, CA 90049; phone: 800-387-2726 or 416-968-2374). Rents private villas. Rentals include a full staff, including a cook. They can also arrange for local transportation.

Hideaways International (PO Box 1270, Littleton, MA 01460; phone: 800-843-4433 or 508-486-8955 throughout the US). Rents luxury beachfront villas, private houses, and condominiums. For $79, subscribers receive two issues per year of their guide to current listings, as well as a quarterly newsletter and discounts on a variety of travel services. For a trial membership of $27.50 for 4 months, members receive one guide and two newsletters.

Rent a Home International (7200 34th Ave. NW, Seattle, WA 98117; phone: 206-789-9377). Rents private villas.

Rent a Vacation Everywhere (RAVE; 328 Main St. E., Suite 526, Rochester, NY 14604; phone: 716-454-6440). Handles moderate to luxury condominiums and villas.

Villa Leisure (PO Box 30188, Palm Beach, FL 33420-0188; phone: 800-526-4244 or 407-624-9000). Rents condominiums, private homes, and villas.

Villas International Ltd. (605 Market St., Suite 510, San Francisco, CA 94105; phone: 800-221-2260 or 415-281-0910). Rents upscale villas and condos.

In addition, a useful publication, the *Worldwide Home Rental Guide,* lists properties throughout Mexico, as well as the managing agencies. Issued twice annually, single copies may be available at newsstands for $10 an issue. For a year's subscription (two issues), send $18 to *Worldwide Home Rental Guide,* PO Box 2842, Sante Fe, NM 87504 (phone: 505-988-5188).

When considering a particular vacation rental property, look for answers to the following questions:

- How do you get from the airport to the condominium?
- If the property is on the shore, how far is the nearest beach? Is it sandy or rocky, and is it safe for swimming?
- What size and number of beds are provided?
- How far is the property from whatever else is important to you, such as a golf course or nightlife?
- If there is no grocery store on the premises (which may be comparatively expensive, anyway), how far is the nearest market?
- Are baby-sitters, cribs, bicycles, or anything else you may need for your children available?
- Is maid service provided daily?
- Is air conditioning and/or a phone provided?
- Is a car rental part of the package? Is a car necessary?

Before deciding which rental is for you, make sure you have satisfactory answers to all your questions. Ask your travel agent to find out or call the company involved directly.

Accommodation Discounts – Several discount travel organizations provide a substantial savings — up to 50% off list prices — on rental accommodations (and some hotels) in Acapulco. Reservations are handled by the central office of the organization, or members may deal directly with the rental agencies or individual property owners. To take advantage of the full selection of properties, these organizations often require that reservations be made as much as 6 months in advance — particularly for stays during the holidays or peak travel periods. Companies that provide discounts on accommodations in Acapulco include the following:

Concierge (1600 Wynkoop St., Suite 102, Denver, CO 80202; phone: 303-623-6775 in Colorado; 800-346-1022 elsewhere in the US). Offers up to 50% discounts on rentals. Annual membership fee is $69.95 per couple.

Hotel Express (3052 El Cajon Blvd., San Diego, CA 92104; phone: 800-634-6526 or 619-280-2582). Offers up to 50% off on rentals. Annual membership fee of $49.95 per family provides discounts on other travel services, but membership is not required for bargains on rental accommodations.

IntlTravel Card (6001 N. Clark St., Chicago, IL 60660; phone: 800-342-0558 or 312-465-8891). Provides discounts on car rental and hotel accommodations throughout Mexico. The $36 annual membership fee covers a spouse as well.

Privilege Card (PO Box 629, Duluth, GA 30136; phone: 800-359-0066 or 404-623-0066). Up to 50% discounts available on hotel accommodations. Annual membership fee is $49.95 per family.

Time Zones, Business Hours, and Bank Holidays

 TIME ZONES: Mexico's west coast operates on central standard time. In winter, if it is 9 AM in Acapulco (central standard time), it is 7 AM in Los Angeles (pacific standard time), 8 AM in Denver (mountain standard time), and 10 AM in New York (eastern standard time). As Mexico does not observe daylight saving time, during the summer when this time change is in effect in the US, add 1 hour to each of the equivalent US times.

Mexican timetables use a 24-hour clock to denote arrival and departure times, which means that hours are expressed sequentially from 1 AM. By this method, 9 AM is recorded as 0900, noon as 1200, 1 PM as 1300, 6 PM as 1800, midnight as 2400, and so on. For example, the departure of a tour at 7 AM will be announced as "0700"; one leaving at 7 PM will be noted as "1900."

One further confusion may arise when you're keeping an appointment with a Mexican acquaintance. Although you may be certain that you have already adjusted your watch and that it is working correctly, your companion may not show up until an hour or more after the agreed time. This is neither unusual nor considered impolite. It is simply a different regard for time than is common in the US. And your trip to Mexico may be even more delightful if you relax and adopt this south-of-the-border attitude.

BUSINESS HOURS: While working hours number about the same as those kept in the US, the times differ considerably. Executives usually begin working at 10 AM and stop for a leisurely, 2-hour lunch around 2 or 3 PM. The afternoon shift runs from about 4 to 7 PM. Mexican stores are generally open from 10 AM to 7 PM.

Most banks are open from 9 AM to 1:30 PM Mondays through Fridays. Key branches of some major banks also may offer additional hours, opening from 4 to 6 PM on weekdays. A few banks may keep even longer hours — staying open from 8:30 AM through 5 PM. Some even may have weekend hours — staying open from 10 AM to 1:30 PM and from 4 to 6 PM on Saturdays, and 10 AM to 1:30 PM on Sundays.

If you are unable to get to the bank, you usually can cash your traveler's checks at money exchanges *(cambios)*. Some are open Mondays through Fridays until 5 PM, and Saturdays until 2 PM. The airport money exchanges are open Sundays as well. (For further information, see *Credit and Currency,* in this section.)

BANK HOLIDAYS: Government offices, banks, and stores are closed on national holidays and often on the days just before and after as well. Many offices (but not banks) close between *Christmas* and *New Year's.* Following are Mexican national holidays and the dates they will be observed this year:

January 1: *New Year's Day (Año Nuevo).*

February 5: *Constitution Day* marks the signing of the constitutions of 1857 and 1915.

March 21: *Birthday of Benito Juárez* honors the man often called the "Abraham Lincoln of Mexico."

April 8: *Holy Thursday.*

April 9: *Good Friday.*

May 1: *Labor Day,* celebrated with parades.

May 5: Anniversary of Mexico's victory over the French at Puebla in 1862.

September 1: The president's state of the union report *(Informe)* and the opening of Congress.

September 16: *Independence Day.*

October 11: *Columbus Day (Día de la Raza)*.
November 2: *All Souls' Day* (known in Mexico as the *Day of the Dead*).
November 20: Anniversary of the Mexican Revolution of 1910.
December 12: *Feast of Our Lady of Guadalupe.*
December 25: *Christmas.*
December 31: Banks closed for annual balance.

Mail, Telephone, and Electricity

MAIL: Almost every town throughout the country has a post office, and while there are not many public mailboxes *(buzónes)* on street corners, there are drops in most large hotels, office buildings, and in front of or in every post office.

All foreign postal service is now airmail. The real problem is how long it takes your letter to get from the post office to the plane: Service in Mexico is known as "Burro Express," and can take up several weeks. The good news, however, is that due to the efforts of the Mexican postal authorities, this system is gradually improving.

If you are planning to send packages to destinations either within or outside the country, be sure to have them registered. The procedure is the same as in the US. If your correspondence is important, you may want to send it via one of the special courier services; *Federal Express, DHL,* and other international services are widely available in Mexico. The cost is considerably higher than sending something via the postal service — but the assurance of its timely arrival is worth it.

Stamps are available at most hotel desks, as well as at post offices; they also are dispensed from vending machines in some hotels, drugstores, transportation terminals, and other public places.

Several places will receive and hold mail for travelers in Mexico. Mail sent to you at a hotel and clearly marked "Guest Mail, Hold for Arrival" is one safe approach. If you do not know what your address will be, have your mail addressed to the nearest post office in care of the local equivalent of General Delivery: *a/c Lista de Correos.* Note that you are expected to specify the branch, district, zip code *(codigo postal)* and city — and, under the best of conditions, this is very risky. Most foreign post offices have a time limit for holding such mail — 30 days is a common limit. To claim this mail, you must go in person to the post office, ask for the local equivalent of General Delivery, and present identification (driver's license, credit card, birth certificate, or passport).

In sending mail to Mexico, avoid using middle names. Mexicans use the paternal and maternal surnames — the paternal is in the middle — and using a middle name could lead to confusion. When inquiring about mail addressed to you, should there be nothing under the first letter of your last name, ask the post office clerk to look for it under the first letter of your first or middle name. If you plan to remain in one place for more than a month, consider renting a post office box *(apartado postal)* in the central post office to eliminate the chance of mail getting lost in local delivery.

If you are an *American Express* customer (a cardholder, a carrier of *American Express* traveler's checks, or traveling on on an *American Express Travel Related Services* tour), you can have mail sent to the *American Express* branch office in Acapulco at 709-1 Costera Miguel Alemán (phone: 74-845550). Letters are held free of charge — registered mail and packages are not accepted. You must be able to show an *American Express* card, traveler's checks, or a voucher proving you are on one of the company's tours to qualify for mail privileges. Those who aren't clients cannot use the service. There also is a forwarding fee of $5. Mail should be addressed to you, care of

American Express, and should be marked "Client Mail Service." Additional information on this mail service is listed in the pamphlet *American Express Travelers' Companion,* available from any US branch of *American Express.*

TELEPHONE: Most large Mexican cities and resort areas — including Acapulco — have direct dialing to the US. Telephones from which this is not possible require the assistance of the international operator, who can connect you. If you are staying in a small town or in a hotel with no phone, use the phones in local stores or larger hotels. And here again, the operator can tell you the charges. Although you can use a telephone company credit card number on any phone, pay phones (called *Ladatel* phones) that take specially designated phone cards are increasingly common.

These phone cards have been instigated to cut down on vandalism, as well as to free callers from the necessity of carrying around a pocketful of change, and generally are sold in various peso denominations. The units per card, like message units in US phone parlance, are a combination of time and distance. To use such a card, insert it into a slot in the phone and dial the number you wish to reach. A display gradually will count down the value that remains on your card. When you run out of units on the card, you can insert another. Phone cards can be purchased at post offices, transportation and other commercial centers, and at designated shops (usually sporting a sign in the window indicating this service).

The procedure for calling Mexico from the US is as follows: dial 011 (the international access code) + 52 (the country code) + the city code + the local number. (The city code for Acapulco is 74; for city codes of other areas, check the front of a telephone book or ask an international operator.) For example, to place a call from anywhere in the US to Acapulco, dial 011 + 52 + 74 (the city code) + the local number.

To call the US from anywhere in Mexico, dial 95 + the US area code + the local number. For instance, to call a number in New York City, dial 95 + 212 + the local number.

To make a call from one city in Mexico to another, dial 91 + the city code + the local number. To call a number within the same city code, just dial the local number.

Note that the number of digits in phone numbers is not standardized throughout Mexico. As making connections in Mexico for either local or international calls sometimes can be hit-or-miss, those who have to make an important call — to make a hotel reservation in another city, for instance — should start to do so as far in advance as possible.

Some important phone numbers throughout Mexico include the following:

Emergency assistance: 915-250-0123 and 915-250-0151 (within Mexico City, do not dial 915)
Long-distance operator: 02 (within Mexico)
International operator: 09 (English-speaking)
Local information: 04
Countrywide information: 01

Hotel Surcharges – Avoiding operator-assisted calls can cut international calling costs considerably and bring rates into a somewhat more reasonable range — except for calls made through hotel switchboards. One of the most unpleasant surprises travelers encounter in many foreign countries is the amount they find tacked onto their hotel bill for telephone calls, because foreign hotels routinely add on astronomical surcharges. (It's not at all uncommon to find 300% to 400% added to the actual telephone charges.)

Until recently, the only recourse against this unconscionable overcharging was to call collect from abroad or to use a telephone credit card — available through a simple procedure from any local US phone company. (Note, however, that even if you use a telephone credit card, some hotels still may charge a fee for line usage.) Now *American Telephone and Telegraph (AT&T)* offers *USA Direct,* a service that connects users, via a toll-free number, with an *AT&T* operator in the US, who will then put the call through at the standard international rate. An added feature of this service is that travelers abroad can reach US toll-free (800) numbers by calling a *USA Direct* operator, who will connect them. Charges for all calls made through *USA Direct* appear on the caller's regular US phone bill. Note that, as we went to press, this service was offered throughout much of Mexico, including Acapulco, but only from the new *Ladatel* pay phones mentioned above. For a brochure and wallet card listing toll-free numbers by country, contact International Information Service, *AT&T Communications,* 635 Grand St., Pittsburgh, PA 15219 (phone: 800-874-4000).

Until such services become universal, it's wise to ask about the surcharge rates *before* calling from a hotel. If the rate is high, it's best to use a telephone credit card; make a collect call; or place the call and ask the party to call right back. If none of these choices is possible, make international calls from local post offices or special telephone centers to avoid surcharges. Another way to keep down the cost of telephoning from Mexico is to leave a copy of your itinerary and telephone numbers with people in the US so that they can call you instead.

A particularly useful service for travelers to non-English-speaking destinations such as Mexico is *AT&T's* Language Line Service. By calling 800-628-8486, you will be connected with an interpreter in any one of 143 languages and dialects, who will provide on-line interpretive services for $3.50 a minute. From the US, this service is particularly useful for booking travel services in foreign countries where English is not spoken — or not spoken fluently. Once abroad — this number can be reached by using the *USA Direct* toll-free (800) number connection feature described above — it will enable you to make arrangements at foreign establishments or to reach emergency or other vital services with which you would other wise have trouble communicating due to the language barrier. For further information, contact *AT&T* at the address above or call 800-752-6096.

■ **Other Resources:** A useful directory for planning a trip is *AT&T's Toll-Free 800 Directory,* which lists thousands of companies with 800 numbers, both alphabetically (white pages) and by category (yellow pages), including a wide range of travel services — from travel agents to transportation and accommodations. Issued in a consumer edition for $9.95 plus tax, shipping, and handling, and a business edition for $14.95 plus tax, shipping, and handling. Both are available from *AT&T* Phone Centers or by calling 800-426-8686. The *Toll-Free Travel & Vacation Information Directory* is a practical directory for use before you leave and on the road. It is available for $4.95 plus $1.50 for postage and handling from Pilot Books, 103 Cooper St., Babylon, NY 11702; phone: 516-422-2225). For quick reference you might want to get a copy of the helpful pamphlet *The Phone Booklet,* which lists the nationwide, toll-free (800) numbers of travel information sources and suppliers — such as major airlines, hotel and motel chains, car rental companies, and tourist information offices. Send $2 for postage and handling to *Scott American Corporation,* Box 88, West Redding, CT 06896).

ELECTRICITY: Mexico's electrical current system is the same as that used in the US — 110-volt, 60-cycle, alternating current (AC) — so US tourists can bring their own electrical appliances from home. If you want to be fully prepared, bring along an extension cord (the electrical outlet may be farther from the sink than the cord on your razor or hair dryer can reach), and, even though most of Mexico now uses standard electrical plugs like those in the US, a wall socket adapter with a full set of plugs will ensure that you'll be able to plug in anywhere. In some areas and establishments, the current may be weak; your electrical equipment still should work, but not up to maximum capacity. So if you use an electric razor, it is wise to pack a manual safety razor, too, just in case.

One good source for sets of plugs and adapters for use worldwide is the *Franzus Company* (PO Box 142, Beacon Falls, CT 06403; phone: 203-723-6664). *Franzus* also publishes a useful brochure, *Foreign Electricity is No Deep Dark Secret,* which provides information about converters and adapter plugs for electric appliances to be used abroad but manufactured for use in the US. To obtain a free copy, send a self-addressed, stamped envelope to *Franzus* at the above address; a catalogue of other travel accessories is available on request.

Staying Healthy

 The surest way to return home in good health is to be prepared for medical problems that might occur on vacation. Accidents can happen anytime, but travelers to Mexico are especially vulnerable to certain illnesses. As is always the case with both diseases and accidents, prevention is the best cure. And in Mexico this adage applies not only to diarrhea or dysentery, but to more serious diseases like hepatitis and typhoid fever. Below, we've outlined some things you need to think about when planning your trip.

BEFORE YOU GO: Older travelers or anyone suffering from a chronic medical condition, such as diabetes, high blood pressure, cardiopulmonary disease, asthma, or ear, eye, or sinus trouble, should consult a physician before leaving home. Those with conditions requiring special consideration when traveling should consider seeing, in addition to their regular physician, a specialist in travel medicine. For a referral in a particular community, contact the nearest medical school or ask a local doctor to recommend such a specialist. Dr. Leonard Marcus, a member of the *American Committee on Clinical Tropical Medicine and Travelers' Health,* provides a directory of more than 100 travel doctors across the US. For a copy, send a 9-by-12-inch self-addressed, stamped envelope, plus postage, to Dr. Marcus at 148 Highland Ave., Newton, MA 02165 (phone: 617-527-4003).

Also be sure to check with your insurance company ahead of time about the applicability of your hospitalization and major medical policies away from home; many policies do not apply, and others are not accepted in Mexico. Older travelers should know that Medicare does not make payments outside the US and its territories. If your medical policy does not protect you while you're traveling, there are comprehensive combination policies specifically designed to fill the gap. (For a discussion of medical insurance and a list of inclusive combination policies, see *Insurance,* in this section.)

PREVENTION AND IMMUNIZATION: Specific information on the health status of any area in Mexico can be secured from its consular services in the US. The Centers for Disease Control publishes a comprehensive booklet, *Health Information for International Travel,* which lists vaccination requirements and other health information for Mexico. To order, send a check or money order for $5 to the Superintendent of Documents (US Government Printing Office, Washington, DC 20402), or charge it to your credit card by calling 202-783-3238. For other health-related publications for travelers, see "Helpful Publications," below.

The US Public Health Service advises diphtheria and tetanus shots for people traveling in Mexico. In addition, children should be inoculated against measles, mumps, rubella, and polio, especially since some of these viruses exist in a more virulent form in Mexico than at home. Inquire at an office of the Mexican Ministry of Tourism about specific immunization requirements. Be sure to ask about any local epidemics (some diseases — like polio — that have been virtually eliminated in the States persist in Mexico) so that you can obtain the proper immunization before departure.

For further information on vaccination requirements, disease outbreaks, and other health information pertaining to traveling abroad, you also can call the Centers for Disease Control's 24-hour **International Health Requirements and Recommendations Information Hotline: 404-332-4559.**

First Aid – Put together a compact, personal medical kit including Band-Aids, first-aid cream, antiseptic, nose drops, insect repellent, aspirin or non-aspirin tablets, an extra pair of prescription glasses or contact lenses (and a copy of your prescription for glasses or contact lenses), sunglasses, over-the-counter remedies for diarrhea, indigestion, and motion sickness, a thermometer, and a supply of those prescription medicines you take regularly.

In a corner of your kit, keep a list of all the drugs you have brought and their purpose, as well as duplicate copies of your doctor's prescriptions (or a note from your doctor). As brand names may vary in Mexico, it's a good idea to ask your doctor for the generic name of any drugs you use so that you can ask for their equivalent should you need a refill. Unless it is an emergency, however, some prescriptions may require the signature of a Mexican physician. (In recent years the Mexican Health Ministry has developed a list of restricted drugs and medicines, which includes certain seasickness tablets, that require a written prescription from a local doctor.)

It also is a good idea to ask your doctor to prepare a medical identification card that includes such information as your blood type, any allergies or chronic health problems you have, and any special information that may aid diagnosis of an emergency condition — for instance, if you have heart problems, a copy of your most recent electrocardiogram. This kit also should include your doctor's name, address, and telephone number, as well as your social security number and information on your medical insurance. Considering the essential contents of this kit, keep it with you, rather than in your checked luggage.

MINIMIZING THE RISKS: Typically, tourists suffer two kinds of health problems in Mexico, gastrointestinal upset and sunburn. And as a number of diseases are contracted through bug bites (see below), some precaution against biting insects is strongly advised. Neither these nor any other health problems or illnesses is inevitable, however, and with suitable precautions, your trip to Mexico can proceed untroubled by ill health.

DIARRHEA AND STOMACH UPSETS: It is very important to take the first few days easy, especially if you land in Mexico City, where the high altitude will be tiring and exacerbate the effect of any alcohol on your system; so drink and eat lightly on arrival.

Fortunately, the vast majority of intestinal disorders encountered during travel represent only a temporary inconvenience, which will go away with rest and time. More serious problems may result, however, from the consumption of drinking water contaminated by a particular strain of *E. coli* bacteria. These bacteria inhabit the human intestinal tract and are transmitted through fecal matter, and from there into plumbing and any unpurified water system. The most frequent result is that scourge of travelers known the world over as Cairo crud, Delhi belly, *la turista,* or, in Mexico, Montezuma's Revenge. Its symptoms are dysentery or diarrhea, accompanied by severe intestinal pain and a foul taste in the mouth.

There is a very simple way to avoid it: Don't drink the water. Brush your teeth with bottled purified water (be sure you're not getting a used bottle refilled with tap water). Don't drink iced drinks where the ice has been made from tap water. And take note that those tempting-looking alcoholic concoctions served in coconuts or pineapples, as well as fruit juices — even in the better hotels — may be diluted with tap water, and thus may be unsafe. As a matter of course, it is wise to stick to bottled carbonated water (ask for *agua purificada* or *agua mineral*) or substitute wine or beer at meals. You also might carry standard GI water purification tablets (tetraglycine hydroperiodide). Just drop one of these tablets in a carafe of water and let it stand for half an hour.

Milk sold in supermarkets and groceries is pasteurized, and therefore safe to drink, but stay clear of raw milk and any other unpasteurized or uncooked dairy products. Also, do not eat unpeeled fruit or any uncooked vegetables. Garnishes of fresh vegetables (even a small amount of shredded lettuce and tomatoes) and salads often have been washed with tap water and can wreak havoc with your gastrointestinal tract the morning after. Stay away from unfamiliar dishes that are hard to identify, as well as creamy or mayonnaise-based dressings that may have been out on serving tables for any period of time. Above all, *do not* buy food from food vendors on streets or beaches.

Be sure to carry along an anti-diarrhea medication and recommended antibiotic in case you do develop symptoms. Before you go, pick up a mild over-the-counter preparation, such as Kaopectate or Pepto Bismol (each is available in tablet as well as liquid form), which, if used according to directions, should have you back on your feet within 12 to 14 hours. An old, favored Mexican remedy is *manzanilla* (chamomile) tea. You also may want to ask your doctor to recommend one of the stronger medications containing an antibiotic. If you are stricken with diarrhea and have no medication with you, have your hotel call a doctor or visit the nearest pharmacy.

■ **A Warning:** While unpleasant and inconvenient, the type of gastrointestinal disorder discussed above is rarely dangerous; however, a much more serious illness, infectious hepatitis (nicknamed the "Big H" by gringos) can be contracted from contaminated food or drinking water, and shellfish. It also can be contracted from dirty hypodermic needles, a risk even in hospitals. Again, care about what and where you eat and — should you need an injection — the use of disposable plastic syringes are the best preventive measures. (If you are a diabetic or require regular injections for any other condition, carry these disposable syringes with you.) An additional measure of protection also can be secured with an immunoglobulin shot from your family doctor before your departure.

■ **Note:** Before you leave for Mexico, check specifically with your local county or state health department, or call the US State Department's *Citizens' Emergency Center* at 202-647-5225 for the most up-to-date information on health conditions and other vital information.

SUNBURN: The burning power of the sun can quickly cause severe sunburn or sunstroke. To protect yourself against these ills, wear sunglasses, take along a broad-brimmed hat and cover-up, and most importantly use a sunscreen lotion.

WATER SAFETY: Mexico's beaches are so beautiful, with sands so caressing and waters so crystalline, that it's hard to remember that the waters also can be treacherous. A few precautions are necessary. Beware of the undertow, that current of water running back down the beach after a wave has washed ashore; it can knock you off your feet and into the surf. Even more dangerous is the riptide, a strong current of water running against the tide, which can pull you out toward the sea. If you get caught offshore, don't panic or try to fight the current, because it will only exhaust you; instead, ride it out while waiting for it to subside, which usually happens not too far from shore, or try swimming away parallel to the beach.

Sharks are sometimes sighted, but they usually don't come in close to shore, and they are well fed on fish. Should you meet up with one, just swim away as quietly and smoothly as you can, without shouting or splashing. Although not aggressive, eels can be dangerous when threatened. If snorkeling or diving, beware of crevices where these creatures may be lurking. The tentacled Portuguese man-of-war and other jellyfish may drift in quiet salt waters for food and often wash up onto the beach; the long tentacles of these creatures sting whatever they touch — a paste made of household vinegar and unseasoned meat tenderizer is the recommended treatment.

Mexico's coral reefs are limited, but still razor sharp. Treat all coral cuts with an antiseptic, and then watch for any signs of infection, since coral is a living organism with bacteria on its surface. If you step on a sea urchin, you'll find that the spines are very sharp, pierce the skin, and break off easily. Like splinters, the tips left embedded in the skin are difficult to remove, but they will dissolve in a week or two; rinsing with vinegar may help to dissolve them more quickly. To avoid these hazards, keep your feet covered whenever possible.

INSECTS AND OTHER PESTS: Insects in parts of Mexico — including the Pacific Coast — can be not only a nuisance but also a real threat, carrying infectious diseases such as malaria. To avoid contact in areas of infestation, do not sleep on the ground and, if possible, sleep under mosquito netting.

It is a good idea to use some form of topical insect repellent — those containing DEET (N,N-diethyl-m-toluamide) are among the most common and effective. The US Environmental Protection Agency (EPA) stresses that you should not use any pesticide that has not been approved by the EPA (check the label) and that all such preparations should be used in moderation. (Use no more than a 15% solution of DEET on children, for example, and apply only to clothing, not directly to the skin.) If picnicking, burn mosquito coils or candles containing allethrin, pyrethrin, or citronella, or use a pyre-thrum-containing flying-insect spray. For further information about active ingredients in repellents, call the *National Pesticide Telecommunications Network*'s 24-hour hotline number: 800-858-7378.

If you do get bitten — by mosquitoes or other bugs — the itching can be relieved with baking soda, topical first-aid creams, or antihistamine tablets. Should a bite become infected, treat it with a disinfectant or antibiotic cream.

Though rarer, bites from scorpions, snakes, or spiders can be serious. If possible, always try to catch the villain for identification purposes. If bitten, the best course of action may be to head directly to the nearest emergency ward or outpatient clinic of a hospital. Cockroaches and termites thrive in warm climates, but pose no serious health threat.

If complications, allergic reactions (such as breathlessness, fever, or cramps), or signs of serious infection result from any of the above circumstances, *see a doctor.*

Following all these precautions will not guarantee an illness-free trip, but should minimize the risk. For more information regarding preventive health care for travelers, contact the *International Association for Medical Assistance to Travelers (IAMAT;* 417 Center St., Lewiston, NY 14092; phone: 716-754-4883). This organization also assists travelers in obtaining emergency medical assistance while abroad (see list of such organizations below).

MEDICAL ASSISTANCE IN MEXICO: Nothing ruins a vacation or business trip more effectively than sudden injury or illness. Fortunately, should you need medical attention, competent, professional doctors, surgeons, and specialists perfectly equipped to handle any medical problem can be found throughout the country. In well-developed and large resort areas such as Acapulco, you will find thorough, well-trained specialists in all fields, hospitals, clinics, and pharmacies with pretty much the same drugs as in the US, some available without a prescription.

If you fall victim to any accident or malady that seems serious, do not hesitate to go to a doctor. The medical care available in Mexico is not very different from that offered in the US. There are private doctors, every kind of specialist, clinics, both private and government hospitals, dentists, optometrists, pharmacies, drugstores, and most medications found in the US. The quality of health care and the sophistication of medical facilities are less certain in rural and remote areas, and for specialized treatment it often is best to arrange for transportation to the nearest metropolitan center.

In an Emergency – If a bona fide emergency occurs, the fastest way to get attention may be to take a taxi to the emergency room of the nearest hospital. An alternative is to dial one of the following numbers for emergency assistance: to summon the police, fire trucks, and ambulances: 915-250-0123 or 915-250-0151 (within Mexico City, do not dial 915). When calling these numbers, state immediately that you are a foreign tourist and then the nature of your problem and your location. Note that ambulance dispatchers may not be bilingual, so travelers with little or no Spanish-language ability should try to get someone else to make the call. You also can dial for the operator and ask for someone who speaks English, although you may need an international operator to place a call to the local emergency service and stay on the line as an interpreter. Most emergency services send out well-equipped and well-staffed ambulances, although ambulances in some areas of Mexico may not be equipped with the advanced EMS technology found in the US and may provide only basic medical attention and be used mainly for transportation.

Non-Emergency Care – If a doctor is needed for something less than an emergency, there are several ways to find one. If you are staying in a hotel or resort, ask for help in reaching a doctor or other emergency services, or for the house physician, who may visit you in your room or ask you to visit an office. Travelers staying at a hotel of any size probably will find that the doctor on call speaks at least a modicum of English — if not, request one who does. When you register at a hotel, it's not a bad idea to include your home address and telephone number; this will facilitate the process of notifying friends, relatives, or your own doctor in case of an emergency.

Any US consul also can provide a list of English-speaking doctors and dentists in the area the consulate serves. (For a list of US consuls in Mexico, see *Legal Aid and Consular Services*, below.) Dialing the emergency numbers (listed above) may also be of help.

Pharmacies and Prescription Drugs – Pharmacies *(farmacias)* are a slight variation on the theme to which you are accustomed. While they're owned and operated by licensed pharmacists who fill doctor's prescriptions and provide the same conventional services as druggists in the US, diagnoses and even drug administration (including injections) are *sometimes* performed by Mexican pharmacists or their assistants. This is not as common as it once was, however, as it is illegal to sell or administer prescription medications in Mexico without a doctor's prescription, just as it is in the US. If your complaint is not serious and you wish to avoid the hassle or expense of consulting a physician, the local *farmacia* will be happy to recommend a (non-prescription) drug, administer it either in bulk or in single doses, and even give or recommend a doctor to give injections.

In some areas, pharmacies may take turns staying open for 24 hours. If none is open after normal business hours, you may be able to have one open in an emergency situation — such as for a diabetic needing insulin — for a fee. Contact a local hospital or medical clinic for information on on-call pharmacists.

■**A word of warning:** The threat of AIDS has made medical professionals and patients alike much more cautious about injections, particularly because reusable syringes and needles are often used in Mexico, and sterilization procedures may be inadequate or inconsistently applied. If you have a condition that may need occasional injections, bring a supply of syringes with you or buy the disposable syringes available without a prescription at most pharmacies in Mexico.

ADDITIONAL RESOURCES: Medical assistance also is available from the various medical programs designed for travelers who have chronic ailments or whose illness requires them to return home:

International Association of Medical Assistance to Travelers (*IAMAT;* 417 Center St., Lewiston, NY 14092; phone: 716-754-4883). Entitles members to the services of participating English-speaking doctors around the world, as well as clinics and hospitals in various locations. Participating physicians agree to adhere to a basic charge of around $40 to see a patient referred by *IAMAT.* To join, simply write to *IAMAT;* in about 3 weeks you will receive a membership card, the booklet of members, and an inoculation chart. A nonprofit organization, *IAMAT* appreciates donations; with a donation of $25 or more, you will receive a set of worldwide climate charts detailing weather and sanitary conditions. (Delivery can take up to 5 weeks, so plan ahead.)

International SOS Assistance (PO Box 11568, Philadelphia, PA 19116; phone: 800-523-8930 or 215-244-1500). Subscribers are provided with telephone access — 24 hours a day, 365 days a year — to a worldwide, monitored, multilingual network of medical centers. A phone call brings assistance ranging from a telephone consultation to transportation home by ambulance or aircraft, or, in some cases, transportation of a family member to wherever you are hospitalized. Individual rates are $35 for 2 weeks of coverage ($3.50 for each additional day), $70 for 1 month, or $240 for 1 year; couple and family rates also are available.

Medic Alert Foundation (2323 N. Colorado, Turlock, CA 95380; phone: 800-ID-ALERT or 209-668-3333). If you have a health condition that may not be readily available to the casual observer — one that might result in a tragic error in an emergency situation — this organization offers identification emblems specifying such conditions. The foundation also maintains a computerized central file from which your complete medical history is available 24 hours a day by phone (the telephone number is clearly inscribed on the emblem). The onetime membership fee, between $25 and $45, is based on the type of metal from which the emblem is made — the choices ranging from stainless steel to 10K gold-filled.

TravMed (PO Box 10623, Baltimore, MD 21204; phone: 800-732-5309 or 301-296-5225). For $3 per day, subscribers receive comprehensive medical assistance while abroad. Major medical expenses are covered up to $100,000, and special transportation home or of a family member to wherever you are hospitalized is provided at no additional cost.

■**Note:** Those who are unable to take a reserved flight due to personal illness or must fly home unexpectedly due to a family emergency should be aware that airlines may offer a discounted airfare (or arrange a partial refund) if the traveler can demonstrate that his or her situation is indeed a legitimate emergency. Your inability to fly or the illness or death of an immediate family member usually must be substantiated by a doctor's note or the name, relationship, and funeral home where the deceased will be buried. In such cases, airlines often will waive certain advance purchase restrictions or you may receive a refund check or voucher for future travel at a later date. Be aware, however, that this bereavement fare may not necessarily be the least expensive fare available and, if possible, it is best to have a travel agent check all possible flights through a computer reservations system (CRS).

If you live in or near New York City, you can take advantage of the *International Health Care Service* (440 E. 69th St., ground floor, New York, NY 10021; phone: 212-746-1601), which provides a variety of travel-related health services, including pre- and post-travel screenings and various inoculations at per-shot rates. Appointments are required for all services. Their *International Health Care Travelers Guide,* a compendium of facts and advice on health care and diseases around the world, can be obtained by sending $4.50 in a self-addressed, stamped envelope to the service.

HELPFUL PUBLICATIONS: A useful publication, *Health Hints for the Tropics,* offers tips on immunization and other preventive measures. It is available for $4 postpaid from Dr. Karl A. Western, *American Society of Tropical Medicine and Hygiene,* 6003 Executive Blvd., Rockville, MD 20892 (phone: 301-496-6721).

Practically every phase of health care — before, during, and after a trip — is covered in *The New Traveler's Health Guide,* by Drs. Patrick J. Doyle and James E. Banta. It is available for $4.95, plus postage and handling, from Acropolis Books Ltd., 13950 Park Center Rd., Herndon, VA 22071 (phone: 800-451-7771 or 703-709-0006).

The *Traveling Healthy Newsletter,* which is published six times a year, also is brimming with health-related travel tips. For an annual subscription, which costs $24, contact Dr. Karl Neumann (108-48 70th Rd., Forest Hills, NY 11375; phone: 718-268-7290). Dr. Neumann also is the editor of the useful free booklet *Traveling Healthy,* which is available by writing to the Travel Healthy Program (Clark O'Neill Inc., 1 Broad Ave., Fairview, NJ 07022; phone: 215-732-4100).

Legal Aid and Consular Services

There is one crucial place to keep in mind when outside the US, namely, the American Services section of the United States Consulate. If you are injured or become seriously ill, the consulate will direct you to medical assistance and notify your relatives. If, while abroad, you become involved in a dispute that could lead to legal action, or if you are stranded abroad without funds, the consulate, once again, is the place to turn. And in the case of natural disasters or civil unrest, consulates around the world handle the evacuation of US citizens if it becomes necessary.

It usually is far more alarming to be arrested abroad than at home. Not only are you alone among strangers, but the punishment can be worse. Granted, the US Consulate can advise you of your rights and provide a list of English-speaking lawyers, but it cannot interfere with the local legal process. Except for minor infractions of the local traffic code, there is no reason for any law-abiding traveler to run afoul of immigration, customs, or any other law enforcement authority.

The best advice is to be honest and law-abiding. If you get a traffic ticket, pay it. If you are approached by drug hawkers, ignore them. The penalties for possession of hashish, marijuana, cocaine, and other narcotics are even more severe abroad than in the US. (If you are picked up for any drug-related offense, do not expect US Foreign Service officials to be sympathetic. Chances are they will notify a lawyer and your family and that's about all. See "Drugs," below.)

In the case of minor traffic accidents (such as a fender-bender), it often is most expedient to settle the matter before the police get involved. If the police do get involved in minor accidents or violations, the usual procedure is for the police officer to say that you must pay a fine. If you explain that you are a tourist, the officer usually will offer to settle the fine on the spot. If you speak the language and feel competent, try to bargain the fine — an experienced hand in Mexico would offer half the amount stated — but wisdom decrees that you do what is necessary to get the matter settled on the spot. Otherwise you will have to pay the fine at the police station.

If, however, you are involved in a serious accident, where an injury or fatality results, the first step is to contact the US consular agent in Acapulco and ask the consul to locate a lawyer to assist you. The US Department of State in Washington, DC, insists that any US citizen who is arrested abroad has the right to contact the US embassy or consulate "immediately," but it may be a while before you are given permission to use a phone. Do not labor under the illusion, however, that in a scrape with foreign officialdom, the consulate can act as an arbitrator or ombudsman on a US citizen's behalf. Nothing could be farther from the truth. Consuls have no power, authorized or otherwise, to subvert, alter, or contravene the legal processes, however unfair, of the foreign country in which they serve. Nor can a consul oil the machinery of a foreign bureaucracy or provide legal advice. The consul's responsibilities do encompass "welfare duties" including providing a list of lawyers and information on local sources of legal aid, assigning an interpreter if the police have none, informing relatives in the US, and organizing and administrating any defense money sent from home. If a case is tried unfairly or the punishment seems unusually severe, the consul can make a formal complaint to the authorities.

The consulate is not occupied solely with emergencies and is certainly not there to aid in trivial situations, such as canceled reservations or lost baggage, no matter how important these matters may seem to the victimized tourist. The main duties of any consulate are administering statutory services, such as the issuance of passports and visas; providing notarial services; distributing VA, social security, and civil service benefits to US citizens; taking depositions; handling extradition cases; and reporting to Washington the births, deaths, and marriages of US citizens living within the consulate's domain.

We hope that none of the information in this section will be necessary during your stay in Mexico. If you can avoid legal hassles altogether, you will have a much more pleasant trip. If you become involved in an imbroglio, the local authorities may spare you legal complications if you make clear your tourist status. And if you run into a confrontation that might lead to legal complications developing with a Mexican citizen or with local authorities, the best tactic is to apologize and try to leave as gracefully as possible. Do not get into fights with residents, no matter how belligerent or provocative they are in a given situation. In a foreign country where machismo is part of the national character, some things are best left unsettled.

The US Embassy is located in Mexico City (305 Paseo de la Reforma Cuauhtémoc, México, DF 06500; phone: 5-211-0042). The US government also maintains consulates general in nine other cities in Mexico; consular agents operate in ten additional cities. There is a consular agent in Acapulco (*Club del Sol Hotel,* Local 8, Costera Miguel Alemán, Acapulco, Guerrero; phone: 74-857207).

You can obtain a booklet with addresses of most US embassies and consulates around the world by writing to the Superintendent of Documents (US Government Printing Office, Washington, DC 20402; phone: 202-783-3238) and asking for publication #744-006-0000-7-W, *Key Offices of Foreign Service Posts.*

The US State Department operates a *Citizens' Emergency Center,* which offers a number of services to US citizens traveling abroad and their families at home. In addition to giving callers up-to-date information on trouble spots, the center will contact authorities abroad in an attempt to locate a traveler or deliver an urgent message. In case of illness, death, arrest, destitution, or repatriation of a US citizen on foreign soil, it will relay information to relatives at home if the consulate is unable to do so. Travel advisory information is available 24 hours a day to people with touch-tone phones (phone: 202-647-5225). Callers with rotary phones can get information at this number from 8:15 AM to 10 PM (eastern standard time) on weekdays, 9 AM to 3 PM on Saturdays. In the event of an emergency, this number also may be called during these hours. For emergency calls only, at all other times, call 202-634-3600 and ask for the Duty Officer.

Drinking and Drugs

DRINKING: There are few laws restricting drinking in Mexico; the establishment of a minimum drinking age (18) is itself a recent development. In fact, the manufacture of alcoholic beverages, from beer to brandy, is one of Mexico's most important industries. Mexican beer is so good that much of it is now being exported to the US, where in some areas it holds its own with American beers — depite its higher imported price. While you're in Mexico, try native brews like Bohemia, Carta Blanca, Corona, Dos Equis, Indio, Negro Modelo, Superior, and Tecate at the source.

Tequila, the national drink, is distilled from the juice of the agave plant, and is the beverage US visitors are most eager to sample. Take it straight, with salt and lime, or in a margarita cocktail, with lime juice and ice, but take it easy. Popular brands include Herradura, Hornitos, José Cuervo, Sauza, Viuda de Romero, and Xalisco.

Mescal is another hard liquor made from the agave cactus, although the taste is quite different from that of tequila; try Gusano de Oro, Gusano Rojo, or Monte Albán. Brandy also is one of Mexico's most popular drinks, and, strangely enough, it often is mixed with Coca-Cola, 7-Up, or mineral water. (Some institutional receptions only serve a choice of brandy and Coke or brandy and soda.) Rum, enjoyed straight, in a daiquiri, or with cola remains a favorite of tourists and residents alike; Bacardi, Castillo, and Potosí all are well regarded.

If you're a wine buff, don't neglect Mexico's wines — they're continually improving. There is a big price difference between Mexican and imported wines in most restaurants. Among the better-known Mexican vintages are Calafia, La Cetto, Domecq, Don Angel, Hammerhaus, Hildago, Padre Kino, Pinson, Los Reyes, San Lorenzo, San Marcos, Santo Tomás, and Urbiñon.

As in the US, national taxes on alcohol affect the prices of liquor in Mexico, and as a general rule, mixed drinks made from imported liquors (such as whiskey and gin) are more expensive than at home. If you like a drop before dinner, a good way to save money is to buy a bottle of your favorite brand at the airport before leaving the US and enjoy it in your hotel before setting forth. Or stick to locally produced beverages. If you are buying any quantity of alcohol (such as a case of tequila) in Mexico, be aware that whether you are bringing it with you or having it shipped, you will have to pay US import duties on any quantity over the allowed 1 liter (see *Customs and Returning to the US,* in this section.)

DRUGS: Another way to avoid legal trouble in Mexico is to avoid the drug scene — completely. Illegal narcotics are as prevalent in Mexico as in the US, but the moderate legal penalties and vague social acceptance that marijuana has gained in the US have no equivalents in Mexico. Due to the international war on drugs, enforcement of drug laws is becoming increasingly strict throughout the world. Local Mexican narcotics officers and customs officials are renowned for their absence of understanding and lack of a sense of humor — especially where Americans are involved.

Despite the government's campaign against it, marijuana still is grown in abundance throughout Mexico and is widely available. It is, however, just as illegal in Mexico as it is in the US, and penalties for selling, growing, and smoking it are just as severe. Opiates and barbiturates and other increasingly popular drugs — "white powder" substances like heroin and cocaine, and "crack" (the cocaine derivative) — also continue to be a major concern to narcotics officials.

The concerted effort by Mexican and other foreign authorities to stamp out drug traffic, with the support and encouragement of the United States, has now become a real war on buyers and sellers in the country — a war that has been — and continues to be — deadly.

Penalties for possession of even small quantities of marijuana range from deportation with stiff fines to jail terms, without bail or appeal. The penalties for other drugs may be even more stringent, and smuggling is dealt with even more severely. It is important to bear in mind that the quantity of drugs involved is of very minor importance.

Do not, under any circumstances, take drugs into, out of, or through Mexico. Persons arrested are subject to the laws of the country they are visiting, and in Mexico these laws and their procedures often are very harsh. Once you are in jail, the best lawyers in the country won't be able to get you out — and neither will the US government. Eventually, at the whim of the authorities, you will be tried and, upon conviction, given a stiff sentence. The best advice we can offer is this: Don't carry, use, buy, or sell illegal drugs.

Those who carry medicines that contain a controlled drug should be sure to have a current doctor's prescription with them. Ironically, travelers can get into almost as much trouble coming through US Customs with over-the-counter drugs picked up abroad that contain substances that are controlled in the US. Cold medicines, pain relievers, and the like often have codeine or codeine derivatives that are illegal, except by prescription, in the US. Throw them out before leaving for home.

■ **Be forewarned:** US narcotics agents warn travelers of the increasingly common ploy of drug dealers asking travelers to transport a "gift" or other package back to the US. Don't be fooled into thinking that the protection of US law applies abroad — if accused of illegal drug trafficking you will be considered guilty until you prove your innocence. In other words, do not, under any circumstances, agree to take anything across the border for a stranger.

Tipping

 Many waiters, waitresses, porters, and bellhops in Mexico depend upon tips for their livelihood. The salaries they receive, if they do receive salaries, are far below the equivalent paid in the US (even with the lower Mexican standards of living taken into consideration). There also are situations in which you wouldn't tip in the US but should in Mexico.

In restaurants, tip between 10% and 20% of the bill. For average service in an average restaurant, a 15% tip to the waiter is reasonable, although one should never hesitate to penalize poor service or reward excellent and efficient attention by leaving less or more. (If you notice a 6% or 15% addition to your bill, this usually is a standard tax, called IVA, not a service charge, and a tip still is in order — if you suspect that a gratuity might already be included, ask.)

Although it's not necessary to tip the maître d' of most restaurants — unless he or she has been especially helpful in arranging a special party or providing a table (a few extra dollars *may*, however, get you seated sooner or procure a preferred table) — when tipping is desirable or appropriate, the least amount should be the current equivalent of $5 in pesos. In the finest restaurants, where a multiplicity of servers are present, plan to tip 5% to the captain. The sommelier (wine waiter) is tipped approximately 10% of the price of the bottle of wine.

In allocating gratuities at a restaurant, pay particular attention to what has become the standard credit card charge form, which now includes separate places for gratuities for waiters and/or captains. If these separate boxes are not on the charge slip, simply ask the waiter or captain how these separate tips should be indicated. Be aware, too, of the increasingly common — and devious — practice of placing the amount of an entire restaurant bill (in which service already has been included) in the top box of a charge slip, leaving the "tip" and "total" boxes ominously empty. Don't be intimidated: Leave the "tip" box blank and just repeat the total amount next to "total" before signing. In some establishments, tips indicated on credit card receipts may not be given to the help, so you may want to leave tips in cash.

If you arrive by air, you probably will find a porter with a cart ready to roll your baggage from customs to the cabstand. He should be paid the current equivalent of about $1 to $2 in pesos, depending on how much luggage you have. If you are traveling by train, porters *expect* a tip of about 25¢ to 35¢ per bag — you might want to go higher. Bellhops, doormen, and porters at hotels generally are tipped at the rate of 50¢ to $1 per piece of luggage, along with a small additional amount if a doorman helps with a cab or car. If you arrive without the right denominations in pesos, tip in US money. (When in doubt, it is preferable to tip — in any denomination or currency — than not to tip.)

If a hotel does not automatically add a service charge, it is perfectly proper for guests to ask to have an extra 10% or 15% added to their bill, to be distributed among those who served them. This may be an especially convenient solution in a large hotel or resort, where it is difficult to determine just who out of a horde of attendants actually performed particular services.

For those who prefer to distribute tips themselves, a chambermaid generally is tipped at the rate of around $1 a day. Tip the concierge or hall porter for specific services only, with the amount of such gratuities dependent on the level of service provided. For any special service you receive in a hotel, a tip is expected — the current equivalent of $1 being the minimum for a small service.

Authorized taxi rates are set either by kilometers traveled or by zone, depending on the city or town; in metered cabs current fares are often posted (especially if there has been an increase in fares and the meter has not yet been adjusted). Many cab drivers set their own unofficial fares, and it is a good idea to ask what it will cost to get to a destination before entering the cab and letting the driver take over. Like so many fees in Mexico, this fare is likely to be negotiable. Cab drivers do not expect tips unless they perform some special service. Cabs that you call by phone are slightly more expensive than those that have meters and you hail in the streets.

In Mexico, you may be offered services by young children in the street. These might include watching your car while you shop and sightsee or cleaning your windshield while you stop at a light. You must be firm with them immediately if you don't want their services; otherwise, when the service is complete give your helper a couple of hundred pesos. Arriving and departing from airline terminals also can turn into a battle royal with youngsters over carrying your luggage.

You also may come across uniformed adult car watchers who earn their livelihoods this way. If you find one near your car, give him the current equivalent of $1 in pesos when you return — once you've unlocked the car and made sure everything is still there. If you park your car in a garage or lot, the parking attendant who returns it to you will expect a comparable tip. Unlike in the US, gas station attendants in Mexico expect a tip, even if they don't clean your windshield or check your oil (you should request these services if you want them); 500 to 1,000 pesos is adequate.

Miscellaneous tips: Ushers in theaters should be given about 50¢ after leading you to a seat and giving you a program. Sightseeing tour guides should be tipped. If you are traveling in a group, decide together what you want to give the guide and present it from the group at the end of the tour ($1 per person is a reasonable tip). If you have been individually escorted, the amount paid should depend on the degree of your satisfaction, but it should not be less than 10% of the total tour price. Museum and monument guides also are usually tipped. Coat checks are worth about 50¢ to $1 a coat, and washroom attendants are tipped — there usually is a little plate with a coin already in it suggesting the expected amount. In barbershops and beauty parlors, tips also are expected, but the percentages vary according to the type of establishment — 10% in the most expensive salons; 15% to 20% in less expensive establishments. (As a general rule, the person who washes your hair should get a small additional tip.)

Tipping aboard ships: Although some cruise lines do have a no-tipping-required policy and you are not penalized by the crew for not tipping, naturally, you aren't penalized for tipping either. Never, however, make the mistake of not tipping on the majority of ships, where it is a common, expected practice. Tips should be paid by and for each individual in a cabin, and the general rule of thumb (or palm) is to expect to pay from 10% to 20% of the total cost of the cruise for gratuities — the actual amount within this range is based on the length of the cruise and the extent of personalized services provided. Allow at least $2 to $5 a day for each cabin and dining room steward. Others who may merit tips are deck and wine stewards, porters, and any others who provide personal service. On some ships you can charge your bar tab to your cabin; throw in the tip when you pay it at the end of the cruise. Smart travelers tip twice during a cruise: about midway through the cruise and at the end; even wiser travelers tip a bit at the start of the trip to ensure better service throughout.

Tipping always is a matter of personal preference. In the situations covered above, as well as in any others that arise where you feel a tip is expected or due, feel free to express your pleasure or displeasure. Again, never hesitate to reward excellent and efficient attention or to penalize poor service. Give an extra gratuity and a word of thanks when someone has gone out of his or her way for you. Either way, the more personal the act of tipping, the more appropriate it seems. And if you didn't like the service — or the attitude — don't tip.

Duty-Free Shopping

Duty-free shops are located in all the major international airports throughout Mexico, including Acapulco. If common sense says that it always is less expensive to buy goods in an airport duty-free shop than to buy them at home or in the streets of a foreign city, travelers should be aware of some basic facts. Duty-free, first of all, does not mean that the goods travelers buy will be free of duty when they return to the US. Rather, it means that the shop has paid no import tax acquiring goods of foreign make because the goods are not to be used in the country where the shop is located. This is why duty-free goods are available only in the restricted, passengers-only area of international airports or are delivered to departing passengers on the plane. In a duty-free store, travelers save money only on goods of foreign make because they are the only items on which an import tax would be charged in any other store.

There is little reason to delay buying locally made merchandise and/or souvenirs until reaching the airport. In fact, because airport duty-free shops usually pay high rents, the locally made goods sold in them may well be more expensive than they would be in downtown stores. The real bargains are foreign goods, but — let the buyer beware — not all foreign goods are automatically less expensive in an airport duty-free shop. You can get a good deal on even small amounts of perfume, costing less than the usually required minimum purchase, tax-free. Other fairly standard bargains include spirits, smoking materials, cameras, clothing, watches, chocolates, and other food and luxury items — but first be sure to know what these items cost elsewhere. Terrific savings do exist (they are the reason for such shops, after all), but so do overpriced items that an unwary shopper might find equally tempting. In addition, if you wait to do your shopping at airport duty-free shops, you will be taking the chance that the desired item is out of stock or unavailable.

Customs and Returning to the US

 Whether you return to the United States by air or land, you must declare to the US Customs official before departing everything you have bought or acquired while in Mexico. The customs check can go smoothly, lasting only a few minutes, or can take hours, depending on the officer's instinct. To speed up the process, keep all your receipts handy and try to pack your purchases together in an accessible part of your suitcase. It might save you from unpacking all your belongings.

DUTY-FREE ARTICLES: In general the duty-free allowance for US citizens returning from abroad is $400. This limit includes items used or worn while abroad, souvenirs for friends, and gifts received during the trip. A flat 10% duty based on the "fair retail value in country of acquisition" is assessed on the next $1,000 worth of merchandise brought in for personal use or gifts. Amounts over $1,400 are dutiable at a variety of rates. The average rate for typical tourist purchases is about 12%, but you can find out rates on specific items by consulting *Tariff Schedules of the United States* in a library or any US Customs Service office.

Families traveling together may make a joint declaration to US Customs, which permits one member to exceed his or her duty-free exemption to the extent that another falls short. Families also may pool purchases dutiable under the flat rate. A family of three, for example, would be eligible for up to a total of $3,000 at the 10% flat duty rate (after each member had used up his or her $400 duty-free exemption) rather than three separate $1,000 allowances.

Personal exemptions can be used once every 30 days; in order to be eligible, an individual must have been out of the country for more than 48 continuous hours. If any portion of the exemption has been used once within any 30-day period or if your trip is less than 48 hours long, the duty-free allowance is cut to $25.

There are certain articles, however, that are duty-free only up to certain limits. The $25 allowance includes the following: 10 cigars (not Cuban), 50 cigarettes, and 4 ounces of perfume. Individuals eligible for the full $400 duty-free limit are allowed 1 carton of cigarettes (200), 100 cigars, and 1 liter of liquor or wine if the traveler is over 21. Under federal law, alcohol above this allowance is liable for both duty and an Internal Revenue Service tax. Note, however, that states are allowed to impose additional restrictions and penalties of their own, including (in Arizona and Utah, for example) confiscation of any quantities of liquor over the statutory limit. Antiques, if they are 100 or more years old and you have proof from the seller of that fact, are duty-free, as are paintings and drawings if done entirely by hand. To avoid paying duty twice, register the serial numbers of watches and electronic equipment with the nearest US Customs bureau before departure; receipts of insurance policies also should be carried for other foreign-made items. Gold, gold medals, bullion, and up to $10,000 in currency or negotiable instruments may be brought into the US without being declared; sums over $10,000 must be declared in writing.

The allotment for individual "unsolicited" gifts mailed from abroad (no more than one per day per recipient) is $50 retail value per gift. These gifts do not have to be declared and are not included in your duty-free exemption (see below). The package should be clearly marked "Not for Sale," and you should include a receipt for purchases with each package. The US Customs examiner usually will accept this as indicative of the articles' fair retail value, but he or she is empowered to impose a duty if he or she feels the goods have been undervalued. The duty owed is collected by the US Postal Service when the package is delivered.

It is a good idea, if you have accumulated too much while abroad, to mail home any personal effects (made and bought in the US) that you no longer need rather than your foreign purchases. These personal effects pass through US Customs as "American goods returned" and are not subject to duty. More information on mailing packages home from abroad is contained in the US Customs Service pamphlet *Buyer Beware, International Mail Imports* (see below for where to write for this and other useful brochures).

DUTY-FREE CRAFT ITEMS: In January 1976, the United States approved a Generalized System of Preferences (GSP) to help developing nations improve their economies through exports. The GSP, which recognizes dozens of developing nations, including Mexico, allows Americans to bring certain kinds of goods into the US duty-free, and has designated some 3,000 items as eligible for duty-free treatment.

This system entitles you to exceed your $400 duty-free exemption as long as the purchases are eligible for GSP status. The list of eligible goods includes a wide range of categories. A useful pamphlet, which identifies GSP beneficiary nations and goods included in the program, is *GSP and the Traveler;* order "US Customs Publication No. 515" from the US Customs Service (Customs Information, 6 World Trade Center, Rm. 201, New York, NY 10048; phone: 212-466-5550). When in Mexico, information about the GSP status of particular items is available from any US Customs office or at the nearest US consulate (see *Legal Aid and Consular Services*).

CLEARING CUSTOMS: This is a simple procedure. Forms are distributed by airline or ship personnel before arrival. (Note that a $5-per-person service charge — called a user fee — is collected by airlines and cruise lines to help cover the cost of customs checks, but this is included in the ticket price.) If your purchases total no more than the duty-free $400 limit, you need only fill out the identification part of the form and make an oral declaration to the customs inspector. If entering the US with more than $400 worth of goods, you must submit a written declaration.

Customs agents are businesslike, efficient, and not unkind. During the peak season, clearance can take time, but this generally is because of the strain imposed by a number of jumbo jets simultaneously discharging their passengers, not because of unwarranted zeal on the part of the customs people.

Efforts to streamline procedures used to include the so-called Citizens' Bypass Program, which allowed US citizens whose purchases were within their duty-free allowance to go to the "green line," where they simply showed their passports to the customs inspector. Although at the time of this writing this procedure still is being followed at some international airports in the US, most airports have returned to an earlier system. US citizens arriving from abroad now have to go through a passport check by the Immigration & Naturalization Service (INS) prior to recovering their baggage and proceeding to customs. (US citizens will not be on the same line as foreign visitors, but this additional wait does delay clearance on re-entry into the US.) Although all passengers have to go through this obligatory passport inspection, those entering with purchases within the duty-free limit may be spared a thorough customs inspection; however, inspectors still retain the right to search any luggage they choose — so don't do anything foolish.

It is illegal not to declare dutiable items; not to do so, in fact, constitutes smuggling, and the penalty can be anything from stiff fines and seizure of the goods to prison sentences. It simply isn't worth doing. There is a basic rule to buying goods abroad, and it should never be broken: *If you can't afford the duty on something, don't buy it.*

FORBIDDEN IMPORTS: Narcotics, plants (unless specifically exempt and free of soil), and many types of food are not allowed into the US. Drugs are totally illegal, with the exception of medication prescribed by a physician. It's a good idea to travel with no more than you actually need of any medication and to have the prescription on hand in case any question arises either abroad or when reentering the US.

Any authentic archaeological find, Spanish colonial art, and other original artifacts cannot be exported from Mexico unless a special permit is obtained before leaving. Without such a permit, these items will be confiscated at the border, and the violator runs the risk of being fined or imprisoned. Mexico also restricts export of gold and silver coins; people interested in such items should check with Mexican Customs. For further information, contact the *Instituto Nacional de Antropología e Historia (National Institute of History and Anthropology),* 45 Córdoba, Col. Roma, México, DF 06700 (phone: 5-533-2263).

Tourists have long been forbidden to bring into the United States foreign-made, US trademarked articles purchased abroad (if the trademark is recorded with US Customs) without written permission. It's now permissible to enter with one such item in your possession as long as it's for personal use.

The US Customs Service implements the rigorous Department of Agriculture regulations concerning the importation of vegetable matter, seeds, bulbs, and the like. Living vegetable matter may not be imported without a permit, and everything must be inspected, permit or not. Approved items (which do not require a permit) include dried bamboo and woven items made of straw; beads made of most seeds (but not jequirity beans — the poisonous scarlet and black seed of the rosary pea), Mexican jumping beans, and some viable seeds; coconut shells (unhusked and empty); cones of pine and other trees; roasted coffee beans; most flower bulbs; flowers (without roots); dried or canned fruits, jellies, or jams; polished rice, dried beans, and teas; herb plants (not witchweed); nuts (but not acorns, chestnuts, or any nuts with outer husks); dried lichens, mushrooms, truffles, shamrocks, and seaweed; and most dried spices.

Other processed foods and baked goods usually are okay. Regulations on meat products generally depend on the country of origin and manner of processing. As a rule, commercially canned meat, hermetically sealed and cooked in the can so that it can be stored without refrigeration, is permitted, but not all canned meat fulfills this requirement. Be careful in buying canned chili, for instance. Chili made with peppers, beans, and meat in itself is acceptable, but the pork fat that often is part of it may not be. (The imported brands you see in US stores have been prepared and packaged according to US regulations.) So before stocking up on a newfound favorite, it pays to check in advance — otherwise you might have to leave it behind.

The US Customs Service also enforces federal laws that prohibit the entry of articles made from the furs or hides of animals on the endangered species list. Don't be tempted by sweaters and other garments made from the fine hair of the vicuña (a relative of the domestic llama and alpaca), which is an endangered species. Also beware of shoes, bags, and belts made of crocodile and certain kinds of lizard, and anything made of tortoise-shell; this also applies to preserved crocodiles, lizards, and turtles sometimes sold in gift shops. Most coral — particularly black coral — also is restricted (although small amounts of coral incorporated into jewelry and other crafts items are usually permitted). And if you're shopping for big-ticket items, beware of fur coats made from the skins of spotted cats. They are sold abroad, but they will be confiscated upon your return to the US, and there will be no refund. For information about other animals on the endangered species list, contact the Department of the Interior, US Fish and Wildlife Service (Publications Unit, 4401 N. Fairfax Dr., Rm. 130, Arlington, VA 22203; phone: 703-358-1711), and ask for the free publication *Facts About Federal Wildlife Laws.*

Also note that some foreign governments prohibit the export of items made from certain species of wildlife, and the US honors any such restrictions. Before you go shopping in any foreign country, check with the US Department of Agriculture (G110 Federal Bldg., Hyattsville, MD 20782; phone: 301-436-8413) and find out what items are prohibited from the country you will be visiting.

The US Customs Service publishes a series of free pamphlets with customs information. It includes *Know Before You Go,* a basic discussion of customs requirements pertaining to all travelers; *Buyer Beware, International Mail Imports; Travelers' Tips on Bringing Food, Plant, and Animal Products into the United States; Importing a Car; GSP and the Traveler; Pocket Hints; Currency Reporting; Pets, Wildlife, US Customs; Customs Hints for Visitors (Nonresidents);* and *Trademark Information for Travelers.* For the entire series or individual pamphlets, write to the US Customs Service (PO Box 7474, Washington, DC 20044) or contact any of the seven regional offices — in Boston, Chicago, Houston, Long Beach (California), Miami, New Orleans, and New York.

Note that the US Customs Service has a tape-recorded message whereby callers using touch-tone phones can get more information on various travel-related topics; the number is 202-566-8195. These pamphlets provide great briefing material, but if you still have questions when you're in Mexico contact the US Customs representative at the nearest US consulate (for the address, see *Legal Aid and Consular Services,* above).

Sources and Resources

Mexican Consulates and Tourist Offices in the US

The Mexican government tourist offices and consulates in the US generally are the best sources of local travel information, and most of their publications are free for the asking. When requesting brochures and maps, state the areas you plan to visit, as well as your particular interests: accommodations, restaurants, special events, tourist attractions, guided tours, facilities for specific sports, and other activities. There is no need to send a self-addressed, stamped envelope with your request, unless specified. Offices generally are open on weekdays, during normal business hours.

Where required, the consulates also issue tourist cards. They also are empowered to sign other official documents — such as commercial and residence visas — and to notarize copies or translations of American documents, which often is necessary for those papers to be considered legal in Mexico.

The Mexican Embassy is located in Washington, DC (1911 Pennsylvania Ave. NW Washington, DC 20006; phone: 202-728-1600). In most cases, however, visitors to Mexico should direct their inquiries and requests to one of the consulates or tourist offices listed below.

Below is a list of Mexican consuls, consulates, and Mexican government tourist offices in the US:

Consuls and Consulates

Albuquerque: Consulate General, Western Bank Bldg., 401 Fifth St. NW, Albuquerque, NM 87102 (phone: 505-247-2139).

Atlanta: Consulate General, 410 S. Tower 1, CNN Center, Atlanta, GA 30303-2705 (phone: 404-688-3258).

Austin: Consulate General, 200 E. Sixth St., Suite 200, Austin, TX 78701 (phone: 512-478-2866).

Boston: Consulate, Statler Bldg., 20 Park Plaza, Suite 1212, Boston, MA 02116 (phone: 617-426-4942).

Brownsville: Consulate, 724 E. Elizabeth St., Brownsville, TX 78520 (phone: 512-542-4431).

Buffalo: Consul, 1875 Harlem Rd., Buffalo, NY 14212 (phone: 716-895-9800).

Calexico: Consul, 331 W. 2nd St., Calexico, CA 92231 (phone: 619-357-3863).

Chicago: Consulate General, 300 N. Michigan Ave., 2nd Floor, Chicago, IL 60601 (phone: 312-855-1380).

Corpus Christi: Consulate, 800 N. Shoreline Blvd., N. Tower, 4th Floor, Corpus Christi, TX 78401 (phone: 512-882-3375).

Dallas: Consulate General, 1349 Empire Center, Suite 100, Dallas, TX 75247 (phone: 214-630-7341).

Del Rio: Consulate, 1010 S. Main St., Del Rio, TX 78840 (phone: 512-774-5031).

Denver: Consulate General, 707 Washington St., Suite A, Denver, CO 80203 (phone: 303-830-0523).

Detroit: Consulate, 600 Renaissance Center, Suite 1510, Detroit, MI 48243 (phone: 313-567-7713).

Eagle Pass: Consulate, 140 Adams St., Eagle Pass, TX 78852 (phone: 512-773-9255).

El Paso: Consulate General, 910 E. San Antonio St., El Paso, TX 79901 (phone: 915-533-3645).

Fresno: Consulate, 905 N. Fulton St., Fresno, CA 93728 (phone: 209-233-3065).

Honolulu: Consul, Control Data Bldg., 2828 Paa St., Suite 2115, Honolulu, HI 96819 (phone: 808-833-6331).

Houston: Consulate General, 3015 Richmond Ave., Suite 100, Houston, TX 77098 (phone: 713-524-4861).

Laredo: Consulate, 1612 Farragut St., Laredo, TX 78040 (phone: 512-723-6360).

Los Angeles: Consulate General, 2401 W. Sixth St., Los Angeles, CA 90057 (phone: 213-351-6800).

Madison: Consul, 141 N. Hancock, Madison, WI 53703-2311 (phone: 608-283-6000).

McAllen: Consulate, 1418 Beech St., Suite 102, McAllen, TX 78501 (phone: 512-686-0243).

Miami: Consulate, 780 NW 42nd Ave., Suite 525, Miami, FL 33126 (phone: 305-441-8780).

Nashville: Consul, 226 Capitol Blvd., Suite 212, Nashville, TN 37219 (phone: 615-244-7430).

New Orleans: Consulate General, World Trade Center, 2 Canal St., Suite 1140, New Orleans, LA 70130 (phone: 504-522-3596).

New York: Consulate General, 8 E. 41st St., New York, NY 10017 (phone: 212-689-0456).

Nogales: Consulate, 60 Terrace Ave., Nogales, AZ 85621 (phone: 602-287-2521).

Norfolk: Consulate, 5121 E. Virginia Beach Blvd., Suite E2, Norfolk, VA 23502 (phone: 804-461-4553).

Philadelphia: Consulate, Bourse Bldg., 21 S. Fifth St., Suite 575, Philadelphia, PA 19106 (phone: 215-922-4262).

Phoenix: Consulate General, 1190 W. Camelback, Suite 110, Phoenix, AZ 85015 (phone: 602-242-7398).

Portland: Consul, 545 NE 47th Ave., Portland, OR 97213 (phone: 503-233-5662).

Richmond: Consul, 2420 Pemberton Rd., Richmond, VA 23233 (phone: 804-747-1961).

Sacramento: Consulate, 9812 Old Winery Pl., Sacramento, CA 95827 (phone: 916-363-3885).

St. Louis: Consulate General, 1015 Locust St., Suite 922, St. Louis, MO 63101 (phone: 314-436-3233).

Salt Lake City: Consulate General, 182 S. 600 East, Suite 202, Salt Lake City, UT 84102 (phone: 801-521-8502).

San Antonio: Consulate General, 127 Navarro St., San Antonio, TX 78205 (phone: 512-227-9145).

San Bernardino: Consulate, 588 W. 6th St., San Bernardino, CA 92401 (phone: 714-889-9836).

San Diego: Consulate General, 610 A St., Suite 200, San Diego, CA 92101 (phone: 619-231-8414).

San Francisco: Consulate General, 870 Market St., Suite 528, San Francisco, CA 94102 (phone: 415-392-5554).

San Jose: Consulate General, 380 N. First St., Suite 102, San Jose, CA 95112 (phone: 408-294-3415).

Seattle: Consulate General, 2132 Third Ave., Seattle, WA 98121 (phone: 206-448-6819).

Spokane: Consul, 12019 E. Sprague Ave., Spokane, WA 99206 (phone: 509-928-7671).

Tampa: Consul, 1717 W. Cass St., Tampa, FL 33602 (phone: 813-254-5960).

Tucson: Consulate, 553 South Stone Ave., Tucson, AZ 85701 (phone: 602-882-5595).

Washington, DC: Consulate, 2827 16th St. NW, Washington DC 20009 (phone: 202-736-1000).

Ministry of Tourism Offices

Chicago: 70 E. Lake St., Suite 1413, Chicago, IL 60601 (phone: 312-565-2786).

Houston: 2707 N. Loop W, Suite 450, Houston, TX 77008 (phone: 713-880-5153).

Los Angeles: 10100 Santa Monica Blvd., Suite 224, Los Angeles, CA 90067 (phone: 213-203-8191).

New York: 405 Park Ave., Suite 1401, New York, NY 10022 (phone: 212-838-2949).

Washington, DC: 1911 Pennsylvania Ave. NW Washington, DC 20006 (phone: 202-728-1750).

Weights and Measures

 When traveling in Mexico, you'll find that just about every quantity, whether it is length, weight, or capacity, will be expressed in unfamiliar terms. In fact, this is true for travel almost everywhere in the world, since the US is one of the last countries to make its way to the metric system. Your trip to Mexico may serve to familiarize you with what may one day be the weights and measures used at your grocery store.

There are some specific things to bear in mind during your trip. Fruits and vegetables at a market are recorded in *kilos* (kilograms), as is your luggage at the airport and your body weight. (This latter is particularly pleasing to people of significant size, who, instead of weighing 220 pounds, hit the scales at a mere 100 kilos.) A kilo equals 2.2 pounds and 1 pound is .45 kilo. Body temperature usually is measured in Centigrade or Celsius rather than Fahrenheit, so that a normal body temperature reading is 37C, not 98.6F, and freezing is 0 degrees C rather than 32F.

Gasoline is sold by the liter (3.8 liters to 1 gallon), but tire pressure gauges and other equipment measure in pounds per square inch, as in the US. Highway signs are written in kilometers rather than miles (1 mile equals 1.6 km; 1 km equals .62 miles). And speed limits are in kilometers per hour, so think twice before hitting the gas when you see a speed limit of 100. That means 62 miles per hour.

The tables and conversion factors listed below should give you all the information you will need to understand any transaction, road sign, or map you encounter during your travels.

CONVERSION TABLES: METRIC TO US MEASUREMENTS		
Multiply	**by**	**to convert to**
LENGTH		
millimeters	.04	inches
meters	3.3	feet
meters	1.1	yards
kilometers	.6	miles
CAPACITY		
liters	2.11	pints (liquid)
liters	1.06	quarts (liquid)
liters	.26	gallons (liquid)
WEIGHT		
grams	.04	ounces (avoir)
kilograms	2.2	pounds (avoir)

US TO METRIC MEASUREMENTS		
Multiply	**by**	**to convert to**
LENGTH		
inches	25.	millimeters
feet	.3	meters
yards	.9	meters
miles	1.6	kilometers
CAPACITY		
pints	.47	liters
quarts	.95	liters
gallons	3.8	liters
WEIGHT		
ounces	28.	grams
pounds	.45	kilograms

TEMPERATURE

$$°F = (°C \times 9/5) + 32 \qquad °C = (°F - 32) \times 5/9$$

APPROXIMATE EQUIVALENTS		
Metric Unit	**Abbreviation**	**US Equivalent**
LENGTH		
millimeter	mm	.04 inch
meter	m	39.37 inches
kilometer	km	.62 mile
AREA		
square centimeter	sq cm	.155 square inch
square meter	sq m	10.7 square feet
hectare	ha	2.47 acres
square kilometer	sq km	.3861 square mile
CAPACITY		
liter	l	1.057 quarts
WEIGHT		
gram	g	.035 ounce
kilogram	kg	2.2 pounds
metric ton	MT	1.1 tons
ENERGY		
kilowatt	kw	1.34 horsepower

Cameras and Equipment

Vacations are everybody's favorite time for taking pictures and home movies. After all, most of us want to remember the places we visit — and show them off to others. Here are a few suggestions to help you get the best results from your travel photography or videography.

BEFORE THE TRIP

If you're taking your camera or camcorder out after a long period in mothballs, or have just bought a new one, check it thoroughly before you leave to prevent unexpected breakdowns or disappointing pictures.

1. Still cameras should be cleaned carefully and thoroughly, inside and out. If using a camcorder, run a head cleaner through it. Always use filters to protect your lenses while traveling.
2. Check the batteries for your camera's light meter and flash, and take along extras just in case yours wear out during the trip. For camcorders, bring along extra Nickel-Cadmium (Ni-Cad) batteries; if you use rechargeable batteries, a recharger will cut down on the extras.
3. Using all the settings and features, shoot at least one test roll of film or one videocassette, using the type you plan to take along with you.

EQUIPMENT TO TAKE ALONG

Keep your gear light and compact. Items that are too heavy or bulky to be carried comfortably on a full-day excursion will likely remain in your hotel room, so leave them at home.

1. Invest in a broad camera or camcorder strap if you now have a thin one. It will make carrying the camera much more comfortable.
2. A sturdy canvas, vinyl, or leather camera or camcorder bag, preferably with padded pockets (not an airline bag), will keep your equipment organized and easy to find. If you will be doing much shooting around the water, a waterproof case is best.
3. For cleaning, bring along a camel's hair brush that retracts into a rubber squeeze bulb. Also take plenty of lens tissue, soft cloths, and plastic bags to protect equipment from dust and moisture.

FILM AND TAPES: If you are concerned about airport security X-rays damaging undeveloped film (X-rays do not affect processed film) or tapes, store them in one of the lead-lined bags sold in camera shops. In the US and Canada, incidents of X-ray damage to unprocessed film (exposed or unexposed) are few because low-dosage X-ray equipment is used virtually everywhere. While the international trend also is toward equipment that delivers less and less radiation, equipment in Mexico tends to be less up-to-date than in some other foreign countries, and is, therefore, less predictable. If you're traveling without a protective bag, you may want to ask to have your photo equipment inspected by hand.

One type of film that should never be subjected to X-rays is the new, very-high-speed ASA 1000; there are lead-lined bags made especially for it — and, in the event that you are refused a hand inspection, this is the only way to save your film. The walk-through metal detector devices at airports do not affect film, though the film cartridges may set them off.

You should have no problem finding film or tapes throughout Mexico, particularly in metropolitan and major resort areas. When buying film, tapes, or photo accessories the best rule of thumb is to stick to name brands with which you are familiar. Different countries have their own ways of labeling camcorder tapes, and although variations in recording and playback standards won't affect your ability to use the tape, they will affect how quickly you record and how much time you actually have to record on the tape. The availability of film processing labs and equipment repair shops will vary from area to area.

■ **A note about courtesy and caution:** When photographing individuals Mexico (and anywhere else in the world), ask first. It's common courtesy. In many of the smaller towns, and even some of the cities, the Indians have superstitions or religious beliefs that photographing them is an insult at best, and at worst, a violation. Furthermore, some governments have security regulations regarding the use of cameras and will not permit the photographing of certain subjects, such as particular government or military installations. When in doubt, ask.

USEFUL WORDS
AND PHRASES

Useful Words and Phrases

 Unlike the French, who tend to be a bit brusque if you don't speak their language perfectly, the Mexicans do not expect you to speak Spanish — but are very flattered when you try. In many circumstances, you won't have to, because the staffs at most hotels, museums, and tourist attractions, as well as at a fair number of restaurants, speak serviceable English, or at least a version of it, which they are usually eager to try — and that means practicing with you. Particularly when you get off the beaten path, however, you will find at least a rudimentary knowledge of Spanish very helpful. Don't be afraid of misplaced accents or misconjugated verbs. Mexicans appreciate your efforts to speak their language and will do their best to understand you. They will also make an effort to be understood.

Mexican Spanish has a number of regional dialects, but the dialect of educated people in Mexico City is regarded as standard, is used on national television, and is understood by almost everybody, even though their local speech may be quite different. Most people can communicate in what is considered "standard" Spanish, and the spelling of standard Mexican Spanish is a very reliable guide to pronunciation.

The list below is a selection of commonly used words and phrases to speed you on your way. Note that in Spanish all nouns are either masculine or feminine, as well as singular and plural, and that the adjectives that modify them must agree in both gender and number. Most nouns ending in *o* are masculine (the corresponding articles are *el* and *uno* or *un*); most nouns ending in *a* are feminine (the feminine articles are *la* and *una*). Plurals are formed by adding *s* (the articles are *los, unos, las,* and *unas*). Adjectives almost always follow nouns in Spanish. Otherwise, word order is very much as in English.

The following pronunciation rules may also be helpful:

The vowel before the last consonant in a word (except *n* or *s*) is accented, unless there is an accent mark on another vowel. When the last consonant is *n* or *s,* the vowel before the preceding consonant is usually accented. In addition:

a is pronounced as in *father*
e is pronounced as in *red*
i is pronounced as in *machine*
o is pronounced as in *note*
u is pronounced as in *rude*
ei/ey are pronounced as in *vein*
oi/oy are pronounced as in *joy*
ai/ay are pronounced like *y* in *by*
au is pronounced like *ou* in *house*

In general, in vowel letter sequences (*ae, ie, ue, ia,* and so on), each letter is pronounced.

Mexican Spanish consonants are pronounced as in English, with these exceptions:

The consonants *b, d,* and *g* are pronounced with the air passage slightly open, producing a softer sound. The consonants *p, t,* and *c/k* are pronounced without the aspiration (the strong puff of breath) that characterizes them in English.

b within words is pronounced like the English *v*

d within words is pronounced like *th* in *other*

g before *e* or *i* is pronounced like a strongly aspirated English *h* or German *ch;* otherwise, as above

h is silent

j is pronounced like a strongly aspirated *h*

ll is pronounced like *y* in *youth*

ñ is pronounced like *ny* in *canyon*

qu is pronounced *k* before *e* or *i: quilo* is pronounced as the English *kilo*

r is pronounced like the casual English *d* in *pedal*

rr is trilled, as in the Scottish *farm*

s and *z* are pronounced *z* within words preceding a voiced consonant (*b, d, g, m, n, r, l*); otherwise they are pronounced as the English *s*

Greetings and Everyday Expressions

Good morning (also, Good day).	*Buenos días*
Good afternoon/evening	*Buenas tardes*
Good night	*Buenas noches*
Hello	*Hola!*
How are you?	*Cómo está usted?*
Pleased to meet you	*Mucho gusto en conocerle*
Good-bye!	*Adiós!*
So long!	*Hasta luego!*
Yes	*Sí*
No	*No*
Please	*Por favor*
Thank you	*Gracias*
You're welcome	*De nada*
I beg your pardon (Excuse me).	*Perdón*
I'm sorry	*Lo siento*
It doesn't matter	*No importa*
I don't speak Spanish.	*No hablo Español.*
Do you speak English?	*Habla usted inglés?*
I don't understand.	*No comprendo.*
Do you understand?	*Comprende?/Entiende?*
My name is . . .	*Me llamo . . .*
What is your name?	*Cómo se llama?*
miss	*señorita*
madame	*señora* (married).
	doña (unmarried).
mister	*señor*
open	*abierto/a*
closed	*cerrado/a*
entrance	*entrada*
exit	*salida*

push	*empujar*
pull	*tirar*
today	*hoy*
tomorrow	*mañana*
yesterday	*ayer*

Checking In

I have a reservation.	*He hecho una reserva.*
I would like . . .	*Quisiera . . .*
a single room	*una habitación sencilla*
a double room	*una habitación doble*
a quiet room	*una habitación tranquila*
with bath	*con baño*
with shower	*con ducha*
with a sea view	*con vista al mar*
with air conditioning	*con aire acondicionado*
with balcony	*con balcón*
overnight only	*sólo una noche*
a few days	*unos cuantos días*
a week (at least)	*una semana (por lo menos)*
with full board	*con pensión completa*
with half board	*con media pensión*
Does that price include . . .	*Está incluído en el precio . . .*
breakfast?	*el desayuno?*
taxes?	*los impuestos?*
Do you accept traveler's checks?	*Acepta usted cheques de viajero?*
Do you accept credit cards?	*Acepta tarjetas de crédito?*
It doesn't work.	*No funciona.*

Eating Out

ashtray	*un cenicero*
(extra) chair	*una silla (adicional)*
table	*una mesa*
bottle	*una botella*
cup	*una taza*
plate	*un plato*
fork	*un tenedor*
knife	*un cuchillo*
spoon	*una cuchara*
napkin	*una servilleta*
hot chocolate (cocoa)	*un chocolate caliente*
black coffee	*un café negro*
coffee with milk	*café con leche*
cream	*crema*
milk	*leche*

tea	*un té*
fruit juice	*un jugo de fruta*
lemonade	*una limonada*
water	*agua*
mineral water	*agua mineral*
carbonated	*con gas*
noncarbonated	*sin gas*
orangeade	*una naranjada*
beer	*una cerveza*
port	*oporto*
sherry	*jerez*
red wine	*vino tinto*
white wine	*vino blanco*
cold	*frio/a*
hot	*caliente*
sweet	*dulce*
(very) dry	*(muy) seco/a*
bread	*pan*
butter	*mantequilla*
bacon	*tocino*
eggs	*huevos*
hard-boiled	*un huevo cocido*
fried	*huevos fritos*
omelette	*torta de huevos*
soft-boiled	*un huevo pasado por agua*
scrambled	*huevos revueltos*
honey	*miel*
jam, marmalade	*mermelada*
orange juice	*jugo de naranja*
pepper	*pimienta*
salt	*sal*
sugar	*azúcar*
Waiter!	*Camarero!/Mesero!*
I would like	*Quisiera*
a glass of	*un vaso de*
a bottle of	*una botella de*
a half bottle of	*una media botella de*
a carafe of	*una garrafa de*
a liter of	*un litro de*
The check, please.	*La cuenta, por favor.*
Is a service charge included?	*Está el servicio incluído?*
I think there is a mistake in the bill.	*Creo que hay un error en la cuenta.*

Shopping

bakery	*la panadería*
bookstore	*la librería*
butcher shop	*la carnicería*
camera shop	*la tienda de fotografía*
delicatessen	*la tienda de comestibles preparados*
department store	*el almacén grande*
grocery	*la tienda de comestibles*
jewelry store	*la joyería*
newsstand	*el puesto de periódicos*
pastry shop	*la pastelería*
perfume (and cosmetics) store	*perfumería*
pharmacy/drugstore	*la farmacia*
shoestore	*la zapatería*
supermarket	*el supermercado*
tobacconist	*el estanquero*
inexpensive	*barato/a*
expensive	*caro/a*
large	*grande*
larger	*más grande*
too large	*demasiado grande*
small	*pequeño/a*
smaller	*más pequeño/a*
too small	*demasiado pequeño/a*
long	*largo/a*
short	*corto/a*
old	*viejo/a*
new	*nuevo/a*
used	*usado/a*
handmade	*hecho/a a mano*
Is it machine washable?	*Es lavable a máquina?*
How much does it cost?	*Cuánto cuesta esto?*
What is it made of?	*De qué está hecho?*
camel's hair	*pelo de camello*
cotton	*algodón*
corduroy	*pana*
filigree	*filigrana*
lace	*encaje*
leather	*cuero*
linen	*lino*
suede	*ante*
synthetic	*sintético/a*
tile	*baldosa*
wood	*madera*
wool	*lana*

brass	*latón*
copper	*cobre*
gold	*oro*
gold plated	*dorado*
silver	*plata*
silver plated	*plateado*
stainless steel	*acero inoxidable*

Colors

beige	*beige*
black	*negro/a*
blue	*azul*
brown	*moreno/a*
green	*verde*
gray	*gris*
orange	*anaranjado/a*
pink	*rosa*
purple	*morado/a*
red	*rojo/a*
white	*blanco/a*
yellow	*amarillo/a*
dark	*obscuro/a*
light	*claro/a*

Getting Around

north	*norte*
south	*sur*
east	*este*
west	*oeste*
right	*derecho/a*
left	*izquierdo/a*
Go straight ahead.	*Siga todo derecho.*
far	*lejos*
near	*cerca*
gas station	*la gasolinería*
train station	*la estación de ferrocarril*
bus stop	*la parada de autobuses*
subway station	*estación de metro*
airport	*el aeropuerto*
tourist information	*información turística*
map	*el mapa*
one-way ticket	*un billete de ida*
round-trip ticket	*un billete de ida y vuelta*
track	*el andén*
first class	*primera clase*
second class	*segunda clase*
smoking	*fumar*
no smoking	*no fumar*

gasoline	*gasolina*
regular	*nova*
premium	*extra*
leaded	*con plomo*
unleaded	*magna sin* or *sin plomo*
diesel	*diesel*
Fill it up, please.	*Llénelo, por favor.*
oil	*el aceite*
tires	*las llantas*
Where is . . . ?	*Dónde está . . . ?*
Where are . . . ?	*Dónde están . . . ?*
How far is it from here to . . . ?	*Qué distancia hay desde aquí hasta . . . ?*
Does this train go to . . . ?	*Va este tren a . . . ?*
Does this bus go to . . . ?	*Va este autobús a . . . ?*
What time does it leave?	*A qué hora sale?*
Danger	*Peligro*
Caution	*Precaución*
Detour	*Desvío*
Do Not Enter	*Paso Prohibido*
No Parking	*Estacionamiento Prohibido*
No Passing	*Prohibido Pasar*
One Way	*Dirección Unica*
Pay Toll	*Peaje*
Pedestrian Zone	*Zona Peatonal*
Reduce Speed	*Despacio*
Steep Incline	*Fuerte Declive*
Stop	*Alto*
Use Headlights	*Encender los faros*
Yield	*Ceda el Paso*

Personal Items and Services

aspirin	*aspirina*
Band-Aids	*curitas*
barbershop	*la barbería*
beauty shop	*el salón de belleza*
condom	*condón*
dry cleaner	*la tintorería*
hairdresser's	*la peluquería*
laundromat	*la lavandería*
laundry	*la lavandería*
post office	*el correo*
postage stamps	*estampillas*
sanitary napkins	*unos paños higiénicos*
shampoo	*un champú*
shaving cream	*espuma de afeitar*

soap	*el jabón*
tampons	*unos tampones higiénicos*
tissues	*Kleenex*
toilet paper	*papel higiénico*
toothpaste	*pasta de dientes*
Where is the bathroom?	*Dónde está el baño?*
toilet?	*excusado?*
MEN	*Caballeros*
WOMEN	*Señoras*

Days of the Week

Monday	*Lunes*
Tuesday	*Martes*
Wednesday	*Miércoles*
Thursday	*Jueves*
Friday	*Viernes*
Saturday	*Sábado*
Sunday	*Domingo*

Months

January	*Enero*
February	*Febrero*
March	*Marzo*
April	*Abril*
May	*Mayo*
June	*Junio*
July	*Julio*
August	*Agosto*
September	*Septiembre*
October	*Octubre*
November	*Noviembre*
December	*Diciembre*

Numbers

zero	*cero*
one	*uno*
two	*dos*
three	*tres*
four	*cuatro*
five	*cinco*
six	*seis*
seven	*siete*
eight	*ocho*
nine	*nueve*
ten	*diez*
eleven	*once*
twelve	*doce*
thirteen	*trece*
fourteen	*catorce*
fifteen	*quince*
sixteen	*dieciséis*
seventeen	*diecisiete*
eighteen	*dieciocho*

nineteen	*diecinueve*
twenty	*veinte*
thirty	*treinta*
forty	*cuarenta*
fifty	*cincuenta*
sixty	*sesenta*
seventy	*setenta*
eighty	*ochenta*
ninety	*noventa*
one hundred	*cien*
one thousand	*mil*

THE CITY

ACAPULCO

(pronounced Ah-ca-*pul*-co)

The mere mention of Acapulco usually causes a string of extravagant images to come to mind. Whether or not you consider these superlatives justified, Acapulco's reputation as an international beach resort borders on legendary. Throughout the year, and especially in the winter, tourists from all over the world descend on the hotel-lined gem of a bay facing the Pacific Ocean, generating a momentum that is in itself a kind of homage to this resort's reputation.

How you personally feel about Acapulco will depend, in large part, on your reaction to the sheer number of tourists around you — over 6 million people visited Acapulco last year. It is definitely not a place for "getting away from it all," if by that you mean getting away from all the other people who are also trying to get away from it all. It is not, in fact, a place where you can get away from much of anything, except the rest of the world's rotten weather and your own daily routine. But if you don't mind sharing the pleasures of the sun — and the flesh — with lots of other similarly inclined folk, the beaches and pools in and around Acapulco can be among the most compelling tourist destinations in the Western Hemisphere.

The prime reason anyone comes to Acapulco is the weather — that perfect weather that simply can't be duplicated in any sun-drenched spot within the same distance of the United States. When a winter-paled body makes its hegira to Acapulco, it knows it's going to return home beautifully browned, sporting an even tan devoid of imperfections.

It is possible to enjoy Acapulco without getting into a hectic round of nightclubs, discos, and parties. You can get up early in the morning and have the eastern beaches all to yourself, although it's common to joke that the only people in Acapulco who get up early in the morning are those who go deep-sea fishing. (*A sun warning:* Be very careful if you have sensitive skin. Two hours on an Acapulco beach in the morning can roast you — to say nothing of the afternoon, when the sun is even stronger.)

In the afternoon, it's far better to take a siesta between 1 and 4 PM. Even Acapulco residents stay out of the sun in the middle of the afternoon. In late afternoon, watch the sunset while sipping tequila concoctions. Places like Pie de la Cuesta Beach, just outside town, are traditional dusk headquarters, though in recent years they've become inundated by native peddlers so you'll now have to venture farther off to escape the harassment of vendors and beggars. After dusk, return to your hotel and get ready for a quiet, leisurely dinner. Acapulco doesn't have to be frenetic.

But for most of the people who come here, Acapulco means party. A lot of people, Mexican as well as foreign, wouldn't be caught anywhere near a beach until one or two in the afternoon, after they've had a chance to sleep off the night before. The afternoon beach used to be Los Hornos, and the morning beach Caleta, but times have changed. Caleta is not as classy (or as clean) as it used to be, and the action has moved farther east, from Los Hornos to La Condesa, which is the stretch of beach between the *El Presidente* and the *Continental Plaza Acapulco* hotels.

There are two things to heed on this stretch of beach: the Pacific Ocean, which can easily toss you upside down, and the swarm of vendors of all ages who work the strip. The surf, however, never discriminates. At Condesa, things don't get going until noon and don't really start swinging until after one in the afternoon. Lunch is served around 2 PM. Take your time. People don't start drifting back to the beach until late afternoon. Dinner in Acapulco is served around 9 or 10 PM.

More than any other Mexican city, Acapulco reeks of sensuality. This, too, accounts for its popularity. Acapulco's sexiness is part of its legend, and one of the first things you're almost bound to notice is that no one ever wears more than bathing trunks or a bikini during the day. People are constantly flaunting their bodies, even on the city's buses or in supermarkets.

At night, the sounds of tropical guitar and rock music drift through the air, mingling with the music of the ocean, the leaves blowing in the soft, humid wind, and the murmur of gentle conversations. There is something languorous in the air, and it can prove disastrous to one's inhibitions. In addition to mellowing people, the sexual atmosphere serves to level differences in social class. There's no way to tell the difference between a genuine jet setter and an Oklahoma secretary or Omaha insurance salesman when everything is pared down to the bare essentials. You can get down to basics very quickly in Acapulco.

The spectacular beauty of Acapulco's bay has been appreciated for centuries, but for years the isolation of the area kept the city from participating in much of Mexico's history. It was founded in 1531 by the Spanish, who cut a sort of horse path through the rugged mountains to it from Mexico City. Today, the drive takes only a few hours on a brand-new superhighway that was blasted through the mountains. It used to take weeks.

A few years after Acapulco was settled, the Spanish built two boats and began sailing up and down the coast making charts of the shoreline. By 1565, they learned (thanks to Magellan's crew) that it was possible to sail *east* from Spain and reach Mexico. Trade routes from the Orient to Mexico were opened, and Acapulco's beautiful harbor came into its own. Luxury items such as silk, porcelain, and ivory were transported by boat from China and Japan to Acapulco, then carried by mule train to Mexico City. From the capital, they were sent on to Veracruz for shipment to Spain. Acapulco soon grew to about 10,000 people (it has more than 1.5 million residents today), but this profitable trade did not go unnoticed by the English pirates. The infamous Sir Francis Drake, among others, began to prey on the Spanish galleons. Acapulco's Fort of San Diego was constructed to defend the port city against pirate raids. Destroyed in 1776 by an earthquake, it was rebuilt and still stands today.

After Mexico's War of Independence began in 1810, trade with the Orient ceased. Acapulco became a forgotten fishing village until a paved road was finally built from Mexico City in 1922, but even then it took another 10 years for it to get its first tentative start as a beach resort. An international port city since 1945, it really came into its own toward the end of the 1950s, when it began to be known as "The Riviera of the West."

Since then, Acapulco's reputation as a resort has dipped and soared like the waterskiers-cum-parachutists who take off from Condesa Beach. At the moment, it is on a plateau after several years of decline — due in part, at least, to the studied opinion of well-heeled travelers that Acapulco was no longer a prime choice among the world's most stylish tropical destinations. The rich and famous still go to Acapulco — religiously, every winter, to soak up sun at their villas in the surrounding hills — but they just don't talk about it the way they used to. More important, the stress of coping with such huge numbers of visitors (and the concomitant growth of the resident population, making Acapulco one of the fastest-growing cities in the world) overtaxed the city's resources.

Several years ago, the Mexican government invested $300 million in restoring and revitalizing Acapulco and the surrounding area. The newly constructed superhighway which joins Cuernavaca and Acapulco cuts the driving time from Mexico City to 3½ hours. Acapulco's main street, Costera Miguel Alemán, is now a well-maintained seaside avenue, and the beaches are better than they've been. The government has made a real effort to clean up its act, literally and figuratively, and to solve the problem of constant harassment by street and beach vendors. For the past several years, the beach around the bay and the main avenues has been cleaned daily. And because the state and municipal governments have set up open-air markets along the beach, and on vacant lots around the city, there are few — if any — encounters with vendors. The new markets are a far cry from the original installations, and have done wonders to help keep the vendors off the streets and beaches. Uniformed "tourist police" also have begun to patrol the Costera and to provide visitors with information. There is still room for improvement, especially in town and up in the mountains, where the majority of people live in substandard conditions. Still, there is too much about Acapulco to be prized and protected for the city to lose its luster entirely. You have only to look down on the city at dusk from the heights of a casita in the luxurious *Las Brisas* hotel complex to appreciate that you are in a unique place. The lights flicker like pearls on an endless necklace, and the dark water provides a muted reflection of the blinking brightness. Outside town, only the most blasé can turn down a ride on an Indian pony down the Revolcadero Beach and beyond.

It may be that Acapulco can regain its former place at the top of the pedestal of resorts that appeal to determined hedonists. Surely if money alone could cure overdevelopment, the city would already be all the way back to its former preeminence. The physical surroundings remain awesomely appealing: Just look at those green mountains rising from the white, sandy beaches surrounding the blue bay on three sides, and listen to the palm trees rustling in the Pacific wind. Add to this more than 300 hotels of every description, dozens of restaurants, nightclubs, discotheques, and beaches with skin diving, snorkeling, water skiing, parasailing, and swimming, and you have Acapulco — a very tempting tropical resort.

ACAPULCO AT-A-GLANCE

SEEING THE CITY: The setting is magnificent, for Acapulco is built where the mountains meet the sea. The first breathtaking view for most people appears at the high point of the hill above the southern border of the city (at the entrance to *Las Brisas* hotel), while they are driving in from the airport. (Airport Road is also known, for good reason, as the Carretera Escénica — Scenic Highway.) And almost every hotel balcony offers an unforgettable view. For a special look, try dining at one of the high-rise, roof garden restaurants, or go parasailing. The nicest time to soak up the scenery is at sunset, when the sky turns bright pink and gold, the city lights begin to twinkle, and the first stars come out.

SPECIAL PLACES: These days the action in Acapulco centers along the Costera Miguel Alemán, the broad avenue that runs along the bay. To the left (as you face the ocean) beyond the southwestern headland is Puerto Marqués and then the open sea, as well as the fashionable *Acapulco Princess* and *Pierre Marqués* hotels. To the right is Caleta, where many of the first hotels were built, and still operate, albeit many in rather run-down fashion now. Since the sea is Acapulco's prime attraction, look first at the beaches. Remember that there are no private beaches in Mexico. All are federal property, and the hotels have no jurisdiction over them. Although the problem of itinerant vendors has been almost completely resolved in Acapulco, they still show up occasionally on the popular beaches, and their petitions can be wearisome, but for safety's sake it's best to avoid completely isolated beaches.

Barra Vieja – A long stretch of beach about 24 miles (38 km) southeast of Acapulco, where Tres Palos Lagoon meets the Pacific. The water on the Pacific side is too treacherous for swimming, but small boats are available for exploring the lagoon, which is fringed with palm and banana trees and populated by tropical birds. *Pescado a la talla* (whole fish charbroiled on a spit) is said to have originated here, and is available at any one of the small restaurants along the beach.

Caleta – Back in the days before air conditioning, when the best hotels were built on the adjacent hillside to catch the breeze, this is where everyone began his day. Caleta was the morning beach. It's not so elegant now, and some segments are polluted, although it does attract the traditionalists and those who like their ocean as calm as a pond. The thing to do at Caleta is rent an inner tube and just paddle around. The small aquarium here, which was opened in 1990 to attract more visitors to this end of town, boasts two well-maintained water slides and is popular with children.

La Condesa – Running from the *Continental Plaza Acapulco* to *El Presidente* hotels, this is the most tourist-infested stretch of sand these days. It's also where the scantiest bikinis are found. One section of the beach is dominated by gays. La Condesa has the most pounding surf on the bay, and up by the Costera are a number of nice luncheon spots with music for dancing.

Los Hornos – Just west of the Costera Miguel Alemán underpass and *Papagayo*

Park, this was once the fashionable spot for late-afternoon sunbathers. The water here is calmer, though not very clean; eateries topped by *palapas* (thatch umbrellas) line the beach.

Icacos – The first stretch of true Acapulco Bay beach as you drive in from the airport. Here the sheltered waters are calm and quiet and the beach is less hectic. *La Palapa* and the *Hyatt Regency* hotels share the sands.

Laguna de Coyuca – A little way beyond Pie de la Cuesta, this primitive freshwater lagoon is a bird sanctuary bordered by coconut palms and full of water hyacinths. The waters teem with catfish, mullet, and snook. The *Maebba Beach Club* offers a tour, including transportation to and from Acapulco proper; a visit to a coconut, pineapple, or banana plantation; a half-hour boat trip on the Coyuca Lagoon; lunch; and a few hours at the club — all for about $26 (phone: 858515).

Pie de la Cuesta – More and more foreign tourists are coming to know about it, so it's no longer the private turf of Acapulco regulars. Swimming is dangerous at this beach 10 miles (16 km) west of the city proper, but it's a wonderful place to order a *coco loco* (perhaps at *Tres Marías* or *Steve's Hideaway*), cuddle up in a hammock, and cement friendships as the sun goes down. Continue to *Club de Playa Maebba,* where visitors can enjoy a buffet and use the pool, tennis court, and hammocks for a small fee. There's also *Cadenas Ski Club,* which offers water skiing and jungle boat rides with delicious meals.

Revolcadero – Out in front of the *Acapulco Princess* and *Pierre Marqués* hotels, and off to either side as well. A favorite of the rich and pampered. Revolcadero is on the open Pacific and is great for body surfing. Indian ponies are available for those who enjoy a canter on the sand. Beware of the sometimes vicious undertow.

Roqueta – The uninhabited island across from Caleta has a small, state-operated zoo with indigenous animals and a certain Robinson Crusoe charm. Boats ferry bathers from and to Caleta throughout the day. There is a direct route that takes about 15 minutes, as well as a more scenic one (this way takes about a half hour longer to get there); buy tickets from the kiosk on the beach. Snorkeling and windsurfing are good, and there are boards for rent. *Aca-Zoo* is open Wednesdays through Mondays from 10 AM to 5 PM. Admission charge to the zoo.

Calandrias – These little horse-drawn carriages, decorated with brightly colored balloons, run up and down the Costera Miguel Alemán, the avenue that skirts the bay. The standard ride is a tour of the town, but *calandrias* also can be hired as taxis. If you're not in a hurry (and who is in Mexico?), they are more fun, albeit more expensive.

Centro Internacional Acapulco – What was formerly the convention center has been completely remodeled and renamed, and is once again a center of urban activity. Folkloric performances held in the plaza on Monday, Wednesday, and Saturday evenings (check with your hotel reservations desk for schedules and details) usually include dinner and an open bar for about $25; the center also offers a movie theater, and occasional special productions in the *Juan Ruiz Alarcón* theater. 4455 Costera Miguel Alemán (phone: 847050).

CICI Park – On the beach, across the street from the *Embassy* hotel, this small, well-maintained amusement park has trained dolphins and seals, a pool with manmade waves, two water toboggans, three dolphin shows daily, several bars and restaurants (including a gigantic seafood restaurant built in the shape of a huge crab), a beach club (accessible from the beach), and seagoing motorcycles. There is also a day-care center where infants and young children will be entertained and cared for by experts while parents play (phone: 841970).

Diego Rivera Mural – A spectacular and little-known mural by one of Mexico's most famous artists surrounds a private home up in the hills of Acapulco. The house is not open to the public, but the mural may be seen by taking the road that leads up to the *Casablanca* hotel (at the gas station about 4 blocks past the zocalo). Bear left at the fork and keep going up; it shouldn't be missed.

Cliff Divers – The Acapulco divers, or *clavadistas,* perform mainly at night. They plunge from a 150-foot cliff into a shallow inlet, and each dive must be perfectly timed to coincide with a wave coming in or the diver risks being crushed on the jagged rocks. There is no trick to it, nor are they in any way faking. The exhibition takes place on the cliffs of La Quebrada, adjoining the *Playa las Glorias El Mirador* hotel. Viewers can sit on the terrace or in the hotel's *La Perla* nightclub and have a drink while watching, or pay a small admission to get closer, but it is a spectacle worth seeing at least once. Shows (one dive per show) are at 1, 7:30, 9:30, and 10:30 PM. The best time to watch is in the evening when divers, with torches in hand, blaze a trail into the waters below. La Quebrada (phone: 831155).

Flea Market – That's what the locals call it (try saying it with a Spanish accent), and it's where handicrafts and Mexican curios are sold. The *Flea Market* is about 5 blocks from the zocalo, and the way is well marked with signs. It's a good place to browse and bargain. Open daily.

El Fuerte de San Diego (Fort of San Diego) – The most historic spot in Acapulco, it was first built centuries ago to protect what was then a major port from pirate attacks (and rebuilt after an 18th-century earthquake). Here the insurgents defeated the royalists in the early 1800s. It has been converted into an interesting museum dedicated to the history of Acapulco from pre-Hispanic times through the conquest of the southern seas, trade with the Orient, piracy, and the War of Independence from Spain. Closed Mondays. Admission charge. The fort is a few blocks to the left of the zocalo, just across from the piers and customs house (phone: 823828).

Papagayo Park – On the grounds of the old *Papagayo* hotel, this delightful 60-acre park straddling Costera Miguel Alemán has cable cars, bumper cars, a Ferris wheel, a carousel, an artificial lake, boats, and a lakeside restaurant.

Plaza Juan Alvarez (The Zocalo) – Getting away from the beaches, this is the heart of Acapulco proper, the main plaza near the piers and docks for deep-sea fishing boats. The zocalo is dominated by the Acapulco Cathedral, an oddity built in 1930, with Byzantine towers and a mosque-like dome. Opposite, at the waterfront, stands a monument to national heroes Guerrero, Morelos, Hidalgo, and Cuauhtémoc (the last Aztec emperor).

Puerto Marqués Village – About 8 miles (13 km) east of the center of the city, along the Carretera Escénica (the Scenic Highway), past *Las Brisas,* where the jet setters sequester themselves in villas with private swimming pools and descend only for an occasional jaunt into town in *Las Brisas*'s famous pink jeeps. At the traffic circle just past *Las Brisas* (in the direction of the airport), turn right and you'll find yourself in the fishing village of Puerto Marqués, where the bay is so calm it hardly shows a ripple. You can rent paddle, sail, and water-ski boats. There are also many seafood restaurants lining the beach and the opposite side of the road. *Pipo's,* one of the best (see *Eating Out*), has a small marina with fishing boats for hire. Punta Diamante, the adjacent headland, is slated to be the next major resort and condominium complex in the area (several large hotel complexes are already being constructed, along with a number of chic condominiums and private homes).

Water Ski Show – Champion water skiers perform daredevil feats in the spectacular *Acapulco Water Ski Show.* Best vantage points for this 45-minute extravaganza — held Tuesdays through Sundays at 9 PM — are at the *Colonial* restaurant (130 Costera Miguel Alemán), or next door at the *Extasis* disco. Admission charge (phone for both: 837077).

Yacht Cruises – One of the best ways to go sightseeing in Acapulco is on the water. Several motor yachts and a catamaran make the 3½-hour cruise around Acapulco Bay,

Puerto Marqués, and La Quebrada cliffs, with a running commentary on the way, for about $35, including lunch or dinner, disco dancing, open bar (local drinks only), and a show in the evening. There are moonlight cruises — even when there's no moon — which include an open bar and performances by Argentine dancers, for about $12. The *Bonanza* and *Fiesta Cabaret* offer morning and afternoon trips, as well as starlight cruises (the stars are almost always out) that include an open bar, music, and dancing; evening departure time is 7:30 PM and return is at 10:30 PM (phone: 831803 or 832531). *Divers de México* runs a 3-hour champagne sunset cruise with a show provided by the divers at La Quebrada, as well as a daytime *Buccaneer* cruise with the crew dressed up as pirates, each for about $25 (phone: 821397/8). No-frills cruises leave at 11 AM and 4:30 PM and cost about $10. A shorter ride can be taken in the glass-bottom boats that leave Caleta all day long and pass over the underwater Shrine of Our Lady of Guadalupe. Tickets for yacht cruises are available at hotel tour desks.

Old Town – This part of the city was the heart of Acapulco before the hotel strip on the Costera took over. Some might argue that it remains the city's soul, and visitors will find another world only a block or so off the Costera. Enter from Azueta at the north end of the Costera and wander among crowded, narrow streets filled with wandering musicians, shopkeepers, and residents. *El Amigo Manuel* restaurant, 1 block off the Costera (31 Benito Juárez; phone: 836981), serves delicious ceviche and grilled grouper filets with crunchy garlic, at a fraction of the cost of a meal in a hotel; take a table upstairs for the breeze, ambience — and view. For shopping that's a world away from the Costera's chic boutiques, head south a few blocks to find the central market on the other side of the wide canal, where blocks and blocks of clothing, crafts, household goods, and curiosities will tempt you.

■**EXTRA SPECIAL:** Costa Chica, the 136-mile stretch of coast southeast of Acapulco, is lined by a paved road that is passable most of the year. (During the rainy months, sections occasionally get washed out.) The road runs through dramatic, uninhabited terrain of lagoons and rocky cliffs. Along this route, in the shadow of the Sierra Madre, several rivers run into the sea. South of the small mining village of Ometepec, Cuajinicuilapa (about 140 miles — 224 km — from Acapulco) is inhabited by the descendants of Bantu tribespeople who were brought to the New World as slaves. The road continues all the way to Guatemala.

SOURCES AND RESOURCES

LOCAL TOURIST INFORMATION: Contact the State Tourist Office (Centro Internacional Acapulco; phone: 847050). It's large and the staff is extremely helpful. The consumer protection bureau, in the same building, can aid in ironing out disputes (phone: 846136); they're open from 9 AM to 10 PM daily. A smaller, but much more helpful, Federal Tourist Office is at Hornos Beach (187 Costera Miguel Alemán; phone: 851041); and several information kiosks line the Costera. There is also an Acapulco Tourist Office (10 Privada Roca Sola; phone: 847621 or 847630).

Local Coverage – The tobacco shop in the *Acapulco Plaza* and most of the other classier hotels sell the *International Herald Tribune,* the *Los Angeles Times, The New York Times, USA Today,* and the English-language *News,* published in Mexico City. They're also available at *Sanborn's* (Costera Miguel Alemán) for considerably less than the hotels normally charge. *Acapulco News* and *Adventure in Acapulco,* local weekly and monthly publications respectively, give tips on local happenings in English.

 TELEPHONE: The area code for Acapulco is 74. When calling from one city to another within Mexico, dial 91 before the area code.

 GETTING AROUND: Airport Limousine – Limos take five passengers to a car. You can pick one up when you get off the plane, and have one pick you up at your hotel. They cost about half the price of a private cab (phone: 852227 or 852332).

Bus – Buses run up and down the Costera all the way from Puerto Marqués to Caleta Beach and are inexpensive. With newer vehicles in operation, service is much improved — but do watch out for pickpockets when it's crowded.

Taxi – Acapulco cabs don't have meters, which means that you have to give the driver your destination and agree on a price before getting in. There are cabstands in front of most of the hotels, and you can ask the doorman about reasonable prices. If you flag down a cab in the street, you'll have to do your own haggling. The going rate should be no more than $2.50 from the Costera area near the *El Presidente* hotel to the zocalo, in the center of downtown. The ride from the *Hyatt Regency,* at the far eastern end of the Costera, to Caleta Beach should cost about $5. No trip within Acapulco proper should cost more than $7, although the fare will be higher when the destination is Revolcadero Beach or Pie de la Cuesta, both a bit out of town.

Car Rental – Many agencies, most visibly *Avis* (phone: 842581), *Dollar* (phone: 843066), and *Hertz* (phone: 856889), rent cars in Acapulco. All have offices at the airport; otherwise just stroll along the Costera. Air conditioned, automatic-transmission cars also are available, but should be reserved well in advance. Jeeps and Volkswagen beetles can be rented as well. *Saad* (phone: 845325 or 843445) rents only jeeps. Be aware, however, that even the costliest cars are likely to be in far worse condition than the exact same make and model routinely rented from companies in the US, and often have just enough gas to get from the airport to town. Be certain to buy insurance when renting an auto; without it, even a small accident can turn into a nightmare.

Motorcycles – Honda Elites may be rented at *Cici* (phone: 841970) for $15 to $20 for up to 4 hours; daily rates are also available. On the beach across the street from the *Embassy* hotel.

 SPECIAL EVENTS: *Carnaval* (Mardi Gras), just before *Lent,* is Acapulco's biggest fiesta. The *International Billfish Tournament* is held in late November or early December; an inter-club tournament is held in February. *Guadalupe Day,* December 12, something of a national holiday, is celebrated with special fervor in Acapulco. December 1 marks the start of the 12-day *International Diving Championship,* which is held at La Quebrada, the cliff at the *Playa las Glorias El Mirador* hotel (74 Quebrada). Also, there are fiestas throughout the year in the many villages near Acapulco. The government tourist office has data about what's in the offing.

 SHOPPING: One of the most popular activities in Acapulco is buying things. Frequent visitors arrive with little more than a toothbrush in their luggage, since resortwear and sports clothes are an Acapulco specialty. Stores also offer a wide selection of Mexico's best handicrafts. For a productive shopping outing, or just some enjoyable browsing, simply stroll Costera Miguel Alemán from the *Fiesta Americana Condesa* hotel to the *Acapulco Malibu*. One of the newest shopping complexes, completely enclosed and air conditioned, is the *Plaza Bahía Mall,* next to the *Acapulco Plaza* hotel. The *Marbella Shopping Center,* done in white marble, is on the Diana Circle. For some of Acapulco's more elegant shops, visit *La Vista Shopping Center* (on Carr. Escénica, 2 miles/3 km before the *Acapulco Princess,* heading toward the airport). Observing the siesta tradition, many shops close in the early afternoon, reopening at 4 or 5 PM. Here are some of the better places to make a purchase:

Aca Joe – Now trying to prosper in the US, it carries stylish casual T-shirts and togs for teens. 117 Costera Miguel Alemán (phone: 848643).

Artesanías Finas Acapulco – Better known locally as *AFA,* it offers a vast selection of handicrafts, jewelry, leather goods, and clothing from all over Mexico. Open daily. Horacio Nelson and James Cook, behind *Baby'O* (phone: 848049).

Benny – At last, a fashionable shop devoted to men. On Costera Miguel Alemán, 15 Horacio Nelson (phone: 841547), and at *La Vista Shopping Center.*

La Colección de Sergio Bustamante – The world-renowned artist's fantastical eggs, animals, and people in ceramics, papier-mâché, and brass are displayed here. 711-B Costera Miguel Alemán (phone: 844992).

Galería Rudic – Paintings and other works of art by the finest Mexican artists. Costera Miguel Alemán and Yañez Pinzón (phone: 841104).

Gucci – Decent knock-offs of the real Gucci shoes and accessories of Italy, at fairly reasonable prices. On the Costera across from the *Galería Plaza* (phone: 862003), at *El Patio Shopping Center* (phone: 840969), and at 4057 Costera Miguel Alemán in front of the *El Presidente* hotel (phone: 844505).

María de Guadalajara – High-quality designer swim- and beachwear with a touch of Latino class. *Galería Plaza,* local 28 (phone: 855073).

Marietta – Eye-catching fashions and accessories for women. In *Torre de Acapulco* on Costera Miguel Alemán (phone: 848853) and at the *Princess* (phone: 843100).

El Mundo de Esteban – Very high-fashion, New York–style clothing for men and women, chic Acapulco wear, lovely hats and tunics, and glamorous evening dress. 2010 Costera Miguel Alemán (phone: 843084).

Polo/Ralph Lauren – Men's and women's sportswear and accessories by the famed designer. Costera Miguel Alemán, across the street from the *American Express* office (phone: 843325).

Ronay – If silver jewelry is your delight, this is the place. 9999 Costera Miguel Alemán, beneath *Carlos 'n' Charlie's* restaurant (phone: 841007).

Rubén Torres – Stunning sportswear for men and women. 1999 Costera Miguel Alemán (phone: 840786).

Suzett's – Striking gold designs, especially in rings with precious stones. At the *Hyatt Regency* (phone: 842888).

Tane – Silver jewelry, flatware, and objets d'art of impeccable design and quality. At the *Hyatt Regency* (phone: 846348), and at *Las Brisas* (phone: 810816).

Taxco el Viejo – A most imaginative silver shop that also sells items in gold, leather, wool, wood, and ceramics. A block from the cliffs from which the famous divers leap, at 830 Quebrada (phone: 837300).

SPORTS: Acapulco is mostly a town for participating, not spectating, but there is something here for virtually every taste.

Boating – Catamarans and other boats of varying size are available for rent on all the bay beaches. The best places to go are Caleta and Puerto Marqués. *Divers de México* (phone: 821397/8) rents private, chartered yachts for about $60 per hour. They also host a sunset cruise (during which you can watch Acapulco's world-famous cliff divers and drink champagne), a moonlight cruise, and a daytime bay cruise aboard a 100-foot replica of a pirate ship.

Bullfighting – Not a sport, aficionados will tell you, but a spectacle. Established matadors perform Sunday afternoons starting at 5 PM during December and *Easter Week*. Hotel travel desks have the details and the tickets. The bullring is near Caleta Beach. Tickets cost from $10 to $25.

Fishing – Deep-sea charter boats leave around 8 AM and return around lunchtime. The Pacific waters yield pompano, bonito, barracuda, yellowtail, red snapper, and shark. A few miles southeast of the city in the Tres Palos Lagoon, and at Coyuca Lagoon near Pie de la Cuesta, you can rent small boats with awnings, and fish for freshwater catfish. *Divers de México* (phone: 821397/8) has nine American yachts, some air conditioned, all Coast Guard–approved and with uniformed crews, costing $220 to $500 per day for 4 to 30 passengers, or $50 per chair. *Club de Esquies Beto* has speedboats, from which five can fish, that rent for $25 per hour, with a minimum of 3 hours, and fishing boats for four for $150 (phone: 822034). Freshwater fishing costs about $35 an hour, including equipment, with a 3-hour minimum.

Golf – There are three courses worth knowing about: the 9-hole public course next to the Centro Internacional (on Costera Miguel Alemán); an 18-hole course at the *Acapulco Princess* (on Revolcadero Beach); and an 18-hole course at the *Pierre Marqués Club de Golf* at the hotel adjoining the *Princess,* also on Revolcadero Beach. All three courses have resident pros and charge greens fees. Reservations for starting times are advised during the winter season. The *Pierre Marqués Club de Golf* is the longest and most challenging; the *Acapulco Princess* layout usually is in the best condition.

Horseback Riding – Revolcadero Beach is the place to go for a canter astride a smallish Indian pony; ask for Mundo or Carlos — they'll take the time to find you the best horses. Some horses are also available at Pie de la Cuesta.

Parasailing – The next best thing to sky diving is going aloft in a parachute pulled by a speedboat. There's no trouble finding the boatmen — they are on every beach. The cost is $10 to $20 for up to 10 minutes. *Be warned:* It can be dangerous.

Scuba Diving – Lessons and equipment are available at all the major hotels. The Arnold brothers run a school, *Hermanos Arnold* (106 Costera Miguel Alemán), in front of *Las Hamacas* hotel (phone: 820788). *Divers de México,* which is owned by a very helpful American woman, has dive packages that include pool instruction and lunch (phone: 821397/8). Most dives are made in the waters off Roqueta Island.

Surfing – Surfing, though limited in Acapulco, is possible at the *Copacabana* and *Princess* hotels' beaches and a half-mile south of the *Princess* at Revolcadero Beach. Although surfing is not allowed in the bay area, inner tubes may be rented at Caleta for paddling around the bay.

Tennis – Acapulco has a number of tennis clubs, some with indoor, air conditioned courts as well as outdoor courts; others have lighted courts for night play. Altogether, there are about 30 courts in town. In addition to those at the *Acapulco Princess, Acapulco Plaza, Las Brisas, Hyatt Regency,* and *Pierre Marqués* hotels, there is a tennis club at *Villa Vera* (35 Lomas del Mar), and at the golf club in town, *Club de Golf Acapulco* (next to the Centro Internacional).

Water Skiing – Acapulco is the ideal place to learn or to perfect skills. Boats are available at all the major hotels. Caleta Beach and Puerto Marqués are especially good places to start since the water is calmer there. Prices run about $25 to $40 per hour. At Coyuca Lagoon visitors can watch demonstrations of barefoot skiing.

Wrestling – Matches are held Wednesday and Sunday nights at the *Coliseo Arena,* which draws a rough crowd. There often is more fighting in the stands than in the ring.

NIGHTCLUBS AND NIGHTLIFE: If traditional Mexican entertainment is what you're after, Acapulco has its share of Mexican fiestas. Slightly corny, but great fun, the fiestas usually feature mariachi music, folkloric dancing, a Mexican buffet, and an open bar. Each place offers some variation on the same Mexican theme. Fiestas at the Centro Internacional Acapulco and the *Marbella Shopping Center* frequently feature the spectacular *Flying Indians of Papantla* and are well worth seeing. Since there is no set schedule, check with your hotel for time and details. Javier de León's excellent folkloric ballet performs (during winter months only) at the *Calinda* hotel (1260 Costera Miguel Alemán). At *Las Brisas*'s *El Mexicano* restaurant, the festivities begin with a *tianguis* (marketplace) of handicrafts and end with a spectacular fireworks display. The fiestas cost $25 to $30 per person, and reservations can be made through most hotel travel desks.

Acapulco really gets going after dark — *well* after dark. The discos don't get crowded until after 11 PM, so one way to get a table is to arrive around 10:30. The big hotels usually have several places to fill the evening hours, depending on your mood, and they often feature live entertainment. *A fashion note:* As casual as Acapulco is both day and night, its nightspots do not look kindly on shorts, old jeans, or bare feet.

Antillano's – Formerly *Cat's,* its main attraction is a laser show in the early hours of the morning. Open Thursdays through Saturdays. 32 Juan de la Cosa, across the street from the *Acapulco Plaza* (phone: 847235).

Atrium – The old *Bocaccio* club has been renamed and redecorated: no tables, no chairs — just bars, a dance floor, and a DJ spinning disco recordings. $25 covers all drinks (except champagne and cognac) and snacks. Closed Mondays and Tuesdays. 5040 Costera Miguel Alemán (phone: 841900).

Baby'O – One of Acapulco's top discos, imaginative and fashionable, it looks like a stylized mud hut from the outside. A pajama party is held annually. Opens at 10:30 PM, and the beat goes on until 5 or 6 AM. Costera Miguel Alemán, out where it begins (phone: 847474).

Delirio's – Once the chic disco *Jackie'O,* it's been renamed but still attracts a young and energetic clientele. Costera Miguel Alemán, at *El Patio Shopping Center* across from the *Continental Plaza Acapulco* (phone: 840843).

Le Dome – One of the port's original discos, its interior is the most compelling attraction. 402 Costera Miguel Alemán (phone: 841190).

Eve – It's practically on the water, and one of the prettiest discos in town. 115 Costera Miguel Alemán (phone: 844777).

Extasis – Built on the water's edge, it offers a great view of the ski show at the *Colonial* next door. 200 Costera Miguel Alemán (phone: 837077).

Extravaganzza – Aptly named, the club is huge, modern, and posh, with an immense glass wall providing an awesome view of the entire bay. Truly spectacular, it shouldn't be missed, even by non-discophiles. Next door to *Los Rancheros* on the Carr. Escénica, headed to *Las Brisas* (phone: 847154 or 847164).

Fantasy – The façade is alight with a cascade of tiny lights; the interior is like a glass ship. Carr. Escénica at *La Vista Shopping Center* (phone: 846727).

Fiesta Cabaret – The floating dinner party aboard this huge trimaran begins with cocktails on the top deck and a cruise around the bay, followed by a formal dinner, a Latin American floor show, and disco music for dancing — a very enjoyable experience. The trimaran leaves from the pier across from the San Diego Fort at 7:30 PM and gets back around 10:30 PM (phone: 831803 or 832531, for reservations).

El Fuerte – This Spanish-style nightclub claims to have the best flamenco show this side of Seville. Shows at 10 and 11:30 PM, except Sundays. Next to *Las Hamacas Hotel,* 239 Costera Miguel Alemán (phone: 837006).

Gallery – A disco where the 11 PM and 1 AM shows feature female impersonators.

The entertainment is surprisingly good. Closed Mondays. 11 Av. Deportes, across the street from the *Holiday Inn* (phone: 843497).

Hard Rock Café – At this south-of-the-border branch, dancing is in air conditioned comfort, day and night, but the live music — and real fun — begins at 11 PM when everyone — waiters and customers alike — gets into the act. Good food too. 37 Costera Miguel Alemán (phone: 846680).

Magic – A selective door policy has made this one disco everybody wants to get into. People come here to be seen as much as to dance. Costera Miguel Alemán at Fragata Yucatán (phone: 848815).

News – One of Acapulco's largest and most popular dance spots, it seats 1,200 people in booths and love seats (no chairs). It's also not unusual to find people dancing on the tables. On the Costera Miguel Alemán across the street from the *Hyatt Regency* (phone: 845904).

La Perla – On the cliffs overlooking the sea, this is a supper club where the floor show is provided by the famed Acapulco divers. There are two orchestras for dancing. The first evening show is at 7:15 PM. La Quebrada (phone: 831221 or 847254).

Poseidon – Some of Mexico's best nightclub performers appear here. At the *Torres Gemelas* hotel, on the Costera (phone: 844828).

Tiffany's – Victorian decor, with plush upholstery and all that. The sound system allows guests seated at tables to actually carry on a conversation. At the *Acapulco Princess* (phone: 843100).

BEST IN TOWN

CHECKING IN: It's best to arrive in Acapulco with a prepaid reservation directly from your hotel, including a written confirmation stating the price. Overbooking is a frequent risk, so if there's trouble, make a scene, demand to talk to the reservations manager, and/or threaten to call the Tourism Ministry (5-250-0123 in Mexico City, day or night). The loudest squeaking wheel usually gets the oil, and noisy, demanding guests usually get service. Winter rates are often more than double summer rates. In winter expect to pay up to $250 for a double room in very expensive hotels, $145 to $175 for expensive, about $100 for moderate, and $70 or less for inexpensive. All telephone numbers are in the 74 area code unless otherwise indicated. When calling from one city to another within Mexico, dial 91 before the area code.

Acapulco Princess – Designed to evoke the most dramatic elements of Mexico's Aztec and Maya heritage, the shape of its main building is pyramidal, with exterior balconies hung with exotic tropical blossoms. Try to arrange for accommodations in this building if you want to be near the action. A fine 18-hole course serves as a prime lure for golfers. There are also 5 swimming pools (one with a bar under a waterfall), a beach, a sauna, 11 tennis courts (6 clay, 5 Laykold), jeeps, parachute rides, 7 restaurants (of which the *Hacienda* is best), a lobby bar, and a disco. 1,019 rooms. Rate includes breakfast and dinner. Airport Rd., 12 miles (19 km) south of Acapulco (phone: 843100; 800-223-1818 in the US; fax: 843664). Very expensive.

Las Brisas – One of the truly unique resort hotels of the world and still our favorite in Acapulco, this striking amalgam of lovely casitas, built in 1957, has been carved into the side of the tallest of the hilltops surrounding Acapulco Harbor, offering a superb view as well as superb accommodations. Privacy is paramount here, and the service is mostly splendid, with a private beach club (at the foot of the steep hill) that satisfies the desire for swimming in the Pacific. There are 300 rooms — including some 1-, 2-, and 3-bedroom suites, as well as 4- to 6-bedroom homes — most with private or semiprivate swimming pools strewn with fresh blossoms each day. Try to arrange for a room with your own pool. There are 2 saltwater pools (at the beach club), 5 lighted tennis courts, water sports, golf and fishing nearby, and private restaurants open to hotel guests only. Rate includes continental breakfast and membership in the hotel's private *La Concha Beach Club,* which serves some of the best ceviche in Mexico. The *Bella Vista* restaurant serves good seafood (see *Eating Out*). Airport Rd., 8 miles (13 km) south of Acapulco (phone: 841580; 800-228-3000 in the US; fax: 842269). Very expensive.

Hyatt Regency – The sight of towering ceiba trees and graceful fountains welcomes guests as they approach. It offers 700 large, comfortable, recently remodeled rooms, a good-size pool framed by palms, water sports at the beach, 5 lighted tennis courts, a pro shop for guests only, 3 restaurants, coffee shop, 2 bars, and exercise classes. Costera Miguel Alemán (phone: 842888; 800-228-9000 in the US; fax: 843087). Very expensive.

Pierre Marqués – Sharing the Revolcadero beachfront (and ownership) with the next-door *Princess,* this place was constructed by billionaire J. Paul Getty and retains its authentic luxurious mien. A shuttle runs between the two hotels. Probably the most underrated of Acapulco's accommodations, its facilities include 3 swimming pools, a pleasant, uncrowded stretch of beach, a true championship golf course (the best around), fishing, tennis, 2 restaurants, and a cocktail lounge. The only drawback: very little shade. There are 341 rooms, including junior and master suites. Rate includes breakfast. Airport Rd., about 11 miles (18 km) south of Acapulco (phone: 842000; 800-223-1818 in the US; fax: 848554). Very expensive.

Continental Plaza Acapulco – An Acapulco landmark, it has a pool surrounding an island, and its beach is enormous. It also has 433 rooms, 3 restaurants, a coffee shop, lobby bar with live music, 2 pool bars, and access to the tennis courts at the *Hyatt Regency.* Costera Miguel Alemán (phone: 840909; 800-88-CONTI in the US; fax: 842081). Expensive.

Fiesta Americana Condesa Acapulco – Next to *El Presidente* on the beach, this large (500-room) hotel — the best on the Costera — has 2 swimming pools, a social program for kids, a lobby bar where live music attracts nighttime crowds, and a restaurant with more tranquil music. Costera Miguel Alemán (phone: 842828; 800-FIESTA-1 in the US; fax: 841828). Expensive.

Sheraton Acapulco – Set on a hillside on secluded Guitarrón Beach on the east end of Acapulco Bay, it has 17 villas comprising 226 rooms and 8 suites. Facilities include 2 pools (one with a swim-up bar), 2 restaurants, and a lobby bar with live music. 110 Costera Guitarrón (phone: 843737; 800-325-3535 in the US; fax: 843760). Expensive.

Villa Vera – A glamorous jet set favorite, the place where the movie stars go and starlets follow. There are 80 spacious rooms, suites, and villas (many of which have private pools), an excellent restaurant, a large hotel pool (with a swim-up bar — this is where they began), Jacuzzi, a fitness center, and 3 clay tennis courts. There's no beach, but guests may use the beach at the *Maralisa.* No children under 16. In town, at 35 Lomas del Mar (phone: 840333; 800-223-6510 in the US; fax: 847479). Expensive.

Acapulco Malibu – This smaller, circular hostelry, with its own tropical garden, offers water skiing as well as its beach and swimming pool. Though the 80 rooms are somewhat on the glitzy side, they're almost always full. 20 Costera Miguel Alemán (phone: 841070; fax: 840994). Moderate.

Acapulco Plaza – Its exterior resembles a funnel-shaped parking garage, but it's more luxurious inside. *La Jaula* bar hangs in the lobby gardens, seemingly suspended in midair. About half of the 1,008 rooms are small; the other half are very comfortable suites. The *Oasis Club* has a pleasant and quiet private Jacuzzi on the third floor; *Club Mirage,* on the second floor, offers more of the same, and also allows children. There's also a tennis club (4 courts on the roof of the shopping center next door), 2 pools, a fine beach, 50 shops in the shopping center next door, a health club, 4 restaurants, and a coffee shop. Service at the front desk is not always friendly. Affiliated with Holiday Inns. 123 Costera Miguel Alemán (phone: 858050; 800-HOLIDAY in the US; fax: 855285). Moderate.

Boca Chica – One of Acapulco's older, smaller places, right on the water, with 2 restaurants (one a sushi and oyster bar) and 2 pools (one is a natural saltwater cove). Snorkeling is at its best here. Rate includes breakfast and dinner. Caletilla Beach (phone: 836601 or 836741; fax: 839513). Moderate.

La Palapa – The 30 floors beneath a scalloped gold crown contain nothing but suites (335) with balconies, indoor bars, and plenty of closet space. Plants give the place an airy feel. The hotel also has a large pool with swim-up bar, water sports center, social program, live music nightly, and an electronic-game room. 210 Fragata Yucatán (phone: 845363; 800-334-7234 in the US; fax: 848399). Moderate.

Paraíso Radisson – Right on Hornos Beach, it has 422 recently redecorated rooms with balconies and satellite TV. There's a pool, cafeteria, a restaurant on the beach, and a rooftop restaurant with a breathtaking view of Acapulco Bay. 163 Costera Miguel Alemán (phone: 855050; 800-333-3333 in the US; fax: 855543). Moderate.

El Presidente – This rather sterile 407-room giant on the beach has 2 swimming pools, a sauna, nightclub, restaurant, 2 bars, and a social program in case you can't find enough to do. 89 Costera Miguel Alemán (phone: 841700; 800-777-1700 in the US; fax: 841376). Moderate.

Ritz – A modern high-rise, it has a pleasant lobby with wicker furniture, pool, restaurant, and video games. Costera Miguel Alemán, at Hornos Beach (phone: 857336; fax: 857076). Moderate.

Tortuga – This peach-colored property, with an atrium from which plants dangle impressively, has 250 large rooms, a swimming pool, 2 bars, and 2 restaurants, including *La Fonda.* Close to, but not on, the beach. 132 Costera Miguel Alemán (phone: 848889; fax: 847385). Moderate.

Acapulco Dolphins – An unpretentious little hotel across from *CICI Park* (a small amusement park), it boasts large air conditioned rooms, a restaurant, a pool, and first-rate service. There also is a rooftop solarium with a Jacuzzi. 50 Costera Miguel Alemán (phone: 846648 or 846678; fax: 843072). Inexpensive.

Autotel Ritz – With 103 rooms, a restaurant, and pool. MAP available. Costera Miguel Alemán and Wilfrido Massieu (phone: 858023; fax: 855647). Inexpensive.

Bali-Hai – One of the advantages of this motel is that guests can enjoy a quiet room in the back and still be right on the main strip. Restaurant; swimming pool. Room service is available. Near the *Acapulco Plaza.* 186 Costera Miguel Alemán (phone: 856622; fax: 857972). Inexpensive.

Etel – Spotlessly clean rooms and 1- to 4-bedroom apartments equipped with air conditioning, fans, and a marvelous view. There is also a pool set in a pretty garden. Up a steep street at 92 Pinzona (phone: 822240). Inexpensive.

Los Flamingos – This is where the film stars of the 1940s came to frolic, and the place is alive with memories. There is a pool, restaurant, and bar. The panoramic view is a constant spectacle. Rate includes breakfast. On a hillside at López Mateos and Flamingos (phone: 820690; fax: 839806). Inexpensive.

Las Hamacas – Across from the beach on the strip, this hostelry offers a pool with bar, garden dining room, and flamenco shows in its nightclub. Of the 160 rooms, those off the pool are nicer and quieter, though they have no view. 239 Costera Miguel Alemán (phone: 837709; 800-421-0767 in the US; fax: 830575). Inexpensive.

Majestic – Up in the hills overlooking the bay, it offers 195 rooms, a pool, parking, and transportation to the Costera. 73 Av. Pozo del Rey (phone: 834710; fax: 821614). Inexpensive.

Playa las Glorias El Mirador – People generally come here to sip cocktails at *La Perla* supper club and watch the cliff divers, but besides the dramatic view, the hotel offers 3 pools, and 160 pleasant rooms with large bathrooms. It's best for those who don't need a beach at hand. 74 Quebrada (phone: 831155; 800-342-AMIGO in the US; fax: 820638). Inexpensive.

Sands – In the center of things, yet tranquil, it has a restaurant, 2 pools, a bar, 2 squash courts, and 59 modest but good-size rooms and 34 bungalows. The staff is pleasant. 178 Costera Miguel Alemán and Juan de la Cosa (phone: 842260; 800-422-6078 in the US; fax: 841053). Inexpensive.

El Tropicano – Just 2 blocks from the beach, this place has 127 rooms and 12 suites, cable TV, 2 pools, restaurants, a garden, and a disco. 20 Costera Miguel Alemán (phone: 841100; 800-528-1234 in the US; fax: 841308). Inexpensive.

EATING OUT: Acapulco has more restaurants than you'll be able to test even during a 2-week stay. Many of the finest are in the best hotels (including the *Hyatt Regency* and the *Acapulco Plaza*). Dining out here is relatively costly. Expect to pay up to $80 for two at those places we've listed as very expensive; $50 to $60, expensive; up to $40, moderate; under $30, inexpensive. Prices do not include drinks, wine, or tips. Most restaurants below accept MasterCard and Visa; a few also accept American Express and Diners Club. All telephone numbers are in the 74 area code unless otherwise indicated. When calling from one city to another within Mexico, dial 91 before the area code.

Casa Nova – With modern decor and a wonderful view of Acapulco Bay, this spot serves pasta, antipasto, and Italian treatments of shrimp and fish. Open daily. Reservations necessary. 5256 Carr. Escénica, across the street from *Las Brisas* hotel (phone: 846819). Very expensive.

Coyuca 22 – A great place for a pre-dinner drink and conversation, it looks like the set of a romantic Hollywood musical extravaganza of the 1940s. You almost expect to see Fred Astaire and Ginger Rogers come dancing around the pool. The menu includes lobster thermidor; a highlight of the decor is a handsome unicorn sculpture by Victor Salmones. Open daily for dinner only. Closed May through October. Reservations necessary. 22 Coyuca (phone: 835030). Very expensive.

Bella Vista – Set atop a hill overlooking the entire city and bay, the prime eating place at the *Las Brisas* hotel provides a wonderful view. Menu items include lobster thermidor, fresh fish, and shrimp served with coconut and rice. Open daily for breakfast and dinner. Reservations necessary. Airport Rd., 8 miles (12 km) south of Acapulco (phone: 841580). Expensive.

Black Beard's (also known as Barbas Negras) – Not surprisingly, the decor is early pirates' den. The menu concentrates on steaks, lobster, chicken, baked potato with sour cream, and a salad bar. It's next to Condesa Beach, and you usually have to wait for a table. Open daily for dinner only. No reservations. Costera Miguel Alemán (phone: 842549). Expensive.

El Campanario – A beautiful bell-tower dining room with colonial decor atop a mountain, with a panoramic view of Acapulco and very well prepared international dishes and seafood. Open daily. Reservations advised. Calle Paraíso (phone: 848830). Expensive.

Dino's – Homemade Italian bread is what makes this place special, and dining on the terrace makes things even more pleasant. You can get some continental dishes, but standard Italian-American fare characterizes most of the menu. Open daily. No reservations. 137 Costera Miguel Alemán (phone: 840037). Expensive.

D Joint – Also known as "DJ's," it's the best place in town for roast beef. An excellent place for sandwiches and chili, too. Open daily. Reservations advised. 79 Costera Miguel Alemán (phone: 843709). Expensive.

Embarcadero – A showplace with a South Seas motif, it offers such temptations as charcoal-broiled mahimahi with rice and bananas. Open daily (closed Mondays in summer). Reservations advised. Costera Miguel Alemán near *CICI Park* (phone: 848787). Expensive.

Hard Times – Trendy and fun, it's a place where you can select your meal from an international menu — or just order tacos and beer. The salad is marvelous, with artichoke leaves, avocado, beets, cauliflower, red cabbage, and much more. As you may have guessed, the motif is Depression era. Dinner only. Closed Sundays. Reservations advised. 400 Costera Miguel Alemán (phone: 840064). Expensive.

Kookaburra – With romantic dining under the stars and a stunning view of the bay, this spot specializes in seafood, steaks, and barbecue. There is also a wonderful ceviche bar (Mexico's answer to sushi). Dinner only. Open 6 PM to midnight; closed Sundays. Reservations advised. Carr. Las Brisas (phone: 841448). Expensive.

Madeiras – A pretty place with terrace dining and a view of the bay, it drips ferns and sophistication. The prix fixe menu includes baby lamb chops, sea bass, red snapper baked in sea salt, Cornish hen, and frogs' legs in white wine or garlic sauce. Dinner only. Closed Sundays. Reservations advised. Carr. Escénica, in *La Vista Shopping Center* (phone: 846921). Expensive.

La Mansión – In a colonial-style setting, it's famous for its steaks grilled on individual habachis at your table. Try the *lomo al jerez* (thick slices of filet mignon marinated in sherry). Open daily for lunch and dinner; Sundays for lunch only. Reservations advised. 81 Costera Miguel Alemán, in front of the golf course (phone: 810796). Expensive.

Miramar – Elegant, yet cozy, it too offers a spectacular view. Diners sit on multilevel terraces, and enjoy fine French fare. The *pato à la naranja* (duck with orange sauce) is crisp and beautifully presented. Closed Sundays during the summer. Reservations necessary. In *La Vista Shopping Center* (phone: 847874). Expensive.

Normandie – Easily the best French restaurant in Acapulco and perhaps in all of Mexico, it is run by Nicole Lepine, a Gallic lady, and her daughter. Open daily. Dinner only. Closed May through October. Reservations advised. In town at Costera Miguel Alemán and Malespina (phone: 851916). Expensive.

Suntory – Operated by a leading distiller of Japanese whiskey, this fashionable place offers authentic Japanese food. Open daily. Reservations advised. 36 Costera Miguel Alemán (phone: 848088). Expensive.

Bananas Ranas – A hodgepodge of Elvis posters, hats, mermaids, and hubcaps provide a fun setting. The menu is fashioned after *Carlos 'n' Charlie's* (i.e., ribs, shrimp, and the like) but the food is better and the prices lower. The music is loud, the lively crowd even louder. Open daily from 1 PM to 1 AM. No reservations. 23 Costera Miguel Alemán, near *La Palapa* hotel (phone: 843252). Moderate.

Beto's – Right on Condesa Beach, it's very popular for breakfast, lunch, live music, and good seafood (see *Quintessential Acapulco* in DIVERSIONS). Open daily. Reservations advised. Costera Miguel Alemán, at Condesa Beach (phone: 840473). Moderate.

Carlos 'n' Charlie's – The atmosphere is lively, but expect to wait in line half an hour or more. House specialties include charcoal-broiled spareribs and stuffed shrimp, and good sangria. Open daily for dinner only. No reservations. 999 Costera Miguel Alemán (phone: 840039). Moderate.

Chez Guillaume – Quiet and elegant, it serves well-prepared continental dishes including seafood crêpes, soufflés, and scampi. The bar attracts an international crowd. Open daily for dinner only. Reservations advised. 110 Av. del Prado (phone: 841231). Moderate.

Fonda Santa Anita – This intimate little spot offers a true taste of *sabor mexicano* (home-cooked Mexican fare), including many dishes such as *flor de calabraza* (pumpkin flower soup). Open daily. Reservations advised. Costera Miguel Alemán, in front of Condesa Beach (phone: 844485). Moderate.

Hard Rock Café – A combination rock 'n' roll hall of fame, bar, restaurant, dance hall, and boutique. The food, everything from shrimp fajitas to filet mignon, is tasty, and portions are generous. Live rock music is played from 11 PM to 2 AM. Service is friendly. There's always a line at the boutique, which sells sportswear bearing the familiar *Hard Rock* logo. Open daily. No reservations. 37 Costera Miguel Alemán, next to *CICI Park* (phone: 846680). Moderate.

Mimi's Chili Saloon – Behind a bird's egg blue façade, it offers hamburgers, burritos, fried chicken, frozen margaritas, and a lovely view of the ocean. Closed Mondays. Reservations advised. Costera Miguel Alemán; next to *Black Beard's* (phone: 843498). Moderate.

Paraíso – Serving delicious red snapper right on Condesa Beach, this spot is similar to, but wackier than, its neighbor *Beto's* (see above). Open daily. Reservations advised. Costera Miguel Alemán, at Condesa Beach (phone: 845988). Moderate.

Shangri-La – An Oriental garden with lily pond and bridge is the setting and, as you might expect, the fare is standard Cantonese. If you can't live without egg foo yong and fried rice, this is your best bet in Acapulco. Open daily for dinner only. Reservations advised. Just off the Costera at 5 Calle Piedra Picuda (phone: 841300). Moderate.

Villa Demos – A beautiful garden restaurant specializing in homemade fettuccine and other Italian dishes, we think it's the most romantic eatery in town. We recommend the veal *piccata*. There is a terrace for outdoor dining, as well as indoor service. Closed Mondays in the off-season. Reservations advised. 6 Av. del Prado, off Costera Miguel Alemán (phone: 842040). Moderate.

Pipo's – There are four of them; each one looks raunchy, but regulars insist that they serve the best seafood on the Mexican Pacific. Open daily. Reservations unnecessary. Across from the sport fishing docks, at 3 Almirante Bretón (phone: 822237); Puerto Marqués (phone: 846343); 105 Costera Miguel Alemán (phone: 840165); and the oldest branch, located on the Airport Road (about 4 miles/6 km south of town; phone: 846036). Branch on the Costera, moderate; all others, inexpensive.

Acapulco Fat Farm – Also known as *La Granja del Pingüe* (The Original Fat Farm), this cozy little eatery is run by high school and college students who formerly lived at the Acapulco Children's Center, an orphanage. The name points to the ice cream, pastries, and pies that are the specialties here, but there's less-fattening fare, too — good soup, sandwiches, and Mexican food. There's a book exchange, and classical music is played all day long. Open daily; no set hours. No reservations. No credit cards accepted. 10 Juárez, 2 blocks west of the zocalo (phone: 835339). Inexpensive.

100% Natural – Fresh vegetable sandwiches, exotic fruit drinks, and other organic goodies are served here. Costera Miguel Alemán, next to the Banco Internacional building (phone: 853982). Inexpensive.

Los Rancheros – Easy to overlook for its hilltop location, this is a good place to sample authentic Mexican food while gazing out at the Pacific. Open daily from 7 AM to 11 PM. Reservations unnecessary. On Carr. Escénica en route to *Las Brisas* (phone: 841908). Inexpensive.

DIVERSIONS

For the Experience

Quintessential Acapulco

Among other things, traveling south of the border doubtless has taught you that the real spirit of Acapulco lies somewhere between the jet set glitz of an all-night disco and a tranquil sunrise on a secluded beach. If you have tried on the requisite number of sombreros, anointed your body with coconut oil to bronze it in the tropical sun, and haggled over a colorful serape at the *mercado,* you've certainly scratched the surface. You may even have donned a pair of water skis, mixed it up with a marlin, eaten an enchilada, and outstared an iguana at Puerto Marqués. But, amigos, until you savor the places and pleasures listed below, you haven't experienced the true meaning of Acapulco.

BREAKFAST AT BETO'S: For many dyed-in-the-bikini sun lovers, morning in Acapulco means breakfast at *Beto's.* For what better way to start the day than lounging under a *palapa* (thatch umbrella) on the golden strands of Condesa Beach, smack-dab in the middle of Acapulco Bay. After partying all night to a rock 'n' roll beat at your favorite disco, try an eye-opening breakfast of *chipachole,* a spicy crayfish stew that is guaranteed to cure even the most cumbersome hangover (although you may develop an ulcer in the process). Though Beto claims to have invented the recipe himself, *chipachole* is actually an old Veracruz tradition. Still, this version of the blistering bouillabaisse is definitely an Acapulco original.

If your stomach isn't strong enough to go one-on-one with *chipachole,* there's another *Beto's* specialty for beach-bound early birds — fresh clams on the half shell. For about $6, you can enjoy a plate of 12 clams garnered from the bay's sandy floor that very morning, still dripping in ocean brine, and accompanied by a bowl of sliced limes. To test a clam's freshness, squeeze the lime juice over it; if it squirms for a few seconds, it's fresh enough to eat. If the clam doesn't move, send it back. Beto will gladly exchange it for a more mobile surrogate. Then add a pinch of salt and a drop or two of Tabasco sauce — sheer ecstasy for the taste buds!

Although the careworn collection of wobbly card tables and rusty chaise longues that pass for *Beto's* seaside dining room are bohemian at best and tawdry at worst, the scenic vista of the turquoise blue bay more than makes up for any shortcomings in the place's furnishings. Acapulco is uncannily serene in the early-morning hours: tropical marimba rhythms provided by a live trio, an occasional bevy of speckled sea gulls, and the pounding of the Pacific lend a sensuality to the atmosphere — reminding you why you chose this place for your escape from the workaday world.

Be aware, however, that by midday (2 PM) much of Condesa is home to Acapulco's gay guests. Those with more heterosexual leanings tend to clear out by lunchtime.

CEVICHE: You've tried sashimi and sushi at Japanese restaurants, but did you know that Mexico has its own version of raw fish? Delicate morsels of red snapper, tuna, shrimp, or crab are marinated overnight in lime juice with finely diced tomatoes and onions, plus chilies, olives, slivers of avocado, and a generous pinch of coriander to produce ceviche, one of Mexico's most delectable appetizers. You can get Acapulco's best ceviche at *Pipo's,* just off the Costera across from the sport fishing docks (3 Almirante Bretón; phone: 74-822237). The decor is a bit gaudy, but the seafood is always fresh and the ceviche is out of this world.

CLIFF DIVERS: Watching these daring young men on ABC's "Wide World of Sports" and seeing them dive in person are two very different things. You can't really appreciate the bravado — or the insanity — of Acapulco's cliff divers until you see the spectacle up close.

Wearing nothing more than spandex bikinis and crucifixes around their necks, the divers at La Quebrada (there are 46 in all) plunge 150 feet headfirst from a craggy cliff into a narrow gorge of ocean only 5 feet deep. And if that weren't enough, they must time their dives perfectly with the comings of the waves or . . . Their compensation for this death-defying act is a handful of change that will feed and clothe their families for one more day.

Why do they do it? Partly, because it's considered a status symbol to belong to this exclusive club of Mexican supermen, partly because it's proof positive of their machismo (very important among Mexican men), and partly because it's an Acapulco tradition. Back in the early 1920s, diving off a high ledge into a foaming broth of ocean was the way local young men sought to impress their intended brides; in 1934, Swiss-born playboy and entrepreneur Teddy "Mr. Acapulco" Stouffer and his movie star wife Hedy Lamarr decided to capitalize on the tradition by erecting a hotel and nightspot where the most spectacular dives were performed. Today, *La Perla* (at *Playa las Glorias El Mirador Hotel,* 74 Quebrada; phone: 74-831155) is still the best spot to watch the divers. They hurl themselves off the cliff at 1, 7:30, 9:30, and 10:30 PM. It's a good idea to arrive at least 30 minutes before the scheduled dive in order to get a good front-row table and have your cocktails served before showtime. The best time to watch is in the evening, when the divers, armed with two oversize torches, blaze a trail, hopefully into an incoming wave.

If you're lucky enough to be in Acapulco during the first 2 weeks of December, you'll have a ringside seat for the annual international diving competitions. Held at La Quebrada, they are climaxed with the December 12 celebration of the Virgin of Guadalupe, the patron saint of divers, whose shrine sits at the top of the cliff (you'll often see divers praying here before taking the plunge).

LAS BRISAS: Privacy is the byword for this exclusive resort. *Las Brisas* (5255 Carr. Escénica; phone: 74-841580) represents the epitome of exclusivity and luxury in Mexico. Straddling an entire mountainside along Acapulco Harbor, this palatial, pink-and-white 300-villa recluse embraces over 750 acres of ravishing landscape. Each cabaña is nestled into its own private garden, sheltered by hedges of bougainvillea and hibiscus; and each offers a spectacular view of the ocean below. On their arrival, guests are welcomed with a personalized mosaic of rose- and mallow-hued flowers spread out on the oversize beds that dominate the spare, elegant rooms. Most of the villas also boast a private swimming pool, generously strewn with ruby-hued hibiscus blossoms and headily scented gardenias. This self-contained haven offers everything you could possibly desire, from 24-hour valet and room service to a secluded beach club at the foot of the hill that's replete with orchid-draped palms and saltwater lagoons. And when you decide to head to town, you can tool around the city in style in one of *Las Brisas*'s trademark pink jeeps.

MARVELOUS MARGARITAS: There's more to a good margarita than a frosty salt-rimmed glass, and no one makes a better one in Acapulco than Chuy Rodríguez, owner of the *Paraíso* restaurant (on Condesa Beach next to *Barbas Negras;* phone: 74-845988). Served in an oversize goblet topped with a stem of bougainvillea, this potent potable is made from the best tequila (Sauza) and imported Cointreau (most places use a local substitute known as Controy that just doesn't provide the same flavor). Rodríguez also maintains that the way you *prepare* the drink definitely affects its taste. Rather than using an electric blender, he insists that the ingredients be blended by gentle shaking in a hand-held mixer, then poured ever so slowly into a chilled glass so as not to "bruise" the tequila. A twist of lime completes the orchestration, and a live marimba band, balmy ocean breeze, and majestic view of the bay to set the mood don't hurt either.

PARASAILING: This sport isn't for everyone, but if you're willing to brave the open sea and the boundless sky all in one fell swoop, parasailing might just be for you. Once you overcome the initial trauma of flying like a kite above a massive body of water, the bird's-eye view is a sight to behold. When soaring 100 feet above the water, the ocean looks like a placid pool, peppered with swimmers, sailboats — and powerboats, launching other would-be "birds" into flight.

Originally called "tow chuting," parasailing is one of Acapulco's oldest and most popular tourist attractions. During the early 1950s, a local fisherman invented this macho-minded sport after watching the splashdowns of space shuttles off the coasts of Florida and California. Strapping a regulation Air Force parachute to his back and tying a series of guide ropes to a speedboat, he instructed his wife to tow him around the bay until he was airborne. Needless to say, the experiment had its ups and downs in the beginning, many of which included serious injuries. But eventually, the fisherman managed to get the bugs out of his contraption, and parasailing began to catch on among the natives. It was only a question of time before tourists took to the chutes as well, and the rest, as they say, is history.

A 10-minute flight around Acapulco Bay costs between $10 and $20, depending on your bargaining powers. Veteran parasailers insist that the winds are best around midday, and for safety reasons, you should try to take off from (and land at) an uncrowded beach with plenty of open space and no major obstacles that could tangle your chute's cords. Even with the best of care, however, accidents do happen, and Mexican courts are not lawsuit happy. Any risk you incur is your own responsibility; in fact, you'll be asked to sign a release before taking off.

SALSA-ING AT EXTRAVAGANZZA: If you think that Acapulco cools off when the sun goes down, you're mistaken. The nightlife in this city is so sultry it sizzles, and nowhere is the temperature more scorching than at Acapulco's newest hot spot, *Extravaganzza* (Carr. Escénica, next door to *Los Rancheros;* phone: 74-847154 or 74-847164). From A to double Z, this place has it all — a suspended 540-square-foot dance floor pulsating with the latest rock and *latino* rhythms, 27-foot-high scenic windows overlooking the entire bay, and an intimate piano bar and champagne lounge with soft, romantic music to tame the spirit and relax the mind. There's also a boutique with fashions designed by the owner, Acapulco disco magnate Tony Rullan.

For those who want to see and be seen, *Extravaganzza* is *the* place to be. It is also where Mexico's crème de la crème rub elbows and mingle among the ordinary folk. That smartly clad teenager sipping a Courvoisier might just be an ambassador's son, and the sensuous brunette doing the lambada in a silver-sequined miniskirt could very well be the star of the hottest Mexican soap opera.

Getting into *Extravaganzza,* particularly on weekends and during the high season (*Christmas* and *Easter* holidays), can be tricky. Here it's not so much a matter of who you are, but who you *look* like you know. Plaid Bermuda shorts, a Hawaiian shirt, and high-top Nikes won't cut the mustard with the doorman, even if you slip him a 20,000-peso note. The dress code is categorically defined and rigidly enforced: Men are expected to wear long pants, closed leather shoes, and a long-sleeve, button-down shirt (which, however, can be open to the navel). *Extravaganzza* dress codes for women call for heels and a dress, but how much or how little else is exposed is strictly up to the individual. Plunging necklines and hip-high slit skirts are standard attire for Acapulco discophiles.

SUNSET AT PIE DE LA CUESTA: Watching the sun disappear into the Pacific Ocean is a memorable sight; but nowhere does it seem quite so resplendent as from Pie de la Cuesta, a 10-mile (16-km) swath of sand 10 miles (16 km) west of the city on Costera Miguel Alemán. Affectionately dubbed Sunset Beach by the locals, this is where Acapulco sun worshipers linger to watch their golden idol fade into the sea. Offshore, the setting sun casts a rainbow of colors — scarlet, aquamarine, and lilac — on the turquoise water. In the deep blue waters of Coyuca Lagoon, the reflection takes on a darker and more somber tone, contrasting majestically with the vivid colors on the ocean surface. At the far end of the horizon, both bodies of water seem to meld into a thin haze of indigo and mauve.

The best way to watch the day draw to a close is comfortably swaying on a hand-loomed hammock that is suspended between two palm trees, sipping a frosty *coco loco* (the milk of a fresh coconut mixed with gin, lime juice, and maraschino liqueur, and served in a coconut shell). Pie de la Cuesta has several beachside restaurants that offer a front-row seat for the sunset spectacle, along with reasonably priced seafood and surprisingly good service. The best is *Tres Marías,* at the east end of the lagoon. If you're ready for a change from the Acapulco staples of red snapper and sea bass, try sampling the house specialty, fresh catfish from the lagoon, charcoal-broiled on a stake with garlic and onions.

STARLIGHT SAILS: It's true what they say about not being able to see the forest for the trees. Up close, Acapulco Bay seems like an endless tier of lofty modern resort hotels, each vying for a place in the tropical sun. But from a distance — out at sea — the beauty of Acapulco still shines, untarnished by crass commercialism. From the deck of a luxurious trimaran, the stark concrete and steel of the resort hotels and the rustic charm of *palapas* harmonize with the green hills that surround the beach. The attraction is undeniable, especially at night.

Acapulco's bay has always been a siren, luring sailors and paradise seekers alike to its sun-drenched beaches and palm-crested shores for centuries. It is this view of the city that probably convinced Spanish navigator Andrés de Urdaneta to build a permanent settlement here in the mid-16th century and to transform the jungle-fringed bay into his country's key port for trade between Mexico and the Far East.

For early risers, there are a number of commercial yachts in Acapulco that offer mini-cruises around the bay, starting at 11 AM. A spicy Mexican buffet and mariachi band create a festive mood, which is echoed in the brilliant colors of the tropical landscape.

But the bay is at its best in the evening. Starlight cruises on the *Fiesta Cabaret* and *Bonanza* trimarans depart from the downtown pier at 7:30 PM nightly for 3-hour tours, and include dinner, live music, an open bar, and a Las Vegas–style cabaret with a definite tinge of *sabor latino.* There's no extra charge for the spectacular view of the city, its lights sparkling like thousands of diamonds beneath a star-studded sky. It's a splendid experience, one that lingers in the memory long after the lights have gone out.

BALLET FOLKLÓRICO: In every Mexican town and village, music and dance express the soul of the people. Pre-Hispanic Mexican music, simple and almost hypnotic, was dominated by percussion and wind instruments, and was designed to accompany dances and religious rites; each of the many Indian cultures had its own dances and costumes. In spite of very forceful efforts by the conquistadores to stamp out all traces of indigenous cultures, music and dance survived, mainly because the Spanish clergy realized that these arts could be used as tools for recruiting the heathens into the church. The dances and music didn't really change; what changed was the name of the god to whom they were dedicated. Slowly, Spanish, French, and other European traditions found expression as part of this multi-cultural heritage. Even today, a church festival isn't considered complete without the performance of brilliantly clad folk dancers.

Although the main Ballet Folklórico school is in Mexico City, there are numerous smaller troupes across the nation that faithfully re-create the country's dance in the style and tradition of their ancestors. In Acapulco, you can enjoy a whirlwind tour of the entire Mexican republic through one of the *fiestas mexicanas* offered at several of the larger hotels during the winter season. The *Calinda* (1260 Costera Miguel Alemán; phone: 74-840410) boasts the best and most complete folklore ballet in town, presented Mondays, Wednesdays, and Fridays during the winter months. Tickets include domestic drinks and a dinner buffet. Reservations are advised. The Centro Internacional Acapulco (also known as the Convention Center) on Costera Miguel Alemán frequently presents folkloric ballet shows throughout the year. Check with your hotel travel desk for information.

DIA DE LOS MUERTOS (DAY OF THE DEAD): Although Mexicans fear and respect death as much as any other peoples, they face it, defy it, mock it, and even toy with it more than most cultures. Never is this more apparent than on November 2, *All Souls' Day* — known in Mexico as the *Day of the Dead* — an eminently Mexican holiday perpetuating a tradition of death and rebirth.

By mid-October, bakeries and markets throughout Mexico are filled with sweets and toys created with death as their theme. Bakeries are piled high with *pan de muerto,* a coffee cake decorated with meringues fashioned into the shape of bones. Children, friends, and relatives are given colorful sugar skulls with their names inscribed on them; death figures shaped from marzipan are on sale at most candy stores. Verses, called *calaveras,* containing witty allusions or epitaphs, are written about living friends, relatives, and public figures, and by the end of October, shop windows take on a macabre air, with shrouded marionettes and other ghoulish-looking figurines heralding the holiday.

On the actual date, families gather in graveyards to picnic and spend the day with their departed, bringing along their loved ones' favorite foods and drink. Graves are decorated with bright orange *zempasuchil* (marigolds), the flower of the dead; *copal,* an incense that dates back to pre-Hispanic cultures, is burned. The celebration begins with prayers and chants for the dead, and usually ends with drinks to the health of the departed. Homes are decorated in much the same way, with tables filled with marigolds and objects of which the deceased was especially fond.

MARIACHI MUSIC: The melodies pervade all of Mexico. Groups of musicians roam the streets of cities large and small, serenading under the windows of apartment buildings and in the doorways of restaurants and shops. Students, carrying guitars and flutes on buses and subways, often play for their fellow passengers in hope of earning a few pesos on the way to and from school. Although every region of Mexico has its own special music, none is more associated with the country as a whole than mariachi (the word comes from the French for "marriage").

During Emperor Maximilian's reign in the 19th century, wealthy Guadalajara families, trying to imitate the customs of the court, hired musicians to entertain their guests. Today, mariachis — made up of at least one vocalist, a guitar, bass, violin, and a trumpet or two — are usually hired to serenade girlfriends or to play at special events (weddings, birthdays, anniversaries). Their vast repertoire consists of such sentimental love songs as "Si Estás Dormida," "Las Mañanitas" (the Mexican equivalent of "Happy Birthday," but sung for almost any special occasion), "Guadalajara," "La

Bamba," or "Cucurrucucu Paloma." The traditional Mexican fiestas frequently held at large resort hotels normally include at least one group of mariachis, and any sizable town will have a few restaurants and bars where they provide the entertainment. Some of the best mariachis — dressed in their close-fitting pants, a pistol hanging from the belt, a bolero-type jacket decorated with silver, and a wide-brimmed hat — congregate in hotel lobbies and restaurants in Acapulco.

MOLE: To an uninformed gringo reading a Mexican menu, an entree of turkey mole conjures up visions of a drumstick topped with hot fudge. Nothing could be farther from reality. The word "mole" comes from the Nahuatl *mulli,* which means "sauce" — and this one is made of more than 30 ingredients — only *one* of which is unsweetened chocolate. Most Mexican housewives pride themselves on preparing the sauce from scratch, a time-consuming recipe that involves at least four kinds of chilies (which have to be seeded, deveined, and roasted), sesame seeds, almonds, peanuts, raisins, prunes, plantains, onions, garlic, coriander, anise, cinnammon, and an infinitesimal amount of the aforementioned chocolate. Traditionally, it is served with chicken or turkey, as a filling for tamales, or as a sauce for enchiladas. If you are served mole in a Mexican household, you know you're an honored guest.

Acapulco's Best Resort Hotels

 Whether your idea of a resort is a place to bake elegantly under the tropical sun, with no greater exertion than raising your wrist to sip a tall, cool drink (remember that the now-famous "swim-up" bar was invented in Acapulco at *Villa Vera*), or whether you prefer a haven that inspires you to play tennis and golf in the morning, go boating or riding in the afternoon, and dance all night, Acapulco has a spot that's absolutely perfect.

Acapulco's resorts provide a playland of fun and games: tennis in the cool of the morning and golfing on verdant greens. Then it's the pleasure of a siesta, followed by fabulous food and an exciting nightlife that just never seems to end.

Some of Acapulco's best resorts are located off the beaten track — worlds unto themselves where guests wrap themselves in cocoons of luxury and service. Others offer superb accommodations and activities right where the action is.

The peak season for Acapulco and most of the coastal resorts is from December 15 through April 15. Those who travel during the off-season (approximately April 15 to December 15) normally can save from 40% to 80% on accommodations. The temperature may be a bit hotter and the crowd a bit less chic, but there will be fewer people, and the lower rates may permit an increase in the level of hotel luxury and the length of stay.

ACAPULCO PLAZA: A complex of three towers near the Diana Glorieta, this high-rise village has 1,008 rooms, all decorated in soft pastel shades, and a gigantic 2-tiered lobby, filled with exotic plants and a waterfall. There's also a thatch-roofed *palapa* hut bar suspended from the roof, reached by a wooden gangplank from the second floor of the lobby. Guests enjoy 11 bars and restaurants, 4 tennis courts, 2 swimming pools, a health club, Jacuzzis, sauna, and water sports on Condesa Beach. When choosing a room, take into consideration that this is one of the liveliest (and consequently the noisiest) resorts in town. Therefore, you might prefer a room facing the ocean or pool. There's also a parking garage and a shopping complex. Information: *Acapulco Plaza,* 123 Costera Miguel Alemán, Acapulco, Guerrero 39670 (phone: 74-858050; 800-HOLIDAY in the US).

ACAPULCO PRINCESS: This comprehensive resort cost more than $40 million to build. The exterior of the main building resembles an Aztec pyramid; the interior looks like a movie set, complete with floral hangings and ample marble. Among the props are a championship golf course, air conditioned indoor tennis courts, outdoor tennis courts, 7 restaurants, a disco, a nightclub, 5 swimming pools, 1,019 rooms — even a bar under a waterfall. The traffic can get a bit hectic between lobby and lounge, but it's well run. In addition, the hotel conducts classes in its *Gourmet Mexican Cooking School,* where, under the guidance of expert chefs, students learn the basics of Mexican cuisine and wine selection, as well as the proper use of ancient utensils, many of which date back to the Maya. Week-long courses — held during the fall — are limited to 20 students; cost, including accommodations, is approximately $600, double occupancy. On Revolcadero Beach, about 12 miles (19 km) out of town on the Airport Road. Information: *Acapulco Princess,* Apdo. 1351, Acapulco, Guerrero 39300 (phone: 74-843100; 800-223-1818 in the US).

LAS BRISAS: Just about the best resort address in Mexico for more than 3 decades, this pink hillside hideaway is among the most luxurious hotels anywhere. Three hundred semi-connected or solitary casitas and ten 4- to 6-bedroom villas climb up the 750 acres of *Las Brisas*'s posh mountainside. There are 200 pools (shared and private), new condominium units, 150 pink-and-white-striped jeeps available for rent, and 5 lighted tennis courts. Continuous jeep service brings guests down to the private seaside *La Concha Beach Club;* the view from the *Bella Vista* restaurant atop the mountain is among the most romantic in the world. The emphasis is on privacy and the recharging of human batteries. Continental breakfast is discreetly delivered each morning to the 300 rooms; there is fresh fruit every day, jeep-borne room service (some guests prefer never to leave their casitas), and fresh hibiscus floating in the pools. The night spectacle of twinkling lights across the bay make this all well worth the price. Information: *Las Brisas,* Carr. Escénica, Apdo. 281, Acapulco, Guerrero 39868 (phone: 74-841580; 800-228-3000 in the US).

HYATT REGENCY: Located near many of the most popular nightspots, this 700-room luxury hotel offers guests enough diversions that they may never want to leave the premises. Besides all the water sports on beautiful Playa Icacos, east of Condesa Beach, the hotel offers a swimming pool, 5 lighted tennis courts, golf privileges at the 18-hole *Acapulco Princess* course, a gym, sauna and steamroom, 3 fine restaurants, 2 bars, a nightclub, fishing, and day trips to nearby Taxco. 1 Costera Miguel Alemán. Information: *Hyatt Regency,* Apdo. 560, Acapulco, Guerrero 39335 (phone: 74-842888 or 800-228-9000).

PIERRE MARQUÉS: The sister resort of the *Princess,* this jewel is the real royalty of the twosome. Originally built by the late J. Paul Getty, it is bordered by a palm-fringed golf course on one side and the Pacific on the other. It also has gardens, terraces, lawns with bungalows, restaurants, bars, 3 swimming pools, water sports and fishing gear, tennis, and shopping — and if that's not enough, there are the more frantic facilities at the adjacent *Princess,* too. Surprisingly elegant and discreet, with 341 rooms, junior suites, and villas. Information: *Pierre Marqués,* Apdo. 474, Playa Revolcadero, Acapulco, Guerrero 39300 (phone: 74-842000; 800-223-1818 in the US).

VILLA VERA: With an exclusive private club atmosphere, yet close to the center of town, this elegant resort has 80 spacious casitas — many with private pools. For those who like to mingle, there is also a large main pool with a swim-up bar; an excellent restaurant; and 3 tennis courts. Located in the hills off Costera Miguel Alemán, it also offers magnificent views. (Guests can use the beach at the *Maralisa,* the villa's sister hotel across on the Costera.) The ambience is sophisticated, and no children under 16 are allowed. Information: *Villa Vera,* 35 Lomas del Mar, Acapulco, Guerrero 39300 (phone: 74-840333; 800-223-6510 in the US).

Best Nightlife

 Acapulco comes alive at night. Almost every hotel has a nightclub — many offering live entertainment and dancing. But to truly get a taste of Acapulco's lively nightlife, strike out on your own. One of the most entertaining nightspots is *Gallery,* a revue of female impersonators. See the likes of Diana Ross, Ethel Merman, and Madonna, among others, at 11 PM and 1 AM every night except Mondays. 11 Av. Deportes, across from the *Holiday Inn* (phone: 74-843497).

For the most part, however, it's the pounding rhythm that gives Acapulco a party-like atmosphere. From salsa to rock 'n' roll, this city offers an international musical menu for most every taste. Dress is a bit more formal at night at Acapulco discos. Men must wear shirts, and women should wear dresses; reservations are advised at most clubs.

BABY'O: Still one of Acapulco's most popular discos, *Baby'O* is a pleasant departure from the city's glittery nightlife scene. The fashionable cave setting with tropical decor is fun and appealing. Open 10:30 PM until dawn. Cover charge. Costera Miguel Alemán at Horacio Nelson (phone: 74-847474).

EXTRAVAGANZZA: One of the shining stars on the night circuit (see *Quintessential Acapulco,* in this section), this is certainly the hottest place in town. Nestled on a mountainside, its blazing neon façade promises — and its interior delivers — a spacious dance floor speckled with strobe lights — and lots of loud music. When you tire of the decibels, step outside and enjoy the dazzling view of Acapulco Bay. Open 10:30 PM until dawn. Cover charge. Reservations advised. Carr. Escénica, near *La Vista Shopping Center* (phone: 74-847154).

FANTASY: Popular with the older crowd who like to dress up, *Fantasy* offers a splendid view of the bay with the added touch of a fireworks display at 2 AM. Cover charge. Reservations advised. Open 10:30 PM until dawn. Carr. Escénica in *La Vista Shopping Center* (phone: 74-846727).

MAGIC: Where chic Mexicans and tourists come to be seen, as well as dance. After midnight, its all-black decor is illuminated by the best laser light show in town. Cover charge. Open 10:30 PM until dawn. Costera Miguel Alemán at Fragata Yucatán (phone: 74-848815).

Acapulco's Best Restaurants

 From fast food on the Costera Miguel Alemán to the exclusive restaurants high on the hills, the choice is as wide as Acapulco Bay itself. Most hotels offer guests a least one restaurant, with some having as many as four, and the variety of food is equally broad: Mexican, Italian, French, Japanese, Polynesian — and fresh seafood, for which Acapulco is famous.

Where you decide to dine will dictate your dress. Formal attire, jackets and ties, are completely unknown in this resort town. Except for open-air eateries on the beach (where anything goes), comfortable resortwear is a safe bet. Here are some of Acapulco's best dining spots:

BLACK BEARD'S: This classic for seafood and steaks is true to its name. Fitted like a pirate ship with maps serving as placemats and figureheads from the prows of boats on the walls, the restaurant — also known by its Spanish name, *Barbas Negras* — has won awards for its excellent food and bar service. Hollywood celebrity guest photos decorate the lounge, where large black barrels serve as tables and authentic ship models hang from the ceiling. The steaks and lobster are every bit as rewarding as the decor. Open daily from 7 PM to 1 AM. No reservations. Costera Miguel Alemán at Condesa Beach (phone: 74-842549).

COYUCA 22: Known more for its views than its continental menu, this dining place is set in a garden of a private hilltop estate. Looking more like a Hollywood movie set of the 1940s (complete with pool) than a restaurant, it serves excellent lobster tails and prime ribs. Open daily from 7 to 11 PM during winter season only. Reservations necessary. 22 Coyuca (phone: 74-835030).

EMBARCADERO: The South Seas comes alive amid wooden planks, hanging vines, and lots of lush greenery. Enjoy Rangoon chicken, deep-fried soy shrimp, and Tahiti tempura, as well as superb steaks. Closed Mondays during summer. Open from 1 to 11 PM. Reservations advised. 25 Costera Miguel Alemán (phone: 74-848787).

KOOKABURRA: An open-air restaurant that offers a splendid view of the bay, as well as an extensive international menu, its specialties include seafood, beef, veal, and pork; there's also an impressive wine list. Open Mondays through Saturdays from 6 PM to midnight. Reservations advised. Carr. Las Brisas (phone: 74-841448).

MADEIRAS: Another fine hilltop restaurant offering French and international dishes. Try coquilles St. Jacques, *huachinango relleño* (stuffed red snapper), baby lamb chops, frogs' legs in garlic, or baked Cornish hen. A prix fixe menu makes this restaurant quite popular. Open Mondays through Saturdays for dinner only. Reservations advised. Carr. Escénica, in *La Vista Shopping Center* (phone: 74-846921).

SUNTORY: A typically serene atmosphere, with meditative rock gardens, tatami mats, and rice-paper screens, it serves such Japanese delicacies as sushi and sashumi. The teak tables have grills set in the center so that you can watch food being prepared. Several prix fixe dinners are offered. Open daily for lunch and dinner. Reservations advised. 36 Costera Miguel Alemán at Icacos Beach (phone: 74-848088).

Shopping at the Source

Almost any regional Mexican craft from handwoven serapes to Indian pottery and fine silver jewelry can be found in the shops on Acapulco's Costera Miguel Alemán and at its open-air markets. In many places, shoppers are expected to bargain for a purchase; to do this, a buyer really should know some basic Spanish, even if it's just a few numbers. (When absolutely necessary, however, body language will suffice.) There are several approaches to bargaining, depending on the place, the item you are after, and your personality. One way to shop is simply to look carefully, decide upon a fair price, and make a firm offer. Or you can offer half to two-thirds of the requested price and argue firmly from there.

Although bargaining is fun, very often the amount in question is so small that it is easier for most tourists to be generous. Bargaining is an art, and you also should know when *not* to practice it. Don't bargain in shops that have the sign *"precios fijos"* (fixed prices), in government shops (often called *Artes Populares*), or in the shops of hotels.

Native crafts are usually less expensive in local markets than in shops. It is better to buy more expensive items — jewelry or gems — in reputable shops. And if someone offers to sell an archaeological relic from a Mexican ruin, turn him down flat. In most cases these "relics" are manufactured by the truckload, and if by some wild chance you are being offered a genuine artifact, the sale is illegal, and the item cannot be exported from Mexico without breaking the law.

Check carefully the quality of any merchandise you are considering buying. Goods are often presented as hand-crafted that are patently machine-made — although if the price is right and the item attracts you, this is certainly no reason to refrain from buying it. But be sure you are paying what the item is worth.

Besides native crafts, Acapulco does have occasional bargains on items produced outside the country. *Warning:* Some expensive items carrying the name of Gucci and other top European designers, and sold in shops of the same name, are *not* the real thing, no matter what you're told — they are imitations made in Mexico and sold through a quirk in Mexican laws.

Certain items are produced or crafted especially well in Mexico, though the areas in which they are found vary. Silver, pottery, woven goods, leatherwork, and copper and tin goods are all uniquely Mexican materials and are worked into enduring art by Mexican craftspeople. Well-made shoes are an excellent buy.

Silver has been plentiful in Mexico since before the Spanish conquest. Silver items should be marked *sterling* or *.925* so that you know that there are not less than 925 grams of pure silver for every 1,000 grams of weight. If you are told that the silver in the jewelry came from local mines, be skeptical. Nowadays, all silver from Mexican mines goes to the central Bank of Mexico, where it is melted into bars and then resold around the country to craftspeople.

Pottery is one of the major crafts of Mexico. There's a lot of it — some of high artistic value — and it's usually inexpensive, but *don't* buy it to cook in and *never* store acidic foods in it, since lead compounds are often used in glazing. Each area of the country has its special designs and materials. Oaxaca pottery is satin black or has an unusual green glaze. You can choose as well from a vast array of Mexico City's modern designs. Lacquerwork and ceramics also are often of high quality. The lacquer is made from *chía* oil (a combination of wild sage and *aje,* the remains of plant lice). Dolomite and other minerals are added to this mixture to produce a lacquer as fine as that made from the sap of the Chinese tree. Lacquer trays usually have polished black backgrounds painted with flowers or gold lacquer.

Serapes, rebozos, blankets, and other woven articles, such as the beautiful bulky sweaters of Toluca, are usually great bargains. They should be handloomed from wool; examine the weave to make sure that other yarns weren't used.

You also should examine leather goods, to make sure that they are pure rawhide, not leather glued to cardboard or plastic. Other native crafts that you will see are *huaraches* (braided sandals), *huipiles* (embroidered dresses), all sizes and shapes of baskets, hammocks, and *piñatas* (papier-mâché figures to be filled with toys and candy).

Copper and tin goods can be found all over Mexico. Copper was once the most popular metal of the Mixtec and the Aztec Indians. Kettles, pots, pans, and pitchers are sold in markets, as well as in the more expensive shops. Again, check for quality — some articles are actually made of iron sprayed with copper-toned paint.

Be wary of gems that are sold as bargains. Jade has not been found in Mexico since the Spanish conquest; turquoise, like all other stones, should only be bought in reputable stores; and gold is not much less expensive in Mexico than in the US. Mexico does, however, have high-quality amethysts and opals and some lovely onyx and black obsidian. Also, coral jewelry is beautiful to look at. But beware: Some species of coral — including all black coral and large chunks of coral fresh from the sea — are protected and cannot be imported into the US.

Acapulco is the home of many working artists and craftspeople, some of whom combine new materials and design with the art of the past to produce original painting, sculpture, weaving, jewelry, and much more. In many ways, Mexico is the perfect place for an artist to live: Life moves slowly and is relatively inexpensive; also, the country's great natural beauty is inspiring. You can see the work of these artists in galleries and shops in towns and cities throughout the country. You are allowed to bring most

Mexican crafts into the US duty-free under the Generalized System of Preferences (GSP) program. For complete details about customs regulations in the US, see *Customs and Returning to the US,* GETTING READY TO GO.

Acapulco has scores of shops selling beautiful resortwear, which is often locally designed and, therefore, less expensive than in the United States. One of the best buys is the *guayabera,* the cotton, pleated-front, long-sleeve sport shirt worn everywhere from restaurants to beaches. There is excellent shopping in a number of boutiques around the zocalo, and along the Costera Miguel Alemán, near the swanky high-rise hotels.

Bullfights: The Kings of the Rings

 If you're truly interested in Mexican culture, you should experience at least one bullfight. The bullfight, a spectacle rather than a sport, dates from before the Christian era. Modern bullfighting originated on the Iberian Peninsula during the 12th century. (On Crete, athletes were known to have hand-wrestled bulls long before the Moors introduced bullfighting to Spain.) The Spanish brought bullfighting to Mexico just 8 years after the conquest, and the first official bullfight in the New World took place in 1529.

Do not attend a fight with the idea of rooting for the bull as though it were the home team, because the bull never wins. Some people find the spectacle of an animal being killed before a cheering crowd thoroughly repugnant. If the idea offends you, don't go. Others consider the bullfight an art form, as much a part of Mexican culture as weaving, pottery work, or onyx sculpture. In any case, the bullfight is certainly a colorful event. Matadors, picadors on horseback, banderilleros, and helpers parade into the plaza accompanied by stirring *pasadoble* music. If the matadors make graceful, artistic passes with their capes or muletas (the red kerchief they wear at the hip when they enter the ring), yell "Olé!" with the rest of the crowd. Should they succeed and make a clean kill with a single sword thrust, wave your handkerchief — you may be rewarded by seeing the judge grant the matador one bull's ear, a pair of ears, or possibly a tail.

At Acapulco's bullring — near Caleta Beach — established matadors perform on Sunday afternoons starting at 5 PM during December and *Easter Week.* Hotel travel desks have the details and the tickets, which cost from $10 to $25 (phone: 74-821181).

A Shutterbug's Acapulco

 If you can get it to hold still long enough, Acapulco is an exceptionally photogenic city. There is architectural variety: Old is juxtaposed with new, ornate with ordinary, and a skyline bristling with the temples of modern tourism is also graced with a 17th-century Spanish fort. There also is natural variety: Luxurious layers of lavender and crimson bougainvillea blanket white stucco walls, a grove of thick coconut palms creates a welcome patch of shade along a talcum white beach, and a tropical sunset sparks the bay ablaze with colors so intense that they defy description. There's human variety as well: Voluptuous jet setters decked out in seductive *tangas* perfect their tans along the beaches, ruddy fishermen in tattered shirts and red bandanas return with their catch, and Nahuatl Indian women hawk their wares of handwoven *huipiles* and native crafts in the local marketplace. The thriving resort city, the shimmering sea, the beaches, the people, and traces of a rich history that has its roots in pre-Columbian times make Acapulco a fertile stomping ground for shutter-bugs. Even a beginner can achieve remarkable results with a surprisingly basic set of lenses and filters. Equipment is, in fact, only as valuable as the imagination that puts it into use. (For further information on equipment, see *Cameras and Equipment* in GETTING READY TO GO.)

Don't be afraid to experiment. Use what knowledge you have to explore new possibil-ities. Don't limit yourself with preconceived ideas of what's clichéd or corny. Just because the Quebrada cliff divers have been photographed hundreds of times before doesn't make them any less worthy of your attention.

In Acapulco, as elsewhere, spontaneity is one of the keys to good photography. Whether it's a sudden shaft of light bursting through the clouds and hitting the bay just so, or fishermen unloading their catch as dawn creeps over the pier, don't hesitate to shoot if the moment is right. If photography is indeed capturing a moment and making it timeless, success lies in judging just when a moment worth capturing occurs and reacting quickly.

A good picture reveals an eye for detail, whether it's a matter of lighting, of position-ing your subject, or of taking time to crop a picture carefully. The better your grasp of the importance of details, the better your results will be photographically.

Patience is often necessary. Don't shoot a view of the azure waters of Coyuca Lagoon in Pie de la Cuesta if a cloud suddenly dims its glow. A rusted old Volkswagen in your shot of a balloon-laden *calandria* (horse-drawn carriage)? Reframe your image to eliminate the obvious distraction. People walking toward a scene that would benefit from their presence? Wait until they're in position before you shoot. After the fact, many of the flaws will be self-evident. The trick is to be aware of the ideal and have the patience to allow it to happen. If you are part of a group, you may well have to trail behind a bit in order to shoot properly. Not only is group activity distracting, but bunches of people hovering nearby tend to stifle spontaneity and overwhelm potential subjects.

The camera or camcorder provides an opportunity, not only to capture Acapulco's varied and subtle beauty, but to interpret it. What it takes is a sensitivity to the surroundings, a knowledge of the capabilities of your equipment, and a willingness to see things in new ways.

LANDSCAPES AND SEASCAPES: Acapulco's spectacular bay and sensuous sun-sets are most often the favorite subjects of visiting photographers, but the city's green spaces and dramatic architecture provide numerous photo possibilities as well. In addition to the San Diego Fort, Papagayo Park, and the jungle of high-rise luxury hotels, be sure to look for natural beauty — flaming canary-yellow royal poincianas that dot Roqueta Island, the well-manicured plots of flowers at the Centro Interna-cional convention center, the bright orange acacias that line the Costera Miguel Ale-mán, and the unassuming fishing boats that skim along the bay are just a few examples.

Color and form are the obvious ingredients here, and how you frame your pictures can be as important as getting the proper exposure. Study the shapes, angles, and colors that make up the scene and create a composition that uses them to best advantage.

Lighting is a vital component in landscapes and seascapes. Take advantage of the richer colors of early morning and late afternoon whenever possible. The overhead light of midday is often harsh and without the shadowing that can add to the drama of a scene. This is when a polarizer is used to best effect. Most polarizers come with a mark on the rotating ring. If you can aim at your subject and point that marker at the sun, the sun's rays are likely to be right for the polarizer to work for you. If not, stick to your skylight filter, underexposing slightly if the scene is particularly bright. Most light meters respond to an overall light balance, with the result that bright areas may appear burned out.

Although a standard 50mm to 55mm lens may work well in some landscape situations, most will benefit from a 20mm to 28mm wide-angle. Acapulco Bay, with its rows of imposing five-star hotels towering in the distance, for example, is the type of panorama that fits beautifully into a wide-angle format, allowing not only the overview, but the opportunity to include people or other points of interest in the foreground. A single flower, for instance, may be used to set off a view of Papagayo Park; or people can provide a sense of perspective in a shot of Icacos Beach.

To isolate specific elements of any scene, use your telephoto lens. Perhaps there's a Byzantine carving in the Acapulco Cathedral that would make a lovely shot, or it might be the interplay of light and shadow on the rippled sand at Barra Vieja. The successful use of a telephoto means developing your eye for detail.

PEOPLE: As with taking pictures of people anywhere, there are going to be times in Acapulco when a camera is an intrusion. Your approach is the key: Consider your own reaction under similar circumstances, and you have an idea as to what would make others comfortable enough to be willing subjects. People are often sensitive to having a camera suddenly pointed at them, and a polite request, while getting you a share of refusals, will also provide a chance to shoot some wonderful portraits that capture the spirit of Acapulco as surely as the scenery does. For candids, an excellent lens is a zoom telephoto in the 70mm to 210mm range; it allows you to remain unobtrusive while the telephoto lens draws the subject closer. And for portraits, a telephoto can be used effectively as close as 2 or 3 feet.

For authenticity and variety, select a place likely to produce interesting subjects. Condesa is an obvious spot for tourists, but if it's local color you're after, visit the downtown market or Caleta Beach, sit at a café on the zocalo and watch the fashion parade, or walk around Papagayo Park, where everyone from overzealous teenagers on roller skates to somber monks reciting their afternoon prayers rove the shady paths. Aim for shots that tell what's different about Acapulco. In portraiture, there are several factors to keep in mind. Morning or afternoon light will add richness to skin tones, emphasizing tans. To avoid the harsh facial shadows cast by direct sunlight, shoot in the shade or in an area where the light is diffused. The only filter to use is a skylight.

SUNSETS: In Acapulco, no hour is more bewitching than sunset, when the last scintillating rays of the tropical sun radiate across the bay, reflecting the entire spectrum of the rainbow in its crystalline waters and the fiery light hits the golden beach, crowning the skyline of glass-encased hotels with clouds of pink and lavender, purple and red.

When shooting sunsets, keep in mind that the brightness will distort meter readings. When composing a shot directly into the sun, frame the picture in the viewfinder so that only half of the sun is included. Read the meter, set, and shoot. Whenever there is this kind of unusual lighting, shoot a few frames in half-step increments, both over and under the meter reading. Bracketing, as this is called, can provide a range of images, the best of which may well be other than the one shot at the meter's recommended setting.

Use any lens for sunsets. A wide-angle is good when the sky is filled with color-streaked clouds, when the sun is partially hidden, or when you're close to an object that silhouettes dramatically against the sky.

Telephotos also produce wonderful silhouettes, either with the sun as a backdrop or against the palette of a brilliant sunset sky. Bracket again here. For the best silhouettes, wait 10 to 15 minutes after sunset. Unless using a very fast film, a tripod is recommended.

Orange, magenta, and split-screen filters are often used to accentuate a sunset's picture potential. Orange will help turn even a gray sky into something approaching a photogenic finale to the day and can provide particularly beautiful shots linking the sky with the sun reflected on the ocean. A pale magenta, as in a fluorescent/daylight correction filter, can add subtle color to dull or brilliant sunsets. If the sunset is already bold in hue, the orange will overwhelm the natural colors, as will a red filter — which can nonetheless produce dramatic, highly unrealistic results.

NIGHT: If you think that picture possibilities end at sunset, you're presuming that night photography is the exclusive domain of the professional. If you've got a tripod, all you'll need is a cable release to attach to your camera to assure a steady exposure (which is often timed in minutes rather than fractions of a second).

For situations such as a folkloric ballet at the Centro Internacional or nighttime cruises along the bay, a strobe does the trick, but beware: Flash units are often used improperly. You can't take a view of the Acapulco skyline with a flash. It may reach out 30 to 50 feet, but that's it. On the other hand, a flash used too close to your subject may result in overexposure, resulting in a "blown out" effect. With most cameras, strobes will work with a maximum shutter speed of 1/125 or 1/250 of a second. If you set the exposure properly and shoot within range, you should come up with pretty sharp results.

CLOSE-UPS: Whether of people or of objects such as hand-painted, lacquered chests, decorated with flowers and animals, that are made in Olinalá, close-ups can add another dimension to your photography. There are a number of shooting options, one of which is to use a 70mm or a 210mm lens at its closest focusable distance. Unless you're working in bright sunlight, a tripod will be worthwhile. If you are very near your subject and there is a good deal of reflective light, it may pay to underexpose a bit in relation to the meter reading.

If you do not have a telephoto lens, you can still shoot close-ups using a set of magnification filters. Filter packs of one-, two-, and three-time magnification are available, converting your lens into a close-up lens. Even better is a special macro lens designed for close-up photography.

The following are some of Acapulco's most photogenic places.

A SHORT PHOTOGRAPHIC TOUR

ACAPULCO BAY: From just about any angle, the glistening waters of Acapulco Bay are breathtaking, but if you really want to overwhelm your friends and neighbors back home, try taking your shot from the top of the hilltop where the exclusive *Las Brisas* hotel caps Guitarrón Point on the Carretera Escénica. From this lofty angle, you can capture the entire bay in all its glory, and with a wide-angle lens, you can also encompass the downtown area with its lineup of sleek luxury liners and quaint fishing boats vying for a place at the docking platform. From this vantage point, you can also photograph the San Diego Fort and, if your lens is wide enough, you'll be able to include a glimpse of the Punta Grifo on the east end of the bay, with its fertile palms and spectacular cliffs cascading with infusions of wild flowers. The best hour for snapping the bay is just before or just after sunset, when the sky's incandescent luster is reflected against the indigo waters of the sea. And for a special touch of tropical allure, try framing your picture to include a hibiscus or acacia blossom in a corner of your foreground.

LA QUEBRADA CLIFF DIVERS: This is a shot that requires quick reflexes and expert timing. If you are not fully familiar with your camera, try setting your focus and exposure ahead of time and framing your image on a tripod so that once the first diver comes into frame, all you have to do is click the shutter and you've got your picture. More adventurous shutterbugs will not be content to limit their vantage point to that provided by the *La Perla* nightclub. It may pose a bit of a trek through some rather weedy terrain, but for a closer look (and shot) of Acapulco's most famous aquatic athletes, you can traipse down almost to the spot where the divers make their perilous plunge. For a less traditional glimpse into the cliff diver's life, you might want to get a shot of him kneeling in prayer at a rustic altar of the Virgin of Guadalupe just before his death-defying leap.

SAN DIEGO FORT: You have to get down to sea level to appreciate this sprawling 10,000-square-meter edifice. The best view is from the corner of Costera Miguel Alemán and Diego de Mendoza. The elevated limestone walls topped with iron cannon tower high above the tallest palms, and the multi-hued bougainvillea that inch their way up the sides of the fort still have not reached the summit of its solitary watchtower. To add perspective to your photograph, try to include a group of people near the fort walls; it will add yet another sense of the gigantic proportions of the exceptional citadel.

PLAZA JUAN ALVAREZ (THE ZOCALO): Opposite the waterfront on the Plaza Juan Alvarez, the Byzantine Acapulco Cathedral — with its mosque-like dome — is a peculiar mixture of Mexican, Spanish, and neo-classical French architecture. The structure itself is a little on the gauche side, but with the right setting, it can be a stunningly interesting — if not necessarily beautiful — photographic theme. The secret is to include an interesting foreground. The stately monument to Vicente Guerrero, José María Morelos, Miguel Hidalgo, and Aztec Emperor Cuauhtémoc, each facing a cardinal point, in the center of the plaza is an obvious choice. Or you might prefer to include a group of Nahuatl women sitting in a corner of the park weaving traditional *huipiles* on their hand-crafted looms. Or why not try to catch a passing *calandria* laden with colorful balloons? People inevitably tend to congregate around the zocalo, and their infinite variety of activities and diversity will more than make up for any lack of architectural elegance in Acapulco's frumpish downtown. The main point to remember is to try juxtaposition.

PIE DE LA CUESTA: If sunsets are your photographic passion, this is the place to indulge yourself. Pie de la Cuesta enjoys not one but *two* resplendent bodies of water where the setting tropical sun is reflected and re-accentuated in shimmering tones of aquamarine and amethyst. Your best bet is to try to frame your photograph to include a portion of the sky, the ocean, and the Coyuca Lagoon. Since no two sunsets are exactly alike, the precise composition and balance of your masterpiece will depend on the moment you decide to snap the shutter. But with the kinds of sunsets that Pie de la Cuesta is famous for, you aren't likely to go too far wrong no matter what angle you choose.

For The Body

Acapulco's Amazing Beaches

 Unless it were to become an island floating freely between the US and Guatemala, it is hard to imagine how Mexico could be any better endowed with coastlines and beaches. Acapulco is a traditional sunning spot and boasts some of North America's most celebrated beach resorts. Here and all along Mexico's Pacific coastline wide, powder-white beaches, a tropical climate, warm waters, and spectacular sunsets (on this coast, the sun usually plunges into the sea with great drama, since most vistas look directly westward) attract thousands of tourists, beachcombers, and vacationing Mexicans all year round, year after year.

Since all beaches in Acapulco are open to the public, visitors can swim and use all the facilities, including those near luxurious hotels (though access to these resort strips may prove awkward or difficult). Beaches that are designated "public recreational areas" are maintained by the government and are much used by *acapulqueños*.

As Mexico's foremost beach resort, Acapulco has more than a dozen beaches of one size or another nestled at the base of the plunging rocks and surrounding cliffs. In light of recent government regulations, beachcombers can look for cleaner beaches sans most of the bothersome vendors selling their wares. Also new are the special tiled traffic-free walkways to the beaches, gardened mini-parks, public telephones, and plenty of changing rooms and showers. A word of caution: It's vital to pay attention to the warning flags posted on Acapulco beaches. The open ocean is especially dangerous, and even in the bay there are strong waves, with riptides and undertows. Red or black flags denote dangerous waters.

The beaches below are our favorite Acapulco strands:

PLAYAS CALETA AND CALETILLA (Caleta and Little Caleta Beaches): A pair of pretty sheltered beaches along the western rim of the bay just beyond the *malecón* and the Fort of San Diego. Known as "the morning beach" because of the early sun, they are ringed with older hotels and resorts and are still popular with traditionalists and Mexican tourists. And although they may not be as serene — or clean — as other more popular spots, they are very often crowded (especially now since they are bisected by the walk to the new *Mágico Mundo Marino* aquarium), and they still offer good swimming. There's also a lot of boat traffic; launches are for rent at the pier, and boats leave regularly for nearby Isla Roqueta. Also for rent are small sailboats, kayaks, and paddleboats.

PLAYA CONDESA: One of the most popular beaches in town, probably because it follows the long strip of the most glamorous hotels, bright beach cafés, and swinging bars. Best bet is to sunbathe here; the waters are rough and there's always a strong undertow. Condesa offers sailboats for rent; there are also rental facilities for windsurfing, parasailing, and water skiing.

PLAYA ICACOS: East of Revolcadero, around a point of land called Punta Guitar-rón, is a small beach providing relatively safe swimming (look for posted flags, however, in front of each hotel). Windsurfing, sailing, parasailing, and water skiing are popular sports here.

PLAYA PAPAGAYO (Parrot Beach): The beach has two names actually, the other being El Morro (The Rock), for the large rock formation just offshore. A beautiful wide strip of sand, Playa Papagayo is in front of Papagayo Parque.

PLAYA PIE DE LA CUESTA: Great spots for watching the sunset, this beach 10 miles (16 km) west of the city is increasingly popular with foreign tourists as well as locals. Beware: The beach suffers from the most dangerous undertows along this section of the coast. Watch, don't swim.

REVOLCADERO BEACH: Within reach of the *Pierre Marqués* and *Acapulco Princess* hotels is this smooth and quiet beach surrounded by jungle foliage. It's right on the open ocean (as opposed to Acapulco's other beaches, on the bay), and the waves here can become foaming breakers, crashing on the sand and retreating with a deadly undertow. The strong waves and current make swimming quite dangerous. Since surfing is prohibited in Acapulco Bay, enthusiastic surfers play their sport here, at their own considerable risk.

PLAYA LA ROQUETA: On Isla Roqueta, this narrow, white-sand beach is a favorite with visitors. Here swimming is safe, in calm and shallow waters. Snorkeling and scuba diving are excellent on the northern side of the island; diving instructors are available. Fishing is good; there also are kayaks for rent.

Scuba and Skin Diving: Best Depths

Some of the most noted skin and scuba diving spots in the world lie off Acapulco's Pacific shores. Warm lagoons, rich with tropical fish and incredible coral deposits of intricate formation and colorful hues, offer ideal underwater experiences.

Every major beach resort in Acapulco rents equipment and offers instruction and organized diving tours. For those who haven't tried skin or scuba diving before, any of the spots listed below would be a good place to begin.

Diving is extremely popular here, though the water in the bay is never as clear as that of the seas along less-developed sections of the Pacific coast or on the Caribbean. The best diving spot in Acapulco is off the shores of Roqueta Island, right in the bay opposite Caleta Beach. *Divers de México* (phone: 74-821397/8), and *Hermanos Arnold* (phone: 74-820788) — both on Costera Miguel Alemán — and the larger hotels offer diving lessons, which start absolute beginners in a swimming pool. Lessons and equipment are also available at the entrance of Caleta Beach. There is fine snorkeling at *Las Brisas* hotel's private *La Concha Beach Club* (phone: 74-841580; 800-228-3000 in the US). Snorkeling instruction and equipment rental are also available; contact the Acapulco Tourist Office (phone: 74-847621 or 74-847630).

Sailing: Acapulco Afloat

 With Acapulco's phenomenal coast, it is not surprising that sailboat races and regattas are held here and all along the Pacific Coast throughout the year. Most resort hotels will rent small sailboats to guests; windsurfing is also popular among locals and visitors alike. For exact dates of regattas and competitions, as well as general information, write to the *Mexican Sailing Federation,* 42 Córdoba, México, DF 06700 (phone: 5-533-3412 or 5-533-4664).

Small sailboats may also be rented at nearby beaches including Playa Caleta, Playa Caletilla, Playa Papagayo, Playa Condesa, and at Puerto Marqués, southeast of Acapulco off Carretera Escénica. One day every month, the bay of Acapulco is covered with sailboats participating in a regatta run by the *Acapulco Yacht Club.* While sailing in Acapulco Bay may be considered easy for some, navigating the more turbulent Pacific waves and currents requires greater expertise and skill. Novices are advised to hire an experienced captain before setting sail. The popular Hobie Cats have gained the nickname "wet cats" by many, and once you try them you'll soon know why. They, too, are available for rent at most beaches. Windsurfing is also a popular sport off most Acapulco beaches. For information, contact *El Colonial,* near the Fort of San Diego (phone: 74-839030).

Tennis

 As with golf, the popularity of tennis is growing by leaps and bounds in Mexico. But although almost all major resorts have tennis facilities, Acapulco remains the tennis capital, with almost perfect weather from October through June.

In addition to hotel courts, a growing number of tennis clubs — often part of golf clubs — have opened their courts to non-members for a fee. Below is a list of hotels and clubs in Acapulco that are known to have good tennis facilities. For more information, write the *Mexican Federation of Tennis* (Federación Mexicana de Tenis), 953 Miguel Angel de Quevedo, México DF 04330 (phone: 5-549-1618 or 5-514-1956).

ACAPULCO PLAZA: Here are 4 clay courts (3 lighted for evening play), atop a shopping center next door. 123 Costera Miguel Alemán (phone: 74-858050).

ACAPULCO PRINCESS: With 2 of the most lavish air conditioned indoor tennis courts anywhere, it offers 11 courts overall. Reservations are necessary. Private lessons are available from local pros Tomas Flores and Juan Téllez or from one of the other instructors. The adjacent *Pierre Marqués,* run by the same management, has 8 courts of its own, and guests also have full access to the *Acapulco Princess* facilities. Airport Rd., 12 miles (19 km) south of Acapulco (phone: 74-843100).

LAS BRISAS: With 300 rooms and a number of 4- to 6-bedroom houses, this resort overlooking Acapulco Bay is one of the best in the world. The 5 hard-surface courts, all lighted, a pro shop, and a tennis and backgammon club are all available to guests. Players must reserve playing time on the courts. 5255 Carr. Escénica (phone: 74-841580).

CONTINENTAL PLAZA ACAPULCO: Shares tennis facilities with the *Hyatt Regency* (below). Costera Miguel Alemán (phone: 74-840909).

HYATT REGENCY: Five lighted, hard-surface courts are available. There is also a good pro shop. Guests who purchase a tennis package can use the courts free of charge — don't forget to reserve playing time, though. 1 Costera Miguel Alemán (phone: 74-842888).

PIERRE MARQUÉS: There are 8 courts, plus the tennis facilities of its sister hotel, the *Acapulco Princess,* which is right next door. Airport Rd., 11 miles (18 km) south of downtown Acapulco (phone: 74-842000).

VILLA VERA: The *Villa Vera Racquet Club* has 3 lighted clay courts. 35 Lomas del Mar (phone: 74-840333).

PRIVATE SPORTS CLUBS: The best courts and the best players are usually found at the private clubs; you may also have some difficulty reserving a court, so ask your hotel to make arrangements for you. A list of Acapulco's best: *Tiffany Racquet Club* (120 Av. Villa Vera; phone: 74-847949), 6 clay courts, 2 lighted; *Club de Golf Acapulco,* across from the *Malibu* hotel (Costera Miguel Alemán; phone: 74-840909), 4 cement courts, 2 lighted.

Good Golf

Although many of the best Mexican courses are part of private country clubs or resort hotel complexes, it is possible to play on some of them. In resort areas such as Acapulco, the best time to tee off is before 9 AM or after 3 PM. At any hotel that is connected with a golf course, or openly offers to secure greens privileges for its guests, few obstacles to entry are found.

ACAPULCO PRINCESS: Ted Robinson designed this shortish, tight, 18-hole golf course, which features many water hazards. Lessons are available. Wayne Sisson is the golf director and Manuel Martinez is the resident pro. Non-guests can play here, and fees during the off-season are a bit lower than in the winter. On Airport Rd., 12 miles (19 km) south of Acapulco (phone: 74-843100).

PIERRE MARQUÉS: Part of the *Acapulco Princess* family, this Percy Clifford 18-hole course, 11 miles (18 km) south of downtown Acapulco, is the longest and one of the best on Mexico's Pacific Coast. Reservations are accepted 2 days in advance, and the season runs from mid-December through mid-April. Wayne Sisson is also in charge here; José Dominiquez is the pro. Guests can enter most of its many tournaments. Playa de Revolcadero, just down the road from the *Acapulco Princess* (phone: 74-842000).

Fishing Acapulco's Rich Waters

Acapulco offers some of the best deep-sea fishing in the world, and American fishermen travel thousands of miles up and down the coast for snook, bass, dorado, striped marlin, sailfish, red snapper, billfish, and shark. Many experienced anglers come here just for the fishing competitions held here each year. There is no problem bringing any kind of fishing gear into the country, and Acapulco has charter boats and fishing gear for hire (figure an average of $275 a day, gear and bait included). See the Acapulco CITY chapter for names and addresses.

Visiting anglers can readily obtain a Mexican fishing permit from Secretaría de Pesca, 269 Av. Alvaro Obregón, México, DF 06700, or from any one of its more than 140 offices throughout the country. Licenses are free for fishing from the shore. There is a charge of $3 a day to $70 for 6 months, for fishing from a small vessel. There are also weekly and monthly rates. Temporary permits are issued for boats and trailers entering Mexico.

More information on fishing in Acapulco, including guides, regulations, fishing seasons, and tournaments, can be obtained by writing to Dirección General de Administración de Pesca, 269 Av. Alvaro Obregón, México, DF 06700 (phone: 5-511-1881).

The fishing spots described below are some of the best in the area.

The city's beaches are only slightly more crowded with people than its waters — sea, lagoon, and river — are crowded with fish. The Pacific is ripe territory all year for big-game fish like marlin, tuna, sailfish, barracuda, bonito, and red snapper. The city's freshwater lagoons — Coyuca, Tres Palos, and Playa Encantada — and the Río Papagayo are good for carp, catfish, and mullet.

Plenty of equipment and lots of fishing boats are available for rent. Deluxe deep-sea charter boats, fully equipped for fishing, cost $220 to $500 per day, depending on the size of the boat and number of participants. The top price is for a fully equipped, air conditioned yacht, suitable for overnight or longer trips. Anglers can make arrangements through their hotel or can try bargaining with boat captains face-to-face — not an uncommon practice and one that can work to advantage, but make sure the price *includes* bait and beer. Most deep-sea boats are docked downtown along the *malecón.* For freshwater fishing, both the Coyuca Lagoon and Tres Palos Lagoon, about 16 miles (25 km) southeast of town, have boats with gear for rent.

An *International Billfish Tournament,* which usually brings catches averaging 90 pounds, is held in Acapulco in November or early December. The inter-club tournament of local fishing clubs is in February.

Acapulco on Horseback

 Along with the Catholic church, lust for gold, and a host of Spanish traditions that were to take root in Mexico and wreak various degrees of havoc for the next 3 centuries, Hernán Cortés reintroduced one thing to Mexico that proved to be an outright blessing: the horse. There were no horses in Mexico when Cortés arrived, though recently discovered cave paintings in northern Mexico indicate that a smaller species once existed, but apparently became extinct. Mexicans are enthusiastic and skilled equestrians, and the tradition of horsemanship is a perfect marriage between the heritage of Spain and the workaday requirements of ranches and farms throughout Mexico's northwestern mountains and plains country.

In Acapulco, where beach riding is a favorite pastime, visitors can test their equestrian talents along some of its beaches. Horses can be rented for about $10 per hour along the sands of Revolcadero Beach near the *Acapulco Princess.* West of town at Pie de la Cuesta, horses are available for rent on the beach at *Tres Marías* (no phone).

DIRECTIONS

Introduction

The pleasures of travel to Acapulco have broadened in recent years, as more and more visitors to this jewel of Mexico's Pacific Coast discover that — if they choose — there's much more to an Acapulco vacation than that which lies along its beaches. Exploring the regions around and beyond the city, a land so rich in archaeological treasures, dramatic history, spectacular scenery, and, yes, even more beaches, has proved pure pleasure for those folks willing to do a bit of roaming on their own.

Both of our routes begin on Acapulco's wide boulevard, the Costera Miguel Alemán, which follows the crescent of the bay past all the luxurious hotels and resorts and the beautiful sandy beaches that are Acapulco's claim to fame. For those who prefer to use Acapulco as a base, each route has at least one day trip, an interesting tour of an area within a day's drive of Acapulco.

History records that Acapulco Bay was discovered early in the 16th century by Hernán Cortés. It was here that Cortés built new ships and launched explorations to the south. He also outfitted the ships that Francisco Pizarro used in his conquest of Peru. Later in the 16th century, Andrés de Urdaneta established this bay as Spain's main port for trade between Mexico and the Orient.

Harassed by pirates and disturbed by the covetous eyes of foreign countries over the centuries, the then-Spanish Viceroy Diego Fernández Guadalacazar commissioned the construction of the San Diego Fort on a hill overlooking the mouth of the bay across from Playa Hornos (it was designed and built by Dutch architect Adrien Boot). In 1776, the fort was completely destroyed by an earthquake; it was rebuilt in 1783. The new fortress, over twice the size of the original, is extant and is on the site of a modern-day Mexican military base. Open to the general public, it is one of Acapulco's few remaining historical attractions.

German naturalist Alexander von Humboldt, who left from Acapulco Bay on many explorations to South America during the early 1800s, called it "the most beautiful bay in the world." Through the years that Cortés's men came and went, and pirates stopped for a spell, only a handful of people actually lived here. The Aztec and Mixtec preferred the more fertile valleys that lie just beyond the mountains, and came to these shores only to catch their quota of fish.

Today, much has changed. New highways have paved the way for modern-day exploration. The government has made the building and improvement of highways a top priority so that, in most areas, it has become virtually impossible to find those narrow, unmarked main roads of yesterday. Secondary dirt roads still exist, but for the most part our routes follow fairly smooth, paved highways.

What follows are the prime driving routes from Acapulco, including the famed Acapulco–Taxco–Mexico City drive. Entries describe the highlights of each route, including useful suggestions for sightseeing and dining, plus descriptions of the driving conditions and approximate timetables for coming and going. *Best en Route* lists suggested accommodations at the best hotels and inns, plus restaurants, along the way. Detailed maps introduce each itinerary and note the major reference points along the route.

We've made our route selections based on our opinions of the most memorable sites and sights along Mexico's Pacific Coast, and inland to the mountains of Morelos and Oaxaca, and the Federal District of Mexico City. It's possible to string two of these itineraries together for more extensive exploration. For those with less time, following a single itinerary will cover the most notable points of interest (and the most attractive accommodations) in a given area.

One word of caution about driving in Mexico: It's always wise for travelers who will be driving on remote country roads to allow sufficient time to reach their destinations well before dark. Driving secondary roads in Mexico after dark is not something we recommend; as a matter of fact, it's a risk we earnestly advise readers to avoid. Naturally, before your journey, be sure your vehicle is in top mechanical condition and include an extra fan belt and quart of oil for good measure. Should your car break down, don't abandon it; Mexico has a wonderful system of "Green Angels" who patrol the highways to help the stranded motorist. They will repair your car on the spot if possible, or tow you to the nearest garage. The only cost to you for simple repairs is for parts and/or gas.

Finally, as anywhere in the world, picking up strangers, camping on lonely beaches, or sleeping in a car in some isolated area can invite serious trouble. It takes only a little common sense, and some very basic planning, to make a driving tour of Acapulco and its environs both a safe and an especially memorable travel adventure.

Acapulco to Oaxaca

If basking in the sun beside a turquoise blue bay by day, sipping margaritas at sunset, and dancing the night away under starlit skies is your idea of heaven, then Acapulco is the place to be. Chances are you may never tire of its sybaritic splendors, but if you do, there's a whole other Mexico just a short drive from your beachfront lounge chair. Our favorite diversion from Acapulco — as we reluctantly ease our way back to the real world — is a visit to the scenic, history-rich region of Oaxaca. The state of Oaxaca is an orgy of contrasts, from cool, forest-covered mountains and lush tropical valleys to a hot, humid coastline of beaches pounded by the Pacific surf. The contrasts are cultural as well as topographical, with ancient Indian ruins lying within sight of old Spanish colonial towns. Oaxaca, the fifth-largest state in the country, also boasts more ethnic groups than any other state except Chiapas. Most of these maintain their original languages, customs, and dress, turning the villages and markets of Oaxaca into an amazing array of otherworldliness. Even geography adds to the exotic atmosphere of the state. The rivers of Oaxaca often overflow their banks during the spring and summer rainy season, minor earthquakes occur frequently, and the state plays host to a diversified wildlife population. Though tapir, jaguars, ocelots, and margays have been severely reduced in numbers by the lumber, oil, and mining industries, they can still be found in some of the forests. Alligators and boa constrictors thrive in the more humid areas in the south.

Two proud cultures dominate the many different ethnic groups in the state (including the Chinantec, Mazatec, Cuicatec, Chocho, Huave, Mije, Trique, and Amusgo) — the Mixtec and the Zapotec, whose civilizations reached great heights in architecture, sculpture, astronomy, and jewelry design long before any Europeans made their way to Mexico. In turns they built the impressive sacred cities of Monte Albán and Mitla.

The state of Oaxaca really represents three major geographical regions: the Valley of Oaxaca, the Isthmus of Tehuantepec, and the Pacific Coast. The valley refers to the part closest to Mexico City and is the cultural, historical, and economic center of the state. The isthmus is where the west coast veers northeast and forms Mexico's narrow belt. The winds of this area are treacherous and the climate is hot and humid. The Pacific Coast, lying south and southwest of Oaxaca City, is not easily accessible from the rest of the state. Thankfully, there is a modern road, Highway 200, from Acapulco that extends along the coast to the beautiful beaches of Puerto Escondido and Puerto Angel, and for those who decide to venture inland to visit the splendid ruins surrounding Oaxaca City, Route 175 is an easy 154-mile (246-km) drive north of Puerto Angel. For those who still crave more sand, the Nine Bays of Huatulco are some 320 miles (512 km) southeast of Acapulco on Highway 200 (65 miles/104 km east of Puerto Escondido).

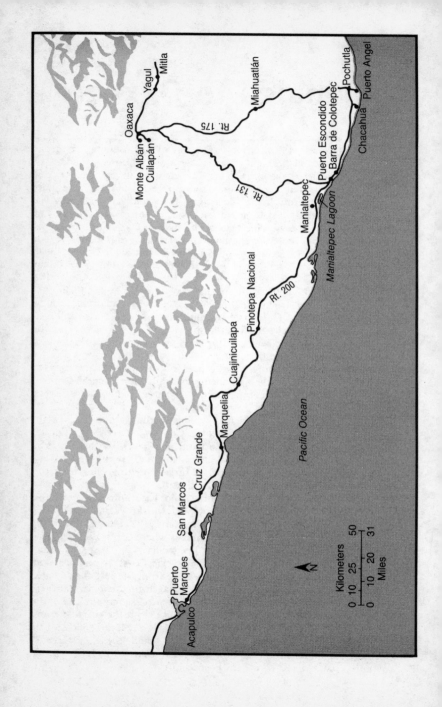

En route from Acapulco – The first leg of this journey follows Highway 200 east to Puerto Escondido, 252 miles (403 km), or approximately 6 to 7 hours, from Acapulco. From town, take the Costera Miguel Alemán east (toward the airport) past Puerto Marqués, a lovely cove lined with luxury hotels and the Punta Diamante (Diamond Point) housing and resort hotel development. From this point, the road leaves the coast and curves inland to the foothills of the Sierra Madre del Sur. There's a brief stretch of not-too-good road here, but it improves before long.

The stretch of coastline between Acapulco and Puerto Escondido, known as the Costa Chica (Little Coast), undergoes a subtle transformation as you head southeast. The harsh beauty of dry, desolate desert alternates with irrigated fields and orchards and tropical ranchland. While there are few settlements, dream beaches, or sites that demand a stop, the landscape and the scenes of daily life along the road are enjoyable. You are likely to see elderly *campesinos* (farmers) urging their burros along the roadside, children knocking almonds from trees with thin sticks, and women prodding herds of skipping goats across the highway. As you approach the state of Oaxaca, increasing Indian influences are visible in the colorful dress of the people, and in the mixture of architectural styles in the villages: Brick homes with red tile roofs give way to adobe houses and more primitive stick–and–mud plaster huts.

Traveling the scenic two-lane highway affords glimpses of the Pacific on the right, and the towering mountains on the left. Pass the village of San Marcos and the tiny hamlet of Cruz Grande and continue for about 24 miles (39 km) to the seaside town of Marquelia, about 98 miles (158 km) from Acapulco. If you travel through here on a Sunday, be sure to stop and sample the produce and handmade crafts on sale at the local market.

A laid-back fishing village renowned for its hospitality to visitors, Marquelia is a great place to sample down-home Guerrero-style cooking. For a few pesos, the only restaurant in town (next to the only pharmacy) will whip up a fresh langoustine and shrimp concoction smothered in enough garlic to ward off vampires for at least 3 weeks. If you pass through here in the morning, you may want to sample the industrial-strength coffee and sweet rolls that are served as the classic Marquelia breakfast. One word of warning: If you plan on visiting Marquelia in the evening, be sure to take along a strong insect repellent. The mosquitoes are huge and omnipresent, particularly during the rainy season. Also worth a detour here is the secluded Pacific beach just 5 miles (8 km) south of town.

Back on Highway 200, drive about 39 miles (63 km) south to Cuajinicuilapa, a village founded in 1562 by freed African slaves; the population today — some 4,000 people — retains much of its original culture. The only place in Mexico with a significant black population, "Cuaji," as it is affectionately referred to by its inhabitants, is unlike the surrounding villages in that most of the thatch huts are round in shape and open into a central meeting circle much like those in Africa.

Continue on Route 200 past the Guerrero–Oaxaca border for 25 miles (40 km) to the Amusgo Indian town of Pinotepa Nacional, an agricultural center whose residents, a minor branch of the Mixtec, tend the land and sell their wares at roadside stall on Sundays. Because of its ideal location midway between the valleys of Chilpancingo and Oaxaca, Pinotepa was a central crossroads in pre-Columbian times. In fact, the name Pinotepa actually means "Palaces of the Outsiders" in Nahuatl, referring to the endless processions of visiting tribes that came to the city to trade their wares during the 13th and 14th centuries. Pinotepa was also a major producer of cacao (chocolate beans), which were the main currency throughout Mesoamerica before the Spanish conquest, making it one of the richest cities in the region. Once the conquistadores discovered the wealth and beauty of Pinotepa in the 1530s, they set out to vanquish the local population and to claim the city as their own. A bloodbath ensued and the native population was almost entirely annihilated. African slaves were brought in to carry out heavy manual labor, and a bustling colonial city was constructed on the ruins of the Mixtec palaces. The elaborate Cathedral of Pinotepa Nacional — which still stands today — was constructed; and for a short time, Pinotepa was the de facto capital of Oaxaca. Nature, however, reclaimed the city from the Spanish intruders through a series of devasting earthquakes and malaria plagues. By the early 19th century, Pinotepa ceased to be a trading center, and as the spirit of the independence movement swept across the territory, the city's past glory faded into oblivion.

Today the city is known for its florid *chilenas* and *tejerones,* the former an erotic courtship dance; the latter a whimsical parody of old age through masked mime. Both of these rituals are carried out in flamboyant style during *Easter* and *Christmas* seasons and during the mid-August celebration of the city's founding. Pinotepa is also renowned for its handwoven *huipiles* (embroidered native dresses), rich with the red and purple tones produced with the natural dyes of the nopal beetle and sea snail. The *Campestre* restaurant alongside the road into town offers good food in pleasant surroundings.

Continue east on Highway 200 for 89 miles (142 km) to Puerto Escondido.

PUERTO ESCONDIDO: A town of 45,000 people on the Pacific Coast in the state of Oaxaca, 252 miles (403 km) from Acapulco, this lesser-known resort is one of the most beautiful, unspoiled, and undeveloped hideaways in southern Mexico.

In fact, a lovely, sweeping view of the resort and its beaches can be seen from the Carretera Costera, the Coastal Highway. A more immediate view is afforded by the *faro* (lighthouse), which can be reached by a 15-minute walk from the main street. Look for a sign that says Camino del Faro; it points the way to the red-and-white tower.

About 95% of Puerto Escondido's population is of Indian descent, and most make their living from fishing or farming. With significant tourism just beginning to stir, it's still possible for a visitor to feel like an intruder here. Inhabitants aren't hostile or cold — it's just that they're gracious without being purposefully ingratiating, going about their lives as if no one with a foreign accent or camera had ever wandered into their midst. Service is inevitably slow (sometimes almost nonexistent), and there's little for visitors to do but enjoy the pristine, quiet beaches, snorkel over the fantastical coral reefs around the bay, and dine on fresh seafood in the town's handful of restaurants. Not yet — not nearly — the superstar resort, Puerto Escondido remains an unsophisticated hideaway; and its largely unpaved streets remain uncrowded, with brand-new cabs often cruising around empty, as though rehearsing for opening night.

Although Puerto Escondido is short on museums, historic houses, parks, and churches, it does have a handful of beautiful beaches, and quite a few lively celebrations. On November 4, its biggest bash, called *November in Puerto Escondido,* features such events as polo burro matches (polo played here on donkeys and using brooms — a sport that originated in Puerto Vallarta), a fishing tournament, exhibitions of parachuting and ballooning, cultural events, a surfing tournament, and a Miss Puerto Escondido beauty contest. Each August, Puerto Escondido's main surfing event, the annual *International Surfing Tournament,* attracts surfers from Mexico, the US, and places as distant as Australia (a bikini contest, in which Miss Surf and Miss Bikini are chosen, is held on the day of the finals).

The state government tourist office (Quinta Pte. y Carretera Postera; phone: 958-20175) has a friendly, helpful staff and offers a very good map, as well as information on hotels and prices.

La Bahía (Main Bay), the half-mile stretch of beach (onto which the town's hotels and restaurants face), is the center of most activities — fishing, swimming, and sunning. Boats also leave here regularly for nearby, popular Puerto Angelito beach — not to be confused with the coast town of Puerto Angel, about 50 miles (80 km) away. The water at the Main Bay is so calm that locals refer to the western end of it as the "Bathtub" or "Kiddie Cove," perhaps also due to its popularity with waders under 3 feet tall.

Also worth exploring is Playa Zikatela (Zikatela Beach), at the east end of Main Bay. This 2-mile stretch of white sand and ruthless waves is considered by some to be one of the best surfing beaches in the world. From sunup to sundown, a dozen or so surfers regularly match their skills against the waves while spectators watch enthralled from the beach. (All but the best swimmers should stick to the sand, however, since the undertow is treacherous here.) Joggers and walkers will also find this beach to their liking; an hour's stroll up and down the shore, followed by breakfast at the *Santa Fe,* is a fine way to start any day. At the far end of the beach is Zikatela Point, a haven for pelicans, sea gulls, sandpipers, and other winged species, as well as for beach- and sunset-loving *Homo sapiens.*

Travel north and you'll be in Puerto Angelito. Protected from the waves by huge rock formations, the Port of the Little Angel offers tepid, tranquil water, two sandy beaches, and coral reefs attractive to snorkelers. There's easy access by boats that leave regularly from the Main Bay at Puerto Escondido; the fare is about $2 each way. Puerto Angelito can also be reached by car: Take the road to the airport, about 1½ miles (2 km) north of Puerto Escondido, then turn left at the sign for Puerto Angelito.

If you're in the mood for an isolated, elongated bit of beach with brilliant white sand, try Playa Bacocho (Bacocho Beach). Here is the place to wallow in solitude and contemplate the open sea. (Don't swim here; the water's too rough.) The *Best Western Posada Real* hotel provides a stunning view of this beach, as well as a path to it.

Shopping in Puerto Escondido is rather limited. There are only a few shops along Avenida Pérez Gazga — *Tanga's* for beachwear, *Casa Artesanal, Tamar,* and *Casa de las Artesanías* are the best — and items are sold at the *Posada Real* and the *Santa Fe.* Most of the *artesanías* (handicrafts) for sale lack real distinction. There are, however, some excellent buys in locally crafted red and white coral jewelry. On Saturday, the big market day, vendors stream in from surrounding communities to sell their wares at the Indian market, the *Mercado Benito Juárez* downtown.

Sports in Puerto Escondido are mostly water-related. Tanks, masks, and flippers may be rented from *Transportación Turística García Rendón* (phone: 958-20114 or 958-20458). Dive trips are available for a flat fee of about $30 per person, not including equipment. Gear is available for rent at the various destinations. Snorkeling equipment can be rented for about $12 per day. Also, fishing boats for rent are about $15 per hour (for a minimum of 3 hours) for one to ten passengers, including rods and bait. There's good snorkeling at Puerto Angelito, but the best diving areas are Puerto Angel and Tangolunda Bay in Huatulco.

Zikatela Beach attracts surfers from all over the world, but since the undertow is so strong, only the most skillful should attempt the waves. No surfboard rentals are available.

Horses can be rented in Manialtepec, Barra de Colotepec, and in the town of Pluma Hidalgo from a man called Alejandro, "El Guapo" (the "handsome one"); inquire at the *Santa Fe* (phone: 958-20170). A typical half-day trip runs the gamut of Mexican scenery, from river crossings and thick jungle undergrowth to stark rock formations and hot springs. *Transportación Turística García Rendón* (phone: 958-20114 or 958-20458) also arranges for horseback riding on the beach, for about $15 an hour.

Puerto Escondido has little nightlife; in fact, if this little fishing village had sidewalks, they would roll up very early. But for those who aren't satisfied counting stars, there's

Bacocho (45 Tehuantepec; no phone), *Pauline* (in the *Fiesta Mexicana,* Blvd. Benito Juárez; phone: 958-20115), *El Sol y la Rumba* (Av. Pérez Gazga; no phone) and *Discotheque Bahía,* on the road to Pochutla. *La Cascada* (Av. Oaxaca) has dancing and a show featuring pop music. For music only, try *Bar Cocos,* adjoining *Cocos* restaurant at the *Posada Real* (Blvd. Benito Juárez; phone: 958-20133 or 958-20237).

Aside from its appeal as a beach and water sports resort, Puerto Escondido is a good base from which to explore this area of Mexico's Pacific Coast. The following sites are within a short drive of the city and can be easily explored in 1 day.

DAY TRIP 1: MANIALTEPEC LAGOON

Some 15 miles (24 km) west of Puerto Escondido on Highway 200 is Manialtepec Lagoon, brimming with tropical birds and surrounded by thick, luxuriant vegetation. Boats depart from the *Alejandria* and *Hamacas* restaurants for a 1½-hour excursion across the lagoon to the ocean, which costs about $10 per person. *Transportación Turística García Rendón* (on Av. Pérez Gazga, in front of *Farmacia Cortés;* phone: 958-20114 or 958-20458) runs an 8-hour tour of the lagoon for about $40 per person, including lunch, boat ride, and ground transportation.

DAY TRIP 2: CHACAHUA NATIONAL PARK

An ideal place to appreciate the region's natural flora and fauna is Chacahua National Park, just 35 miles (56 km) northwest of Puerto Escondido. Declared a protected ecological zone by presidential decree in 1937, Chacahua extends over 14,000 acres of tropical rain forests and mountain ranges, and includes three breathtakingly beautiful natural lakes that are ideal for fishing and swimming. Many endangered species, among them the white-tailed deer and wild boar, thrive in this state park. This is also the best place in Mexico to see the exquisite — and rare — black orchid. The park extends to the seashore and enjoys over 14 miles (22 km) of fine sandy beaches and tranquil inlets and coves for fishing. Those interested in exploring the area should consider the guided tour offered by *Transportación Turística García Rendón* in Puerto Escondido (phone: 958-20114 or 958-20458); the 8-hour trip through the park includes ground transportation and a boat ride. Cost is $30 per person.

BEST EN ROUTE

CHECKING IN: For such a small town, Puerto Escondido has a fair number of hotels. Expect to pay about $80 for a double room in a hotel listed as expensive; $50 to $75, moderate; $25 or less, inexpensive. During the low season, summer through fall, rates are likely to drop about 25%. Most hotels accept MasterCard and Visa; a few also accept American Express and Diners Club.

Best Western Posada Real – More typically resort-style, this hotel isn't as quaint as some of the others in town, and guests must walk down a cliff to get to the beach; but the staff is delightfully friendly and helpful. There are 100 air conditioned rooms, *Cocos* restaurant (see *Eating Out*), 3 bars, 2 pools, tennis, live music nightly, and lovely grounds. Blvd. Benito Juárez (phone: 958-20133 or 958-20185; fax: 958-20192). Expensive.

Villa Sol – One of Puerto Escondido's newer places, it offers 72 rooms, 24 junior suites, and 12 two-bedroom master suites with refrigerators, along with free transportation to the beach, a pool, restaurant, and bar. 2 Loma Bonita, Fracc. Bacocho (phone: 958-20402 or 958-20061; fax: 958-20451). Expensive to moderate.

Aldea Bacocho – About a half mile (1 km) from the beach, this place has 28 units distributed between a 3-story building and some small wood chalets. The rooms are furnished in colonial style and decorated with lots of Mexican crafts. There are delightful gardens, a pool, and a restaurant. 5 Av. Monte Albán (phone: 958-20335). Moderate.

Paraíso Escondido – This former hacienda has 20 rooms, all on the small side, but with whitewashed brick walls and tasteful furnishings, they're still tempting. The rooms upstairs have balconies with an ocean view; downstairs accommodations have porches and face the small pool. There's also a restaurant with bar service, *El Tecolote*. It's just a short walk to the beach. No credit cards accepted. 10 Calle Unión (phone: 958-20444). Moderate.

Santa Fe – The front door opens onto Main Bay, and the back door leads to Zikatela Beach. There are 40 air conditioned rooms, a small pool, and a fine dining area (see *Eating Out*) overlooking sand and surf. It contains authentic Mexican touches throughout: tiles from Puebla and Dolores Hidalgo, traditional ironwork and fabrics from Oaxaca, blown glass from Tlaquepaque, and furniture typical of Guadalajara and Puebla. Calle del Moro (phone: 958-20170; fax: 958-20260). Moderate.

Loren – Simple, clean, and basic, it has 24 rooms with fans. 507 Av. Pérez Gazga (phone: 958-20057). Inexpensive.

El Mirador – Another one of Puerto Escondido's basic but pleasant places, it has 85 rooms, a restaurant, and parking. 113 Carr. Costera Pte. (phone: 958-20129). Inexpensive.

Nayar – Two blocks uphill from the beach, there are 36 rooms, some with balconies, and the restaurant (see *Eating Out*) overlooks the town. No credit cards accepted. 407 Av. Pérez Gazga (phone: 958-20113). Inexpensive.

Las Palmas – It's simple, but clean and comfortable, with 40 rooms, a pleasant palm-filled courtyard, and a restaurant — an excellent place to start the day with a typical Mexican breakfast. Boats to Puerto Angelito can be rented right out front. Av. Pérez Gazga (phone: 958-20230). Inexpensive.

Rincón del Pacífico – A small place on the beach, with 24 rooms decorated cheerily in yellow and white, plus 4 junior suites with air conditioning, TV sets, and refrigerators. It is well maintained, and the atmosphere is very pleasant. It also has a restaurant (see *Eating Out*). 900 Av. Pérez Gazga (phone: 958-20056). Inexpensive.

Villa Marinero – Situated close to the beach, each of the bungalows here is equipped with 2 bedrooms with fans, a small living room, and a kitchenette. Apdo. 16, Cerro el Marinero (phone: 958-20180). Inexpensive.

EATING OUT: Puerto Escondido is not known for elaborate dinners or polished service, but the seafood is almost always good. Expect to pay up to $40 for two in those places listed as moderate, and less than $25 at an inexpensive spot. Prices do not include wine, tips, or tax. Most restaurants listed accept MasterCard and Visa; a few also accept American Express and Diners Club. Unless otherwise noted, all restaurants are open daily. Reservations are unnecessary at all places.

Cocos – This informal restaurant set in an open-sided *palapa* on the beach features seafood and a spectacular view. In the *Best Western Posada Real* hotel, Blvd. Benito Juárez (phone: 958-20133 or 958-20185). Moderate.

Fonda del Gourmet – A huge warehouse decorated with 15-foot oars, anchors, shells, and fishing nets, setting a nautical stage. Specialties include shrimp in orange sauce and a seafood brochette. This spot is open in time to serve typical Mexican breakfasts. Closed Wednesdays. Av. Marina (phone: 958-20995). Moderate.

Hostería del Viandante – At this little *palapa*-topped pizzeria, one of the most popular spots in town, there is sometimes a wait for a table. The menu includes a dozen varieties of pizza, as well as lasagna, spaghetti, and enormous salads. Rock 'n' roll music sets an upbeat mood. Av. Pérez Gazga (phone: 958-20671). Moderate.

Las Mariposas – Indoor or outdoor candlelight dining, an international menu, a guitarist, and a closing time of midnight (unusual in this sleepy town) are the draws here. Just up the hill from Av. Juárez (phone: 958-20197). Moderate.

Santa Fe – Those who are tired of *huevos rancheros* for breakfast might drop by this gracious restaurant for a vegetarian treat of homemade yogurt with granola or tofu hot cakes with fruit. The menu is basically vegetarian, but seafood — lobster, shrimp, squid, abalone, and oysters — also is offered. In the *Santa Fe* hotel, Calle del Moro (phone: 958-20170). Moderate.

Sardina de Plata – Well-prepared seafood and a magnificent view of the sea. There's also a swimming pool. 512 Av. Pérez Gazga (phone: 958-20328). Moderate.

Spaghetti House – Hands down, the best Italian food in town. What better way to enjoy your pasta than with a spectacular view of the ocean and a bottle of Mexican Chianti-style wine. Be sure to try the cheese-garlic bread. El Andedor Azucenas on the main beach (phone: 958-20005). Moderate.

Los Crotos – The service may be the slowest in town, but the prices and the food — *camarónes con frutas* (shrimp and fruit in a cream sauce) and *pescado con camarónes* (fish smothered in shrimp) — are worth the wait. 512 Av. Pérez Gazga next to *Transportación Turística García Rendón* (phone: 958-20025). Inexpensive.

La Perla – Simple and filled with plants. Seafood is the specialty. In town on Calle Tercera Pte. (phone: 958-20461). Inexpensive.

Poncho at the Rock Away Palapa – Hot dogs, hamburgers, steaks, and spaghetti are served under a *palapa* across the street from Playa Zikatela. No credit cards accepted. At Calle del Morro (phone: 958-20668). Inexpensive.

La Posada Loren – Rustic, but serving good, basic Mexican food. Av. Pérez Gazga (phone: 958-20448). Inexpensive.

Rincón del Pacífico – In the hotel of the same name, with the same pleasant atmosphere and service. Seafood, naturally, and steaks. 900 Av. Pérez Gazga (phone: 958-20448 or 958-20193). Inexpensive.

Siete Regiones – This huge place specializes in typical Oaxacan fare from, as the name implies, the seven regions of the state. There's no extra charge for the fine view. No credit cards accepted. On Av. Pérez Gazga near *Los Crotos* (phone: 958-20551). Inexpensive.

La Terraza – Seafood, as could be expected, as well as Mexican and international dishes and a lovely view. No credit cards accepted. In the *Nayar Hotel,* 407 Av. Pérez Gazga (phone: 958-20113). Inexpensive.

En route from Puerto Escondido – Continue east on Highway 200 to Puerto Angel. Just past the village of Barra de Colotepec, the highway curves for some 43 miles (69 km) to the market town of Pochutla, and the junction of Route 175, which leads north to Oaxaca. Pochutla really has little to offer, but about 8 miles (12 km) along the southern spur of Route 175, tiny Puerto Angel is worth a short detour.

PUERTO ANGEL: Though this small fishing community lacks the charm and ambience of its neighbor, it does offer visitors several attractions. Look for Playa del Panteón (Cemetery Beach), with its small graveyard with brightly painted tombstones, and Zipolite Beach, about 5 miles (8 km) out of town — one of the few nudist beaches in

Mexico (beware of the undertow). Perched on a hill above town, the *Angel del Mar* offers a fine view and adequate lodging (see *Best en Route*).

En route from Puerto Angel – Rejoin Route 175 at Pochutla and head north for another 146 miles (234 km) to Oaxaca (about a 4-hour drive). The road — surrounded by the Sierra de Miahuatlán — can be treacherous here; be on the lookout for falling rocks. On the ascent are numerous signs warning "Zona de Niebla" (Fog Zone). If you do encounter fog, drive carefully and keep your headlights' high beams on.

About 85 miles (136 km) from Pochutla, past tiny little settlements and magnificent mountain views, is Miahuatlán de Porfirio Díaz, whose population of over 10,000 makes it seem more like a large city than a small town. Although it has little to offer in the way of tourist attractions, it is renowned throughout Mexico for its exceptional mescal. In fact, some Mexicans contend that the mescal from Miahuatlán is the "cognac of all mescals." For those not accustomed to the taste, however, this potent potable may taste more like fire water than Martell. If you are feeling adventurous, stop at one of the local cantinas (there are plenty from which to choose) and order "un dorado" (a golden aged mescal). It will be served with a plate of salty red powder which is actually ground worms. A real *mexicano* will take a big pinch of worm powder with every slug of mescal, but no one will be offended if you opt instead to take yours straight.

Continue north from Miahuatlán on Route 175 for 42 miles (67 km) to Ocotlán, Oaxaca's cutlery capital. The Mixtec residents of this village have been making high-quality steel swords, knives, and machetes since the mid-1700s and have passed their smelting and tempering secrets from generation to generation. There are currently about 50 family-operated smelters in Ocotlán which still produce their work on a piece-by-piece basis. Examples of these fine knives and swords have found their way into museums in the United States, Europe, South America, and Asia. Among Ocotlán's notable former clientele are Porfirio Díaz, Charles de Gaulle, and Che Guevara. You can get a hand-etched sword or knife here starting at about $150. Prices vary depending on the number of times the piece has been tempered, the quality of the steel, the craftsmanship — and your particular bargaining skill. For an additional fee, you can also get an engraved rosewood, ebony, or bone sheath for your prized weapon.

About 10 miles (16 km) north of Ocotlán, Route 175 mets with Route 131, the unfinished roadway from Puerto Escondido. From here, it's a smooth 9-mile (14-km) drive to the city of Oaxaca.

As you approach within a half mile (1 km) of the Oaxaca city limits, watch for the shop of *Alfarería Doña,* where some of the best black Oaxacan pottery is sold. Continue on Route 175 into Oaxaca.

BEST EN ROUTE

CHECKING IN: The ongoing development of Puerto Escondido and its environs is changing the face of this area from day to day. Accommodations here are varied: Near the beaches are everything from luxurious hostelries offering posh rooms and scenic views of the Pacific to inexpensive, no-frills places with no air conditioning. Visitors to the state of Oaxaca who prize comfort will be pleasantly surprised with very fine accommodations at prices considerably lower than their US counterparts. Expect to pay about $40 to $65 for a double room in these moderate places.

PUERTO ANGEL

Angel del Mar – On a cliff commanding a spectacular view of Puerto Angel, this 42-room hostelry has a restaurant, a bar, a pool, and water sports for guests. The sunsets are simply beautiful (phone: 958-40397). Moderate.

Soraya – Across from the main pier, some of its 40 rooms have air conditioning or ceiling fans; all have terraces with lovely views of the bay. Convenient to the center of town, it boasts a restaurant and parking for guests (no phone). Moderate.

POCHUTLA

Costa del Sol – With 20 rooms (air conditioned or ceiling fan), this hotel is probably the best choice in town. 47 Lázaro Cárdenas (phone: 958-40318). Moderate.

OAXACA: High on the vast plateau of the Oaxaca Valley, Oaxaca is an Indian and colonial city surrounded, like all the valley, by the beautiful Sierra Madre del Sur. Outside the ring of the mountains are the jungles of Chiapas to the southeast, the Pacific Ocean due west, and the Gulf of Mexico to the northeast.

But within the high, protective wall of the Sierra Madre is the plateau world — 5,000 to 6,000 feet above sea level in the city and rising to 9,000 feet in the surrounding mountains. The city, the capital of the state of Oaxaca, has a population of 300,000; the state, more than 3.2 million, almost all of whom are Indians. *Oaxaqueños,* as the natives are called, are mostly descendants of the Zapotec and Mixtec Indian tribes, whose tiny villages dot the valley and mountainside. At the Saturday market, you will hear their languages spoken more often than Spanish.

As part of their legacy, these two great cultures, which first flourished in the area hundreds of years before Christ, have left the magnificent ruins at nearby Monte Albán, Mitla, and Yagul. All within a 25-mile radius of Oaxaca, these rich archaeological zones bear witness to an elaborate and highly religious civilization that was well versed in astronomy and had a system of writing that may be the oldest on this continent. In the late 15th century, however, they were conquered by the Aztec; when the Spanish arrived in the area in 1521, they found it under the grip of Montezuma's empire. Replacing the Aztec fort with their own stronghold, the Spanish named the site Antequera. But in 1529 a city was founded and the name changed to Oaxaca, which derives from an Indian word meaning "forest of gourd trees."

The city was spared the worst ravages of Spanish rule. There was no gold or silver to be mined, so Spain's interest in it was purely aesthetic. Cortés fell in love with the area, claimed much of the land for himself, and planned to build an estate fitting his title of Marqués del Valle de Oaxaca. The estate was never built (Cortés died in Spain in 1547), but his descendants kept the property until the 1910 revolution; the name lingers on in odd places — like the sign outside an old hotel or the label on a bottle of mescal.

As with most Mexican towns today, life begins in the zocalo, or main plaza, and Oaxaca's is especially lovely, with its grand old trees and delicate gazebo-shape bandstand. The ideal places from which to view the lively comings and goings of the plaza are the sidewalk cafés under the Spanish colonnades around the square. Relax here with a drink or a cup of coffee, sit back, and let the world come to you. And it will. In the evening, from around 8 to 10 PM, the tempo picks up, and whenever there is a big band concert, it seems the whole town turns up for the show.

However, for the best view in town, head to Cerro del Fortín, the hill north of Oaxaca that rises 350 feet above the city. To get there take García Vigil, cross the zocalo, and continue on Miguel Cabrera to the *periférico.* Cross the bridge and take the right fork. On its lower slope is the statue of native son Benito Juárez, the Zapotec Indian who became President of Mexico, and an open area from which to look out. Slightly farther up a short dirt road at the top of the hill is a pyramidal monument to the flag of Mexico.

From both spots the view is magnificent; the hill directly south is Monte Albán, which is also a fine place from which to see the city and countryside. There you will also find the magnificent ruins of an ancient Indian community, and the present descendants walking with their goats down the hillside (see *Day Trip 1: Monte Albán,* in this section).

It won't take you too long to realize that Oaxaca is an amazingly unspoiled city; rich with 16th-century architecture, over 2 dozen churches, two excellent museums, a colorful, active zocalo, a large outdoor Indian market, good shopping — and proximity to the archaeological ruins, which make for fascinating side trips. In addition, Oaxaca has managed to conserve its traditions and customs. Known for its colorful fiestas, the town often fills to capacity during a holiday. One of the most popular is *Lunes del Cerro* (Monday of the Hill), held in late July. Among the festivities are the *Guelaguetza,* a celebration dedicated to the god of rain and fertility, featuring music, magnificent costumes, and dances — including the famous *Danza del las Plumas* (Indian Feather Dance); the selection of the "goddess" Centeocihuatl (not for her beauty but for her knowledge of the customs and traditions of her region); and the *Bani Stui Gulal,* meaning "reenactment of the past," which tells the story of the Aztec and Spanish conquests and portrays the battle between the Zapotec and the Mixtec in which Donaji, the last Zapotec princess, was taken hostage and decapitated. The ceremonies are held on the Cerro del Fortín, on Route 190 about a mile (1.6 km) east of the Avenida Madero turnoff, and in the city; reservations are necessary for the main performance (book well in advance — no later than May; reservations can be arranged through US travel agents).

There is always something to see, even if it is only from an outside café along the zocalo. When you get tired of sitting, there are wonderful places to move on to, and when you get tired of moving, there is always an equally wonderful place to sit. It is in many ways the quintessential Mexican city.

For information about getting around Oaxaca and its environs, there is a tourist office (Cinco de Mayo and Morelos; phone: 951-64828), and there are information booths at the airport, in front of the *Regional Museum of Oaxaca* (the one here is closed Mondays), and at Monte Albán.

Certainly one of the gayest and liveliest squares in all of Mexico, the Plaza de Armas (zocalo) offers a gazebo bandstand, numerous tree-shaded benches, outdoor cafés in all directions, hawkers, public scribes, Indians, *oaxaqueños,* tourists, students, old and young, rich and poor. Musical concerts are performed evenings at 7 PM and on Sundays at noon, and wandering street musicians can often be heard at random hours. It is a marketplace, social gathering, and cultural event that should not, and really cannot, be missed.

A very old and weathered church, the Basílica de la Soledad (Basilica of Solitude) is famous not for its structure (Calle Independencia, on the Plaza de la Danza — Plaza of the Dance) but for the statue of La Virgen de la Soledad (Virgin of Solitude), who is the patron saint of Oaxaca and is considered to have great healing powers. The famous legend attached to her arrival in the city is prominently represented on glass panels in the religious museum at the rear of the church. During the 17th century a pack train arrived in town with one more mule than the muleteer could account for. When the train got to the modern site of this church, the extra mule suddenly fell down and died. It was found to be carrying the incredible stone statue of the Virgin, and the people immediately decided to build a church to commemorate this miraculous event. The church was built in 1682. The statue is robed in a jewel-encrusted black velvet cloak, with a large pearl hanging on its forehead. It also has several changes of clothes for various religious occasions.

The Cathedral of Oaxaca, built in 1535, was a gift from the King of Spain to the city of Oaxaca. Situated on the north side of the zocalo, its original lovely baroque façade remains intact in spite of various alterations. The clock, although several hundred years old and made with all wooden works, still keeps good time.

Founded by the Dominican Fathers in 1570, the Church of Santo Domingo is an exquisite example of baroque art and a favorite with the natives of Oaxaca. While the outside is certainly worth a close look, it is the interior that stands out as a truly exceptional work of art: covered in gold scroll and polychrome reliefs set against a white background, with paved tile floors, massive gold chandeliers, and incorporating 11 chapels, including the lovely Chapel of the Virgin of Rosario (off to the right as you enter). The church, located at Calles Gurrión and M. Alcalá, is one of a kind and should not be missed.

Step into the converted convent attached to the Church of Santo Domingo (Calle M. Alcalá) and you'll discover the *Regional Museum of Oaxaca,* with its series of rooms quietly arranged around an open courtyard. There are themes for each space, including regional arts and crafts, costumes, and archaeological artifacts. On the second floor, behind a heavily vaulted door, are the incredible, priceless jewels found at the excavation sites at Monte Albán in 1932. These objects, which date back to AD 500 and display considerable technical sophistication, include ornate filigree work, alabaster vessels, and jade and bone carvings of an earlier Indian culture, either Zapotec or Mixtec. Closed Mondays. Admission charge (phone: 951-62991).

The spectacular *Rufino Tamayo Museum of Pre-Hispanic Art* (usually called the *Rufino Tamayo*) traces the development of art in Mexico from 1250 BC to AD 1500. The 2,000 art objects that make up this collection were donated to the city by native *oaxaqueño* muralist and painter Rufino Tamayo and his wife, Olga. They are exhibited in a beautifully restored colonial mansion (at 503 Morelos) redesigned by Tamayo. Each gallery is arranged to represent a specific culture: Olmec, Totonac, Zapotec, Mixtec, Maya, Nayarit, and Teotihuacan. Closed Tuesdays. Admission charge; Sundays no charge (phone: 951-64750).

Driving along Porfirio Díaz (named after another native son who became President of Mexico), past the *Misión de los Angeles* hotel, stop at the impressive Fuente de las Siete Regiones (Fountain of the Seven Regions). A tribute to the natives of the region, it includes six statues of Indian women in regional garb and is topped by a figure of a male dancer from Teotitlán del Valle, wearing a plumed headdress.

Standing 4 miles (6 km) east of Oaxaca in Santa María el Tule is the Tule Tree, a huge ahuehuete cypress tree estimated to be over 2,000 years old. Some 140 feet high, with roots buried more than 60 feet in the earth, the tree (on Tehuantepec Highway en route to Mitla) is the traditional sentry for the town of Santa María, and is larger than the church in front of which it stands.

As for shopping, there are a number of items that are unique to Oaxaca, and a number of places where they can be purchased. The famous dark green pottery of the nearby village of Atzompa is available at excellent prices in Oaxaca, as are the Miró- and Picasso-inspired wall hangings from Teotitlán, and the black unglazed pottery of Coyotepec. Cotton and woolen shawls, blouses, bags, blankets, heavy serapes, and hammocks are all well made in this area, as are baskets and fine steel hunting knives and machetes with ornate hand-carved handles and engraved blades. Many pieces of jewelry on sale in Oaxaca are reproductions of pieces found at Monte Albán — including necklaces, earrings, and pendants of gold, jade, and seed pearls.

For a true shopping experience, make Saturday your market day. This is when merchants from all the neighboring communities come in, wearing their native costumes and speaking their various dialects of Zapotec, to sell their wares at the arts and crafts *tianguis* outside the *Central de Abastos.* All the different types of mole (sauce) are available in the *Veinte de Noviembre* market (at Veinte de Noviembre and Aldama). Behind the market is *Mayordomo,* a chocolate mill where Oaxacan chocolate can be specially blended to taste with almonds, sugar, and cinnamon. Considered one of the most colorful and interesting of all Mexican markets, it is worth a visit whether or not you are interested in buying.

Alfarería Jiménez – Carries mostly pottery, brightly colored and handmade, including pitchers, plates, serving dishes, and vases. It's possible to watch the artisans at work here. 402 Zaragoza (phone: 951-62102).

Aripo – Ten rooms are filled with rugs, pottery, weavings, and ornaments, primarily from Oaxaca. You can watch craftspeople at work on wooden looms. 809 García Vigil (phone: 951-69211).

Artesanías Cocijo – Pottery, wood, and tinware. 117 Calle Leona Vicario (phone: 951-68081).

Casa Brena – This textile store and weavers' workshop has pottery as well. Walk to the rear — listening for the slapping of the looms — to see people spinning the yarn and dyeing the cloth. 700 Calle Pino Suárez (phone: 951-50222).

El Diamante – A selection of tinware, pottery, jewelry, and other local crafts. Behind the cathedral, at 106H Calle García Vigil (phone: 951-63983).

FONART – Clothing, metal ornaments, and ceramics are the wares here. The selection and prices are quite good. In a red and white building at 116 M. Bravo (phone: 951-65764).

Galería de Arte de Oaxaca – A wonderful collection of works by contemporary Mexican artists, some well-known and some yet to be discovered. 102 Calle Trujano, downtown (phone: 951-69719).

Mercado de Artesanía – A clean market with well-displayed crafts, where weavers can be seen at work, it's open daily. Some items are 50% less than at other places, but bargaining is a must. Corner of Calles J. P. García and Zaragoza (no phone).

El Oro de Montealbán – Reproductions of pre-Hispanic jewelry made on the premises. Plazuela Adolfo C. Gurrión (phone: 951-64528 or 951-64946).

El Palacio de las Gemas – Regional gold jewelry with pearl and coral inlays, as well as a large collection of semi-precious stones. Corner of Calles Morelos and M. Alcalá (phone: 951-69596).

Productos Típicos de Oaxaca – Though unimpressive from the outside, this group of shops set around a sculpture garden is packed with quality pottery, textiles, handmade toys, and tin figures. They will ship items too big to carry home. 602 Av. Belisario Domínguez (phone: 951-52263).

Taller de Artes Plásticos Rufino Tamayo – The exhibition and sale of paintings, sculptures, and graphics produced by local artists in a workshop bearing the name of one of Oaxaca's most famous native sons. 306 Murguía (no phone).

Tianguis – A wide selection of native textiles, as well as other native handicrafts. Portal de Clavería, on the zocalo (phone: 951-69266).

Victor – In a 17th-century monastery, it carries crafts as well as woven clothing. 111 Porfirio Díaz (phone: 951-61174).

Yalalag de Oaxaca – A tasteful selection of Indian and contemporary crafts, native clothing, and Josefa designs. 104 M. Alcalá (phone: 951-62108).

Sports fans should not leave Oaxaca without attending a Mexican-style rodeo. *Charreadas* are held in the *Lienzo Charro.* There is no schedule, but events are always well posted around town.

Swimming pools in Oaxaca are available at most of the large hotels and at the few resorts just outside town.

And tennis facilities can be found at the *Misión de los Angeles* (phone: 951-51500) and the *Victoria* (phone: 951-52633). *Club de Tenis Brenamiel* (at Km 539.5 of the International Hwy.; phone: 951-41815) has 10 lighted, hard-surface courts.

Although the city closes up early, it hardly means the people retire. Most of the hotels have cocktail lounges. In particular, the *Victoria,* on the edge of town (at Km 545, Rte. 190), has a lovely bar with a great view of the city and live music from 7:30 PM to midnight every night except Monday. Discos include *Yonke Video Disco* (at the *Misión Park Inn Oaxaca*) and *Chaplin's Disco* (508 Av. Independencia). *El Corcel Negro* (at the *Fortín Plaza*), *Kaftan*'s and *Tanilaoo* (at the *Misión de los Angeles*) have live music for dancing. And as expected, there is the nightlife on the zocalo, where music is heard from 7:30 to 8:30 PM nightly. People promenade, and lively socializing continues until 11 PM. *El Sol y La Luna* (Sun and Moon) restaurant and coffeehouse (105 Calle Murguía) is a lively gathering place with music every night. At *Los Guajiros* (303 Calle Alcalá) there's dining and dancing to salsa and Latin American jazz nightly from 9 PM to 1 AM. The *Monte Albán,* on the plaza, has a very fine nightly show of regional dances; it's free to guests. On Thursdays at 8 PM the *Misión de los Angeles* (102 Calzada Porfirio Díaz) features folkloric dancing. A *Guelaguetza,* along with a lavish Oaxacan buffet, is presented Fridays at 7 PM in the *Stouffer Presidente* (300 Av. Cinco de Mayo; phone: 951-60611).

Oaxaca is an excellent base for exploring the nearby ruins at Monte Albán, Cuilapán, Tlacochahuaya, Yagul, and Mitla. Travelers can take guided tours, or visit on their own at their leisure. Each of these tours can comfortably be covered in 1 day.

DAY TRIP 1: MONTE ALBÁN, CUILAPÁN

Overlooking the Oaxaca valley from a flattened mountaintop 5½ miles (9 km) south-west of Oaxaca (follow Miguel Cabrera to the *periférico;* cross the Atoyec River bridge and take the right fork) is Monte Albán, once a Zapotec holy city of more than 40,000 people covering 25 square miles, and now one of the most magnificent archaeological ruins in all Mexico. The Zapotec leveled the area in about 600 BC. The buildings are carefully arranged on a perfect north–south axis, with the exception of one structure, thought to have been an observatory, which is more closely aligned with the stars than the poles. The oldest of the four temples is the Temple of the Dancers, so named because of the elaborate carved stone figures that once covered the building. They are naked and distorted in strange positions, and have since come to be thought of not as dancers but as patients in what might have been a hospital or school of medicine. Then sometime around 1,000 years ago, the Zapotec were conquered by the Mixtec, an enemy tribe. These new inhabitants never lived in Monte Albán, but used it as a city of the dead, a massive cemetery of lavish tombs. More than 160 have been discovered, and in 1932 Tomb 7 yielded a treasure unequaled in this hemisphere. Inside there were more than 500 priceless Mixtec objects, including gold breastplates; jewelry made of jade, pearls, ivory, and gold; and fans, masks, and belt buckles of precious stones and metals. All are now on view at the *Regional Museum of Oaxaca.* The ruins are open daily until 5 PM (until 4 PM during the rainy season); most of the drive is straight up, tortuously slow, and splendidly scenic. Return over the Atoyec River bridge and take the left fork to Cuilapán.

Another very different type of ruin is located at Cuilapán, a Mixtec village, about 3½ miles (5 km) southwest of Monte Albán. Here, in 1555, a group of Dominican friars began work on a massive monastery, but the project was never completed. Today, it has deteriorated into an odd combination of functioning parts and crumbling ruins. The walls of the basilica (which is in use) hold the tombs of what was perhaps the last of the Zapotec and Mixtec royalty, the Mixtec Prince of Tilantongo and his wife Cosijopi, daughter of the King of Tehuantepec.

In its heyday, Cuilapán was the hub of the cochineal (red dye) industry, so important in the development of Mexico's traditional textiles. Long before the Spanish invasion, the Zapotec Indians used this dye, which is derived from the fried female cochineal mite. After they laid their eggs on cactus pads, the mites were gathered and dried for marketing. And it is from them that the rich and enduring scarlet dyes are obtained. During the colonial period, the Spanish crown had a monopoly on cochineal, and vast Oaxacan haciendas were built around the industry. The Spanish took their monopoly so seriously that anyone caught removing the cactus from Spanish territory was sentenced to death. Only the Spanish were allowed to export it, which they did, and scarlet soon became the rage in Europe. Even the resplendent red coats of the British army were dyed with cochineal.

In January 1979, Pope John Paul II made this stop one of the most emotional of his 8-day visit to Mexico. Hundreds of thousands of barefoot peasants trekked into the town to get a glimpse of the pontiff, who put on a native hat and picked up a little girl in a moving scene captured by a news photographer and sent around the world. Local officials welcomed the pope with a *Guelaguetza,* a traditional ceremony in which natives don 3-foot-high fan-shaped hats decorated with streaming ribbons and dance to the haunting beat of a single drum.

Three miles (5 km) farther down the same road is Zaachila, a rustic, pastoral village — and the last capital of the Zapotec nation. There is an archaeological site at the edge of town that is only partially excavated. What has been unearthed so far in the way of clay figurines, gold plate, carved reliefs, and royal remains is quite fascinating, and much more is yet to be revealed. Reverse the route for your return to Oaxaca.

DAY TRIP 2: TLACOCHAHUAYA, YAGUL, MITLA

About 12 miles (19 km) southeast of Oaxaca on Route 190 is a turnoff to the right for the Zapotec town of Tlacochahuaya. Follow the dirt road 5 miles (8 km) to the zocalo. Here you will find El Convento de San Gerónimo Tlacochahuaya, founded by Dominican monks in 1558. Its dour exterior with its two stone pillars was constructed from the ruins of indigenous temples; careful examination reveals many pre-Columbian glyphs. Once inside, the huge, austere building takes on a less somber mood with white archways painted with colorful Indian flower and animal motifs — reflections of the Zapotec influence even today. The highlight of the convent is a 17th-century baroque gold-leaf foot organ adorned with many images of angels. The instrument's pipes are uniquely crafted so that the mouth of each angel appears as the vented air hole. Unfortunately, the organ no longer works and cannot be repaired since replacement parts are no longer available. But just seeing this ponderous instrument, you can imagine how it must have sounded echoing its Gregorian choruses through the Oaxaca Valley hundreds of years ago.

Return to Route 190 and continue southeast 7 miles (11 km) to Yagul, a group of pre-Columbian ruins. Not as elaborate as Monte Albán but set in a lovely spot on top of a hill, Yagul is certainly beautiful and interesting enough to make it worth the trip. This city is predominantly a fortress that's set slightly above a group of palaces and temples; it also includes a ball court and more than 30 uncovered underground tombs. Continue on Route 190 to Mitla.

Plan to spend most of the day at Mitla, 5 miles (8 km) southeast of Yagul (24 miles/38 km from Oaxaca). These fascinating ruins are a complex of ceremonial structures started by the Zapotec but taken over and heavily influenced by the Mixtec. The name, derived from an Aztec word, *mictlán,* means "place of the dead." The architecture here is totally different from that of any of the other ruins in the area. The walls of stone and mud are inlaid with small stones cut into geometric patterns, forming a mosaic that is Grecian in appearance. Unlike other ancient buildings in North America, there are no human figures or mythological events represented — only designs. Another unique feature of Mitla is the fact that it was still in use after the Spanish conquest of Mexico. A trip here can be nicely combined with a stop at the famous Tule Tree mentioned above, just 4 miles (6 km) east of Oaxaca, and the *Frissell Museum of Zapotec Art,* just off the plaza in Mitla. This museum, which is also a regional research center of the University of the Americas, is in an 18th-century hacienda and houses a fine collection of Zapotec artifacts; all are labeled in English and clearly trace the development of the Zapotec-Mixtec empires. It also houses the rustic *La Sorpresa Inn,* which has a restaurant that serves hearty country cooking, traditional Oaxacan barbe-cues, and mescal cocktails (see *Eating Out*). (The restaurant is open daily from 8 AM to 6 PM; the museum is open daily from 9 AM to 6 PM.) Adjoining the ruins is a small handicrafts market. About a half mile (1 km) from the museum, the ruins can be reached by following the main, paved street, which is lined with small clothing shops. Return to Oaxaca on Route 190.

BEST EN ROUTE

CHECKING IN: In Oaxaca, expect to pay $80 to $125 for a double room in the expensive category; about $50 to $75 in a moderate hotel; and $20 to $40 for one in the inexpensive range. Most hotels accept MasterCard and Visa; a few also accept American Express and Diners Club.

Stouffer Presidente – Beautifully restored, this unexpected jewel was formerly a convent, built in 1576. A serene atmosphere still prevails in the shelter of its sun-dappled patios and small enclosed gardens. There is, however, now a reason-able complement of modern conveniences to the 91 rooms, including TV sets, a heated pool, dining room, and cocktail lounge. This place is worth a visit even if you don't spend the night here. Jazz is played in the bar every night but Tuesdays from 9 to midnight. On Friday nights there is a buffet of traditional Oaxacan dishes; the evening also includes performance of regional dances. 300 Cinco de Mayo (phone: 951-60611; 800-HOTELS-1 in the US; fax: 951-60732). Expensive.

Victoria – Surrounded by terraced grounds and well-kept gardens, this sprawling, salmon-colored luxury complex is perched on a hill overlooking the city. Ameni-ties include a very good dining room (see *Eating Out*), tennis court, heated pool, disco, and picture-perfect bougainvillea vines. Rooms, bungalows, and suites are available; ask for one with a view. At Km 545 of Rte. 190 (phone: 951-52633; 800-223-9868 in the US; fax: 951-52411). Expensive.

Fortín Plaza – Located on the Cerro del Fortín, this modern, 6-story property hostelry affords a magnificent panoramic view of the city. Each of the 100 pleasant rooms has a TV set and a telephone, and there's a pool, coffee shop, restaurant, and live music and dancing at *El Corcel Negro.* Av. Venus and Calz. Héroes de Chapultepec (phone: 951-57777; 800-826-6842 in the US; fax: 951-51328). Moder-ate.

Hacienda la Noria – An 85-room hostelry, 13 blocks south of the zocalo, it has 2 swimming pools, a restaurant, and ample grounds. *Periférico* at 100 Calle La Costa (phone: 951-67555; fax: 951-65347). Moderate.

Misión de los Angeles – Nestled into a mountainside just above the city, this 155-unit complex boasts an exceptional view of Oaxaca as well as a giant aviary filled with native tropical birds. There is also a first-rate restaurant (see *Eating Out*) and a very large pool. It's a fine walk from here along Avenida Juárez to the Fountain of the Seven Regions. 102 Calz. Porfirio Díaz (phone: 951-51500 or 800-221-6509 in the US; fax: 951-51680). Moderate.

Misión Park Inn Oaxaca – A modern, 154-room hostelry to the north of town renowned for its tranquil gardens, it has big, spacious rooms, a swimming pool, restaurant, bar, and disco. 15 Jalisco, in San Felipe del Agua (phone: 951-50100 or 800-437-PARK in the US; fax: 951-50900). Moderate.

Calesa Real – Comfortable and pleasant, it has 77 units (8 with balconies), a small pool, dining room, and cocktail bar. 306 Calle García Vigil (phone: 951-65544; 800-826-6848 in the US; fax: 951-67232). Inexpensive.

California – Near the *Misión de Los Angeles,* this modern place has 32 rooms with balconies, good food, and friendly service. 822 Calz. Héroes de Chapultepec (phone: 951-53628). Inexpensive.

Gala – A few steps from the zocalo, this hotel has 36 rooms that are painted in soft pastel colors and are tastefully furnished, with large tiled bathrooms. 103 Calle Bustamente (phone: 951-42251; fax: 951-63660). Inexpensive.

Las Golondrinas – This place has 24 spacious, but simply furnished, rooms. Breakfast is served from 8 to 10 AM outside, under the trees. Corner of Palacios and Calle Tinoco (phone: 951-68726). Inexpensive.

Margarita – About a mile (1.6 km) from downtown, this motel offers 60 units, a swimming pool, a garden, tennis, a dining room, and a cocktail lounge. 1254 Madero (phone: 951-64100; fax: 951-61133). Inexpensive.

Marqués del Valle – Right on the plaza and in the middle of things, with 95 rooms. The ground-floor restaurant serves a good breakfast, from bananas and cream to hotcakes. 1 Portal de Clavería (phone: 951-63295; fax: 951-69961). Inexpensive.

Mesón del Rey – A nice little surprise of a hotel, only a block and a half from the zocalo, it offers 22 rooms, a cozy lobby, and cordial staff. No credit cards accepted. 212 Calle Trujano (phone: 951-60033). Inexpensive.

Parador Plaza – This attractive new hotel in downtown Oaxaca has 59 rooms surrounding a delightful patio. The decor is modern Mexican — white walls with colonial accents, regional crafts, and tiled floors, and there's a restaurant. 103 Calle Murguía (phone: 951-64900; fax: 951-42037). Inexpensive.

Principal – Modest with only 17 rooms, it charms with geranium-filled clay pots on the balconies and skylights in the bathrooms on the top floor. The lobby has an excellent map of the town. No credit cards accepted. 208 Cinco de Mayo (phone: 951-62535). Inexpensive.

Señorial – With pool, roof garden, and cocktail bar open until 10 PM, this is one of the most conveniently located hostelries in Oaxaca. The one drawback is the thin walls separating its 127 rooms. 6 Portal de las Flores (phone: 951-63933; fax: 951-63668). Inexpensive.

Trebol – The entrance to this property, set amid some rather shabby shops, belies the sparkling cleanliness within. The 14 rooms are small but comfortable, built around a sunlit patio, and there is a restaurant and laundry service. No credit cards accepted. 201 Calle Flores Magón (phone: 951-61256; fax: 951-40342). Inexpensive.

EATING OUT: There are three specialties for which Oaxaca is known: mole sauce, tamales, and mescal. Mole is a spicy, multi-ingredient sauce made with chocolate, and served with chicken and pork, that can be found throughout Mexico, but in Oaxaca it is made darker, thicker, and usually tastier because Oaxacan chocolate is very special. Local tamales are even more special. Moister than elsewhere in Mexico, flat and rectangular, they are wrapped in a banana leaf rather than the usual corn husk. The most common fillings are chicken and mole sauce, and it definitely should be sampled. Mescal, the local alcohol, is made from the maguey cactus (as is tequila), but with a different distilling process and altered taste. The bottle often contains a dead worm; aficionados eat bits of it while drinking the mescal, not unlike the way tequila drinkers lick salt. When eating in restaurants, expect slow service and a bill of around $40 for dinner for two in places we call expensive; about $25 in the moderate range; and under $15 in an inexpensive place. Prices do not include drinks, wine, or tips. Most restaurants accept MasterCard and Visa; a few also accept American Express and Diners Club. Unless otherwise noted, all restaurants are open daily.

El Asador Vasco – Try the Oaxacan version of mole sauce here — steamy, black, and marvelous on chicken, or the *cazuelas* — small casseroles of baked cheese, mushrooms, and shrimp in garlic. It's easy to order too much. Dining is elegant and the bar comfortable, but the waitresses can be dour. There's a show every night at 9 PM. Reservations advised. One flight up at Portal de Flores on the zocalo (phone: 951-69719). Expensive.

Catedral – A local favorite, it is nicknamed the "House of Filets," with no less than 11 tenderloin cuts from which to choose, as well as regional dishes, hamburgers, sandwiches, and a variety of soups. Guadalajara artist Miguel Angel España's paintings fill one of the pleasant dining rooms. Live entertainment at dinner. Reservations unnecessary. A block from the zocalo, at 105 García Vigil (phone: 951-63285). Expensive.

Mi Casita – Many consider this the best place to enjoy true Oaxacan cooking. The actual dishes are displayed here, so you can see what your food looks like before you order it. It is especially famous for *chapulines* (grasshoppers), but there are also more conventional Oaxacan dishes such as enchiladas with chicken and spicy mole sauce. Try to get a table by the window (*Mi Casita* is 1 flight up). Closed Thursdays. Reservations advised. On the south side of the zocalo at 616 Calle Hidalgo (phone: 951-69256). Expensive.

El Refectorio – The refectory of the original convent and the adjoining patio have been combined into a charming setting for continental and Oaxacan dishes. Fridays in the chapel there's a *Guelaguetza,* at which a Oaxacan buffet is served. Reservations advised. At *Stouffer Presidente* (phone: 951-60611). Expensive.

El Sol y La Luna – This lively spot is a combined restaurant, coffeehouse, and gallery, with only 10 tables inside and another 5 on the terrace. It's worth the wait for an inside table to hear the music that begins at 9 PM every night. Pizza, salads, Italian dishes, and good chocolate-covered crêpes are on the menu. Open from 7 PM to 1 AM. Closed Sundays. No reservations. 105 Calle Murguía (phone: 951-62933). Expensive.

El Tule – A hotel dining room that serves excellent continental and Mexican food (chicken in mole sauce is a specialty) and offers a fascinating view of the city below (mist-shrouded in the morning; streetlight-sprinkled at night). Reservations advised. At the *Victoria Hotel,* Km 545, Rte. 190 (phone: 951-52633). Expensive.

Del Vitral – It's a lovely mansion complete with European chandeliers and stained glass windows. Specialties include the traditional Oaxacan moles and such exotic regional specialties as *nido de grillo,* a basket of tortillas, fried grasshoppers, and guacamole. There's live music in the afternoons and evenings. Reservations advised. 201 Guerrero (phone: 951-63124). Expensive.

Ajos & Cebollas – Although the name of this popular restaurant and bar translates as "garlic and onions," these aren't the edible items for which it's known; chicken curry and veal parmesan are more likely choices. There are three separate dining areas whose ceilings grow increasingly low as you move from one to the next — part of the strange and appealing decor. The intimate bar boasts a peppery house cocktail made with mescal, and live music is provided by a trio. Reservations advised. No credit cards accepted. 605 Av. Juárez, across from Paseo Juárez (phone: 951-63793). Moderate.

Alameda – The good food (mole and Oaxacan-style stuffed peppers), service, and decor (especially the indoor patio), as well as the reasonable prices, make this a very agreeable place to dine. Reservations advised. Two blocks from the zocalo at 202 J. P. García (phone: 951-63446). Moderate.

Antequera – Set in the *Misión de los Angeles* hotel, it features a pleasant dining room. Dinner is finished by 10 PM. Reservations advised. 102 Calz. Porfirio Díaz (phone: 951-51500). Moderate.

Los Guajiros – An offshoot of *El Sol y La Luna* (see above), it serves the same type of food, but the real specialty here is the music: salsa and Latin American jazz. There's dining — salads and Italian dishes — and dancing from 9 PM to 1 AM. Closed Sundays. Reservations advised. 303 Calle Alcalá (phone: 951-65038). Moderate.

La Morsa – A large, open-air *palapa* (thatch-roofed tent) serving excellent seafood and steaks. Closed Sundays. Reservations advised. 240 Calz. Porfirio Díaz (phone: 951-52213). Moderate.

Los Pacos – This restaurant is a local favorite for well-prepared regional dishes, including the ubiquitous *mole negro* and *chiles rellenos de quesillo* (poblano peppers filled with a Oaxacan cheese resembling string cheese). Its bar is open from 6 PM to 1 AM and features live music Wednesdays through Saturdays. Closed Sundays. Reservations unnecessary. 108 Av. Belisario Domínguez (phone: 951-53573). Moderate.

El Biche Pobre – The hands-down favorite for local dishes (there are about seven types of mole) and Oaxaca's famous tamales. Closed Wednesdays. Reservations unnecessary. Mártires de Tacubaya and Abasolo (no phone). Inexpensive.

Casa Elpidia – Simple but clean, this place is where the *oaxaqueños* flock for good regional food, including *mole negro* and the daily fixed-price specials. No reservations. No credit cards accepted. 413 Calle Miguel Cabrera (phone: 951-64292). Inexpensive.

La Flor de Oaxaca – One block from the zocalo, it's where all the *oaxaqueños* come for breakfast, lunch, or dinner — or simply for a cup of hot chocolate. It's an especially good place to sample a true Oaxacan breakfast. Reservations unnecessary. No credit cards accepted. 311 Armenta (phone: 951-65522). Inexpensive.

La Sorpresa – The specialty in this 18th-century mansion is typical Oaxacan barbecue — marinated, tender, and pungent lamb and chicken. No reservations. In Mitla, near the plaza (no phone). Inexpensive.

■**Note:** Many cafés line the zocalo; among the best are *El Jardín* and *Del Portal.*

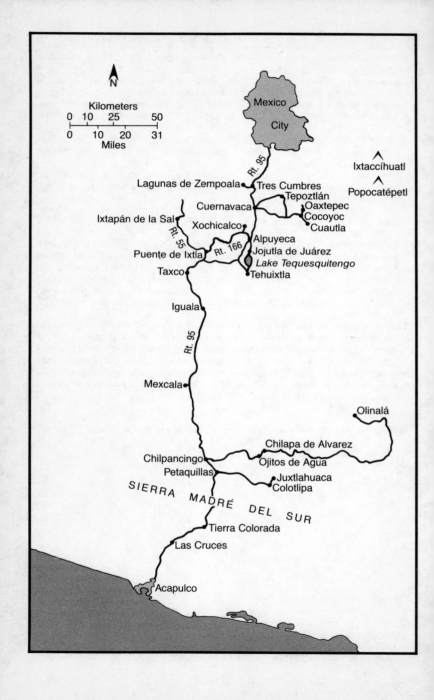

Acapulco to Mexico City

One of the most traveled routes in Mexico is Route 95, the north–south road between Acapulco, the Pacific Ocean resort, and Mexico City, the capital. A trip that embraces three states, it passes through the Sierra Madre mountain range and into the temperate valley of Cuernavaca, known as the "city of eternal springtime." The trip can also be extended to include Taxco, the colonial showpiece of the state of Guerrero and the nation's silver capital for over 4 centuries. There are also suggested stopovers at mountain lakes, ancient caves, beautiful resort areas, and a spa along the way. Though the 255-mile (408-km) trip can be made in 5 to 6 hours (traveling mostly on a two-lane road), if time allows, we suggest more scenic alternatives, such as a stop at the ancient spa at Ixtapán de la Sal. The first leg of the route — from Acapulco to Taxco — is a scenic 3½-hour drive along a superbly maintained, four-lane toll road that zips across the southern Sierra Madre range and offers sweeping views of the fertile mountain valleys. This brand-new highway, a hallmark in Mexican engineering, has reduced the travel time between Acapulco and Cuernavaca by nearly half. The trip from Taxco to Cuernavaca should take no more than 90 minutes. The last leg of the journey is actually the quickest, just 1 hour to the capital. For the portion of the drive from Taxco to Cuernavaca and on to Mexico City, there is a choice of continuing north on Route 95, the old free mountain road, or joining Route 95-D, the newer and faster four-lane divided toll road just south of Taxco in Iguala. We suggest the more scenic Route 95. Both routes begin to parallel each other north of Taxco at the small town of Amacuzac.

Much of this country is Aztec in culture, with many Indians still speaking their original language, Nahuatl, rather than Spanish. While several of the resorts and hotels listed in *Best en Route* cater mostly to Mexican tourists, they are more than happy to extend their hospitality to Americans and other foreign visitors. If time is short and you want a mix of ocean, mountains, cities, villages, and recreational areas, this offers a fine driving route.

En route from Acapulco – Leave Acapulco on Route 95, the four-lane highway that begins at the Glorieta Diana traffic circle on Costera Miguel Alemán. This intersection is situated between the *Continental Plaza Acapulco* and *Condesa del Mar* hotels. The highway runs through Acapulco's crowded residential area, past busy outdoor market stalls, and just beyond the city limits turns into two lanes of winding mountain roadways; in about 15 miles (25 km) is the tiny settlement of Las Cruces and five small villages, each named for its distance (in kilometers) from Acapulco. Practice a little Spanish as you drive by: *Treinta* (30), *Cuarenta* (40), *Cuarenta y Dos* (42), *Cuarenta y Cinco* (45), *Cuarenta y Ocho* (48). There are rows of stands along the highway in these towns which sell fresh coconuts. For about $2, a vendor will slice the top of one open with an oversize machete, stick in a plastic straw, and let you savor the milk. The coconuts are usually too young to have much meat, but the cool nectar is a pleasant refresher.

The road curves sharply as it climbs 1,100 feet toward the town of Tierra Colorada, of interest only for its colorful groves of red papaya. Ten miles (16 km) ahead on Route 95, between the small towns of El Ocotito and El Rincón, is the small *Los Ches* restaurant, a pleasant spot to stop and refresh while taking in the view. Just ahead is the summit of the Sierra Madre del Sur, rising to 4,400 feet; the rocks here actually appear green, because of their high copper content. Now the road begins to wind down to the village of Petaquillas, which leads to the caves of Juxtlahuaca. Those who wish to tour the caves should inquire in Petaquillas about the condition of this road. (Primarily a jeep road, it's rough, but passable in the dry season.) We suggest hiring a guide; inquire at the tourist office in Chilpancingo, 4 miles (6 km) ahead on Route 95, the capital of the state of Guerrero.

GRUTAS DE JUXTLAHUACA (Caves of Juxtlahuaca — pronounced Whoosh-tlah-*wah*-kah): In Petaquillas, take the rough side road east for 30 miles (48 km) to the village of Colotlipa. From here, it's a comfortable hike to the magnificent caverns of Juxtlahuaca. Among the largest in Mexico, these caverns contain Olmec cave paintings of humans and snakes estimated to be from the first millennium before Christ, and, therefore, some of the oldest yet discovered in North America. Remarkably, the bright yellow, red, and black cave paintings have not faded over the centuries. There are also several caves that are home to thousands of vampire bats and a rare species of giant spider. Footpaths connect the principal chambers, but the going is treacherous, with little illumination. An underground lake is in one cave. Old clothes, practical footwear, and anything waterproof will be appropriate because of the spray from subterranean waterfalls. These caves are very beautiful and exciting, but lest we have not yet made the point clear, let it be stressed again: Don't try it on your own. Admission charge.

Return to Route 95 and head north 4 miles (6 km) to Chilpancingo, and the small village of Chilapa de Alvarez.

CHILAPA DE ALVAREZ: A worthwhile detour is to the small village of Chilapa de Alvarez. From Chilpancingo follow the paved road east for about 19 miles (30 km), then take a left a few miles beyond Ojitos de Agua onto a gravel road for 2 or 3 miles (3 to 5 km) to Chilapa. This tiny but very interesting town is noted for the beautiful handloomed rebozos, or shawls, that are made here. Chilapa is also renowned for its Sunday market, one of the largest in the nation. You'll find bargains in all sorts of native handicrafts ranging from ceramics to woodcarvings. Be sure to check out the 16th-century Augustine convent in the center of town. Shaped in the form of a cross, this ornate baroque-style structure's façade is adorned with figures of Juan Diego, the first Mexican ever canonized, and images of the Virgin of Guadalupe. In late June, the town takes on a particularly festive mood, as locals dress up in Renaissance costumes and reenact the 13th-century Spanish war between the Moors and Christians with a fascinating dance ritual. Chilapa is one of the last places in Mexico where the dance is still performed in its original form; people flock here annually to observe this extraordinary event. It is also a takeoff point for a much more adventurous trek by horse to the mountain village of Olinalá, home of some of the most unique and elaborate lacquerware made in Mexico. Return to Route 95 and visit Chilpancingo.

CHILPANCINGO: The state capital of Guerrero, this town is primarily an agricultural center, home to a large university, and has a significant place in Mexico's history. It was here that the first Mexican Congress convened in 1813. Three brothers, Nicolás, Leonardo, and Victor Bravo, all heroes of the War of Independence, were born here. Moreover, Chilpancingo boasts the honor of being the first sovereign capital in all of Latin America, having been declared independent from Spain by José María Morelos y Pavón in 1813. During the revolution the city served as a hotbed of political unrest; it was taken by Emiliano Zapata in 1911. More recently, Chilpancingo is the birthplace of Rodolfo Neri Vera, Mexico's first astronaut, who participated in a US space mission in 1984.

In colonial times, Chilpancingo reached its economic zenith as a major stopover for caravans of silver, gold, ivory, silk, spices, and other luxury items that were traded between Mexico City and Manila from the port of Acapulco. The wealth and riches that this commerce brought helped to pay for the construction of the stately capital building and the solemn Asunción Cathedral. Much of of these two grand structures has been destroyed by the seven major earthquakes that have rocked the Chilpancingo Valley in the last century, but steel and cement reinforcements have not marred their historical significance.

The city's glorious past dates far earlier than colonial times. Chilpancingo, which means "Place of the Wasps," was inhabited as far back as 100 BC by the Olmec, who apparently drew the cave paintings in Juxtlahuaca and also constructed crude rock pyramids along the banks of the Río Azul. Later, the region was occupied by the Yope and Mexica cultures; both left vestiges of their heritage behind. Cave paintings and simple pyramidal mounds are visible on the south edge of town.

Because it is blessed with gentle winds, Chilpancingo enjoys a temperate climate. In fact, German naturalist and explorer Alexander von Humboldt once described the city as having "the most perfect climate in Mexico." And although the French novelist Jules Verne may never have set foot on Mexican soil, he must have taken Humboldt's word that the city was a temperate paradise. In one of his works, Verne refers to "the immense plains of Chilpancingo, where the finest climate in Mexico can be found."

The city center, which is closed to vehicular traffic, is concentrated around the Government Palace, City Hall, and the cathedral. The church opens onto a large plaza that comes alive with music and dancing every weekend. The entire zocalo is shaded by giant jacaranda and elm trees, interrupted only by a modern-style sculpture-mural celebrating the nation's struggle for independence. Across from the capital building is the *Anthropology Museum,* housed in a massive courtyard with a wall-to-wall mural depicting the history of the area. Inside are pre-Columbian artifacts and mementos from the independence period.

Off to the right of the state capital stands the *House of Deputies,* well worth a visit if you can convince the guard to let you sneak a peek inside. The 2-story mahogany and marble building is crowned by a beautiful overhead stained glass mosaic with portraits of four of the city's greatest heroes. Inaugurated in October of 1990, this extraordinary feat of architecture cost over $2 million.

Also of interest in Chilpancingo is the state zoo, with over 270 species of birds and mammals indigenous to the region, many of which are rarely found in captivity.

Although not on most tourist itineraries, Chilpancingo is a pleasant stopover and offers two first class hotels (see *Best en Route*).

En route from Chilpancingo – Continuing north on Route 95, the highway follows the Río Zopilote, passing the unnumbered road to Mexcala, where adventure-seekers can take a rafting expedition downriver. A word of caution: Be sure the expedition *returns* to Mexcala. These rafting trips often leave tourists in

Ciudad Altamirano. Information about the return trip should be checked out carefully in Mexcala *before* you leave.

Leaving Mexcala, continue north on Route 95 for 31 miles (50 km) to Iguala, the area's most important agricultural center. Just 9 miles (15 km) before Iguala on the left of the highway is *Sendi Stop*, a combination convenience store, fast-food stand, and rest stop. Run by the privately owned *Turi Star* luxury bus company, which provides service between Acapulco and Mexico City, it offers spotlessly clean restrooms, safe food, a kids' playground, and a well-equipped pharmacy stocked with plenty of Dramamine for the drive into the Sierra Madre. There also is an enclosed parking area, and well-landscaped grounds for stretching your legs.

IGUALA (pronounced Ee-*gwah*-lah): Just 22 miles (35 km) south of Taxco on Route 95 lies Iguala. Set in a fertile valley, it is surrounded by beautiful mountains. Every Friday is market day, when Indians from the surrounding countryside pour into Iguala to sell their produce. Pineapples, cantaloupes, watermelon, peanuts — and mangoes, for which this city has become famous — fill the the marketplace with luscious colors and smells. Baskets and pottery are also on sale, and occasionally the amethysts for which the state of Guerrero is famous. The zocalo of this town is filled with beautiful tamarind trees; and the town church standing nearby is quite lovely and worth a visit.

Iguala has a special place in Mexican history, because it was here that the flag of Mexico was created. In 1821, Agustín de Iturbide combined his troops with those of the rebel leader Vicente Guerrero, for whom the state is named; and in celebration he ordered Melchor Ocampo, a local tailor, to design and deliver a flag within 24 hours. He returned with the red, white, and green flag that is still in use today, and the main plaza, known as the Plaza de la Bandera (Plaza of the Flag), commemorates this event with a vast momument. On it are inscribed the words "Here the consummation of Mexico's independence from Spain was proclaimed on February 24, 1821." The act was known as the Plan of Iguala, which Iturbide composed (in Taxco). The monument is surrounded by 32 tamarind trees (one for each Mexican state) — a gift from the Chinese government — that encircle the Mexican flag. If you happen to pass through Iguala in December, look for the horse fair, which attracts traders from all over the country. Iguala is also the capital of the mask making region of northern Guerrero State. Ordinary and recently carved masks can be purchased for as little as $10; antique masks, a rare few made of silver, can cost $500 and up.

En route from Iguala – Route 95 passes through the village of El Naranjo before reaching the side road to Old Taxco. To the right is the famous Spratling silver factory, which welcomes visitors (check the tourist office for more information). The ascent on the Sierra Madre road into Taxco is dramatic, affording picturesque views of white stucco with red-brown tile houses stacked on the hillside. Hard to miss, too, are the magnificent Santa Prisca church towers overlooking the quaint cobblestone lanes that crisscross the city — all part of the charm of this silver city in the sky.

TAXCO (pronounced *Tahs*-coe): Nestled high in the folds of the Sierra Madre, 170 miles (273 km) north of Acapulco, sits a treasure town full of silver. Aladdin with his magic lantern couldn't conjure up a more charming place: a village of silversmiths perched on a mountain. Halfway between Acapulco and Mexico City, Taxco is a natural overnight stop for drivers, and if you pamper yourself you'll plan to spend two nights.

Taxco slumbered away until 1930, untouched by modernization because of the lack of decent roads or highways. Even today, civilization's inroads have not seriously altered the classic, almost fairy-tale quality of this town of 200,000 people. Cobblestone streets still weave around the hills, over their tops, and along their gently curved sides. There is no such thing as a paved street in Taxco. White and pink stucco houses, with balconies filled with flowering plants, line the narrow thoroughfares. It is an artist's paradise, and if the Mexican government has its way, that's how the town will remain: Taxco is one of several Mexican towns that have been declared national monuments.

Residents of the surrounding mountains live in whitewashed adobe houses capped with red tile roofs, the houses clinging to the sides of cobbled streets that twist their way to the main plaza, the zocalo. The 20th century is tolerated in Taxco, but not encouraged.

It seems that the ground floor of every other building in town contains a silver shop; there are more than 250 in all. There are textile and clothing stores and tin and curio shops, too, but in Taxco silver is king.

An American actually brought silversmithing to Taxco. William Spratling first came here around 1930, a tourist before there were tourists in Mexico, just after a new highway had opened up the long-isolated mining town. Don Guillermo, as he was known, found that the supposedly played-out mines were still producing enough to allow people to smelt silver in backyard furnaces; they were selling it by the pound to whomever they could. At the time, Spratling taught at Tulane University in New Orleans, but he decided to give up the academic life in favor of creating his own line of silverware in Taxco. He opened his shop on June 27, 1932.

The business prospered; Spratling took in local youths and taught them the trade. His design integrated ancient Indian motifs into jewelry, which was snapped up by buyers from Texas to New York. Many of his apprentices went on to open silver shops of their own, some good, some not so good.

All of these silver shops, combined with the charm of the town itself, helped make Taxco one of Mexico's first major travel destinations, and so it remains today. Many travelers come back year after year to spend their entire vacations in Taxco. In fact, the town has a fair-size community of retired Americans — the ultimate test of a compatible climate and atmosphere.

There are those who grumble that Taxco has become too touristy, and truth to tell, there was a time in Taxco's recent past when it often appeared there were more foreigners than natives around the zocalo. Since the new toll road opened in 1989, though, you're likely to find just as many Mexican tourists as foreigners. It is the rare visitor who regrets having made the trip. Taxco is Old Mexico as everyone expects it to be.

Before the area was discovered by the Spaniards in the early 1500s, its name was Tlachco, which means "place where the ball is played" in Nahuatl, an Indian language. Taxco is the Spanish adaptation of that name. Although remote, Taxco played a significant role in Mexico's history. Montezuma I conquered the region in 1455. Cortés, the Spanish conqueror, who took control of the country in 1521, had an intuitive sense about silver and gold — he seemed to have an invisible dowsing rod that enabled him to detect these metals even from a distance. Shortly after his conquest of Mexico City in 1521, Cortés sent two of his captains to Tlachco/Taxco to investigate its mineral resources. They struck silver, and in 1529 the Spanish moved into the area. The boom proved short-lived, however, and by 1581 only 47 miners were required to work Taxco's mines. When no new veins were discovered after the first mine opened in 1529, the city got a reputation as a played-out source. Its essentially Spanish nature, however, was confirmed; it remained firmly royalist — loyal to Spanish royalty — in the later wars of independence.

But early in the 18th century a wandering Frenchman, Joseph de la Borde (later changed to the more Mexican José de la Borda), undeterred by Taxco's reputation, struck a very rich vein of silver and started Taxco's golden (or should it be silver) age. A religious man (he had a daughter who became a nun and a son who became a priest), de la Borda built one of Mexico's most beautiful churches in Taxco, the Santa Prisca, in gratitude to God for his good fortune. He explained his generosity quite simply: "God gives to Borda, Borda gives to God." Apparently, he wasn't far wrong, because after his death in 1778 the silver boom died. Taxco was no longer of much interest to anyone. Politically, it certainly was inactive. The residents preferred quiet and relative solitude to the excitement that neighboring Cuernavaca generated. Taxco sided with the pro-Spanish royalists in the 1810 War of Independence, and managed to repel an attack by revolutionaries in 1811. Soon after, however, the town was vanquished.

Even today, the town holds pretty much to its old ways. During *Holy Week,* at *Easter,* parades are held daily. On *Good Friday,* Taxco residents reenact Christ's carrying of the cross. A man wears a crown of thorns, and penitents drag chains and go through rituals of mortification of the flesh. But apart from that touch of solemnity, Taxco residents like festivities. Almost every night, somebody shoots off fireworks to celebrate a wedding, a birth, a birthday, or a saint's day. It is a joyous place to visit.

A spectacular view of Taxco can be enjoyed while riding the aerial tramway to and from the *Montetaxco* hotel — an experience no visitor should miss. The tram may be boarded near the main highway, Route 95 (called Avenida J. F. Kennedy in town), by the arches near the northern entrance to town; the round-trip fare is about $3.50. The views from the hotel itself are breathtaking, as are those seen from the *De la Borda* (on Av. J. F. Kennedy), overlooking the town; *Rancho Taxco* (14 Soto la Marina); *La Ventana de Taxco* restaurant (in the *Hacienda del Solar Hotel,* Km 89.5 on Rte. 95 south of town); and the *Pagaduría del Rey* restaurant (Cerro de Bermeja). The Carretera Panorámica, or Panoramic Highway, delivers what its name promises.

Most of Taxco's places of interest are within walking distance of each other. But in the process of getting from one to another, you'll come across lush patios filled with geraniums, cerise and orange bougainvillea, intricately carved doors, ornate ironwork, and cages of exotic singing birds.

For those who prefer a guided tour, both the federal (phone: 762-21525) and state (phone: 762-22279) government tourist offices are helpful; both are in the *Convention Center,* across the street from the former Hacienda del Chorrillo. There also are information booths at both entrances to town. Young boys wearing white shirts and brown ties at Plaza Borda lead tours under the auspices of the tourist office and expect only a tip in return.

Situated on the zocalo, Santa Prisca church is Taxco's most important landmark. Built between 1751 and 1758 by Frenchman José de la Borda as an expression of thanks to God, the twin, 130-foot baroque towers and richly carved stone façade are impressive in their own right, but the blue tile dome and pink exterior walls of the church also account for this place's popularity with visiting photographers, both professional and amateur. Inside, there are 12 altars, gold altarpieces, and original paintings by artist Miguel Cabrera from the colonial era in the sacristy. The church was vandalized in the spring of 1991, with over $3 million in gold and silver religious artifacts stolen. Fortunately, the thieves overlooked Santa Prisca's most valuable treasures: four 18th-century oil paintings by Spaniard Andrés Barragán, which had been recently discovered in a storeroom and restored to their original beauty. These works, and most of the remaining gold relics, are on display — although they are now heavily guarded.

Directly behind Santa Prisca is the *Museo Guillermo Spratling* (William Spratling Museum). The American who gave so much to Taxco was a great collector of pre-Columbian artifacts, many of which are on display here. Downstairs is devoted to the life of New York–born Spratling, and to silver mining. There are also fine exhibits on local history, photos of *Semana Santa* (Holy Week) festivities, and samples of silver ore. The 3-story museum was originally funded by Spratling himself before his death in 1967. Open Tuesdays through Sundays. Admission charge (phone: 762-21660).

Also on the zocalo is Casa Borda, built by José de la Borda in 1759. Its front section is 2 stories high, but the back rises 5 stories. This is due to the slope of the land rather than eccentric architecture. Originally, José de la Borda lived in only half the house, and the other half was donated to the priests of the local church. Today it is the City Hall and also houses a silver shop. Open daily. No admission charge (phone: 762-20018).

Count Cadena, a friend of José de la Borda, built his house, Casa Figueroa, in 1767. It's also called the House of Tears, because the count, a local magistrate, made the Indians who could not pay their fines do the work on it. It became Casa Figueroa because Fidel Figueroa, a modern Mexican artist, restored the house in 1943 and used it as a studio and art gallery, which now exhibits his works. At press time, the house was closed indefinitely for renovations; check first with your hotel desk or the tourist office (phone: 762-22279). If the house is open, take the tour to see the secret stashes, tunnels, and even a room where women hid during the 1910 revolution. On the western end of the zocalo (no phone).

Better known as *Casa Humboldt,* the delightful *Museo del Virreinato* (Museum of Colonial Art; 6 Calle Juan Ruiz Alarcón) is notable for the fine details on the doors and windows, as well as for its façade of bas-relief plaster. The overall style is Moorish. Originally built by Juan de Villnueva in the 18th century, it was renamed in honor of explorer and scientist Baron Alexander von Humboldt, who was a guest on the night of April 5, 1803, during the period of his extensive explorations in the Americas. During this century, *Casa Humboldt* has served as a hotel and, more recently, as a government-run handicrafts shop. At press time, it was being converted into a noteworthy museum of colonial art that was scheduled to open early this year. Admission charge.

Don't miss the Convent of San Bernardino de Sena on the Plazuela del Ex-Convento. Originally a Franciscan monastery founded in 1592, this building was destroyed by fire in 1805 but restored in 1823. Today it is a public grade school and considered a historic site because it is here that the revolutionary Plan of Iguala was drawn up by Agustín de Iturbide in 1821. Open daily.

Adjacent to the tram to the *Montetaxco* hotel, on the grounds of the former Hacienda del Chorrillo, stands the Instituto de Artes Plásticas (Modern Arts Institute). These buildings are a fine example of modern architecture well integrated into a very natural setting. It's possible to visit the workshops here. No admission charge (phone: 762-23690).

During a stay in Taxco, be sure to visit its beautiful *Convention Center.* This facility was built on the site of a 450-year-old hacienda near the stone aqueduct at the northern entrance to the city. The center has a large outdoor amphitheater and an auditorium, and also serves as the state tourist office (phone: 762-22279).

Prize-winning works in silver by local artisans can be seen at the *Museo de la Platería* (Silver Museum). Open daily. No admission charge. It is located on Plazuela de los Artesanos (phone: 762-21645).

Another noteworthy attraction, a short distance from the city, is *Zoofari,* a wild-animal park with more than 100 species of birds and animals from all over the world. The part of the park where the animals roam freely must be visited by car. There is also a wide selection of pets for sale, rides on ponies and dwarf mules, a restaurant, a handicrafts shop, and clean restrooms. Open daily. Admission charge. About 20 miles (33 km) east of Taxco on Rte. 95 (no phone).

For the truly adventurous, the Caves of Cacahuamilpa (*Grutas,* or grottoes, is what everybody calls them since no one can pronounce Cacahuamilpa) are less than an hour's drive north of Taxco. The astounding formations in this vast network of caves are aptly named: Sleeping Lady, The Hunchback, The Asparagus, The Snail, The Dawn, and The Champagne Bottle (for further information see *Day Trip 1: Caves of Cacahuamilpa,* below).

When it comes to celebrations, nowhere in the world is there anything quite like Taxco's *Holy Week.* It begins on *Palm Sunday* with a procession. Daily parades follow, but by *Holy Thursday* it becomes a show that involves the whole town from noon until after midnight. The forecourt of the Santa Prisca church is transformed into the Garden of Gethsemane with guardian angels, Roman soldiers, and centurions. Then there is a reenactment of the Washing of the Feet, the Last Supper, the betrayal of Jesus by Judas, and Jesus' imprisonment in Nicholas Temple. At 11 PM Pontius Pilate reads the sentence and washes his hands. While all this is going on, candlelit processions enter the town from surrounding villages. The crowds, many of them masked, black-gowned penitents bare to the waist, swell to 2,000 or 3,000. Some in the procession carry heavy wooden crosses, others have their arms and backs laced with spiky branches of thorn, and you may see some carrying studded metal thongs with which they flagellate themselves. It is an incredible sight. On *Good Friday,* the Road to Calvary is reenacted. Christ, bearing his cross, passes through the zocalo around noon. The Crucifixion takes place at the Convent of San Bernardino. Christ is tied to the cross, and taken down at 4 PM. The observance ends at midnight with a Procession of Silence, in which hooded men dressed in black flowing robes parade in total silence. Nothing is heard but the weird sound of shuffling feet. On *Saturday* morning, church bells ring out after 2 days of silence to mark the Ceremony of the Resurrection. On Sunday, there is a final procession at 5 PM. You must make hotel reservations for *Easter* months in advance.

The city's other major annual event is the *National Silver Fair,* which takes place during the last week in November. All the silversmiths submit their best work for highly prized awards. A cultural festival held in mid-May, *Jornadas Alarconas,* honors one of Mexico's greatest dramatists, Juan Ruiz Alarcón; he lived in Taxco and wrote many of his important works here. Other holidays with parades and fireworks include February 2, *Fiesta de la Candelaria;* February 5, *Fiesta of the Patron Saint of the Silversmiths, Felipe de Jesús;* February 18, the *Fiesta de la Santa Prisca; Fiesta de Vera Cruz,* held in March; May 3, *Fiesta de la Santa Cruz;* September 24, *Fiesta de la Virgen de las Mercedes;* and, of course, *Corpus Christi Day* and pre-*Lent Carnaval Week.* On the Monday following the *Day of the Dead* (November 2), the whole town takes off for a picnic held in Huixteco (north of Taxco), where everyone eats *jumiles* (small insects very much like cockroaches, said to be delicious). It has become known as *Fiesta de los Jumiles.*

For shoppers, silver is *the* thing in Taxco. Anything from a small, inexpensive ring to a complete silver service or tea set is available. There are silver shops all over town, but the heaviest concentration is around the main plaza and near the north entrance to town on Avenida J. F. Kennedy, near the *Posada de la Misión.* Taxco also mines amethyst, tourmaline, nephrite, garnet, topaz, and various kinds of agates and opals. At the public market, just off the zocalo, shawls, *huaraches* (braided sandals), straw products, leather goods, pottery, woodcarvings, bark paintings, and seed, bean, and nutshell jewelry are sold. Silver is also available in the market, but it is advisable to buy it in reputable shops.

Los Castillos – The silversmiths who are renowned for their "wedding" of silver, copper, and bronze are now doing extraordinary work in ceramics and silver inlays. Ask to visit their workshop. 10 Plazuela de Bernal (phone: 762-20652 or 762-21988).

Elena de Ballesteros – A large, beautifully displayed selection of silver and gold jewelry. On the zocalo at 4 Calle Celso Muñoz (phone: 762-23767).

Galería de Arte Andrés – A silver shop run by the eponymous Andrés Mejía Alvarez, a very personable gentleman who is producing some of the most innovative and impressive work in town. 28 Av. J. F. Kennedy (phone: 762-23778).

Gracias a Dios – Stunning Tachi Castillo jackets with appliqués of brightly colored ribbons. Also, a selection of regional crafts. 3 Plazuela de Bernal (phone: 762-20086).

Huarachería Los Angeles – Carries a wide variety of sandals and other comfortable shoes. Near the *Platería Rancho Alegre,* on Av. J. F. Kennedy (no phone).

El Mineral Joyeros – Some outstanding works of craftsmanship can be found here, including prize-winning pieces and silver and gold jewelry set with semi-precious stones. The shop itself is designed to look like a mine. 1 Plaza Borda (phone: 762-21878).

Pineda's Taxco – Owner Herlindo Pineda displays beautiful pieces in enameled silver. 1 Plaza Borda (phone: 762-23233).

Spratling – William Spratling's traditional designs made in silver from traditional molds. Km 17, Hwy. to Iguala (phone: 762-20026).

Virgilio – Exclusive designs in gold and precious stones. On Miguel Hidalgo in front of the San Nicolás church (phone: 762-20624).

For sportsmen (and women), Taxco offers enough diversions to please competitive — and spectator — tastes. Taxco proper has no *Plaza de Toros* for bullfighting, although bullfights are often held at a small bullring about 3 miles (5 km) from the city (ask at the tourist office for specific details).

The *Montetaxco* hotel (Rte. 95; phone: 762-21300) has a 9-hole golf course open to the public.

For equestrians, mounts are available at the *Montetaxco* (phone: 762-21300).

For a quick dip, the *Montetaxco, Posada de la Misión, Hacienda del Solar, Posada las Palmas,* and *Loma Linda* hotels have swimming pools.

Tennis fans can head to the courts at the *Montetaxco, Posada de la Misión,* and *Hacienda del Solar.*

After-dark activities abound in this mountain town. Discotheques have sprung up all over Taxco, among them *Donde* (on the zocalo; no phone); *Bugambillias* (below *Los Arcos* hotel at 6 Juan Ruiz Alarcón; phone: 762-21836); *La Plazuela* (34 Av. J. F. Kennedy, near *Elena de Ballesteros* jewelers; phone: 762-23976); and *Windows* disco-bar at the *Montetaxco* (Rte. 95), which is the liveliest place in town. Mexican musicians often entertain at *Paco's Bar* and *Berta's. Paco's* is bigger and livelier, but *Berta's* is a landmark — it's named for the owner, whose fortune was made when she invented the drink of tequila, soda, lime, and honey that bears her name. *Berta's* place is on the zocalo, next to Santa Prisca church, and *Paco's* overlooks the lively street scene on the opposite side of the zocalo. For something a little out of the ordinary, buy a $15 ticket for Tony Reyes's show at the *Montetaxco* (Rte. 95). Transportation, two drinks, a performance of the *Voladores de Papantla* (Flying Indians from Papantla), music, and dancing are included in the price. On Saturday nights, the *Montetaxco* hotel hosts a Mexican Fiesta with a show and lavish buffet of regional dishes, followed by a fireworks display.

Taxco is a good base for those who would like to explore this area further. The following destinations can easily be seen on a day trip from the city.

DAY TRIP 1: GRUTAS DE CACAHUAMILPA (Caves of Cacahuamilpa)

About 25 miles (40 km) east of Taxco is the Route 55 junction, and the Guerrero-Morelos border. Take Route 55 north 15½ miles (25 km) and follow the signs leading to the Caves of Cacahuamilpa (pronounced Cah-cah-wah-*meel*-pah). They rival their northern neighbors at Carlsbad in size and in variety of formations. Stalactites, stalagmites, arches, and boulders are lighted in the more central caves for easier exploration, and while guided tours are available either for groups or private parties, much of the caverns has not been investigated. Weekends sometimes have fairly heavy traffic, with people coming and going on the buses from Mexico City and Cuernavaca, but the caves are large and fascinating. Tours are given daily from 9 AM to 4 PM, and there is a sound-and-light show. Concerts are occasionally held in the caves — a real treat. For details, check with the tourist office in Taxco (phone: 762-21525). Take Route 55 south and join Route 95 west back to Taxco. For those who would like to continue on this route, follow Route 55 north to Ixtapán de la Sal.

DAY TRIP 2: IXTAPÁN DE LA SAL

Take Route 55 north from Taxco about 60 miles (100 km) to the mineral water spa at Ixtapán de la Sal. Set in a verdant valley surrounded by mountains, the picturesque village of Ixtapán (pronounced Eex-*tah*-pahn) has small pastel stucco houses and a 16th-century church that once served as the headquarters for French troops.

IXTAPÁN DE LA SAL: Long before the Spanish conquistadores set foot on Mexican soil, the Aztec used to travel over Mexico's mountainous terrain to plunge themselves into these mineral waters. Aztec shamans claimed the waters of Ixtapán — which in Nahuatl means "on the salt" — were endowed with magical qualities, and could heal the sick and relieve the aches and pains of the aged. Even those with incurable illnesses believed they could find temporary relief in the warm pools of Ixtapán.

When Hernán Cortés and his band of conquerors pillaged Tenochtitlán in search of gold and silver, they somehow overlooked the large jugs of water the Aztec had carried back from the spring. And with the destruction of the Aztec city, the secrets of Ixtapán's waters were buried in the annals of history for several centuries. In fact, it was not until the 19th century that Carlota, the wife of Emperor Maximilian, rediscovered them. At least once a month, the Belgian-born empress and her entourage would trek by horseback to Ixtapán de la Sal in order to replenish their spirits and rejuvenate their bodies.

Modern-day pilgrims who visit here will find this a welcome respite along the route. Aside from the waters, there are two excellent hotels (see *Best en Route*), a public park, golf, tennis, and a complete range of water sports. If time allows, a full day — or more — will refresh even the most weary spirit. To return to Taxco, take Route 55 south and join Route 95 west back to the city.

BEST EN ROUTE

CHECKING IN: Taxco is one of the major destinations on the Mexican tourist trail, so it's a good idea to make reservations well in advance, especially if you intend to visit during festival time. Expect to pay over $70 for a double room in a hotel listed as very expensive; up to $70 in an expensive one, $40 in moderate; and $30 or less in an inexpensive place. Most hotels accept MasterCard and Visa; a few also accept American Express and Diners Club.

CHILPANCINGO

Jacarandas – A modern, 70-room complex at the far south end of town set in a spacious garden of jacaranda trees, this government-owned and operated property boasts a splendid view, an oversize swimming pool, but no TV sets or phones in the guestrooms. This service is a bit slow, but the rooms are large and comfortable, as well as extremely clean. Av. Circunvalación (phone: 747-24444). Moderate.

Parador de Marqués – This colonial-style establishment is almost as old as the city itself. More centrally located than the *Jacarandas,* it has a restaurant that offers good simple fare and a small disco off the lobby. Km 276.5 Acapulco–México Hwy. (phone: 747-26773). Moderate.

IXTAPÁN DE LA SAL

Ixtapán – This longtime favorite hostelry has 250 junior suites and chalets, thermal and freshwater pools, Roman baths, tennis, private pools, old-fashioned Swedish massage, a large spa, movies, a playground, horseback riding, and a small — but very challenging — 9-hole golf course. No credit cards, but the hotel does accept traveler's checks. (The *Balneario Nuevo Ixtapán* public baths, which used to belong to the owner of the *Ixtapán,* offers thermal pools and a scenic train ride through beautiful gardens. Avoid weekends, when it is very crowded.) Blvd. Las Jacarandas and Diana Circle (phone: 724-30304); in the US, 800-223-9832). Expensive.

Kiss – This family-oriented 40-unit establishment is run by a Hungarian-born couple of the same name. Its restaurant offers down-home Yiddish cooking that runs the gamut from matzoh ball soup to fresh apple strudel. The accommodations are not as posh as the *Ixtapán* across the street, but neither are the prices. A favorite weekend getaway for the Mexico City crowd. Blvd. Las Jacarandas and Diana Circle (phone: 724-30901). Moderate.

TAXCO

Montetaxco – Set on a steep mountainside overlooking Taxco, with a welcome sign that reads *"Está Ud. en el cielo. Disfrútelo"* ("You're in heaven. Enjoy it"). There are 156 rooms and suites, each with a color TV set and air conditioning, and 32 villas (for four to six people) with kitchenettes. Its facilities and services include a cable car, a heated swimming pool, Swedish massage, steambaths, tennis, golf, horseback riding, a disco, and 3 restaurants (see *Eating Out*). On Fridays, Saturdays, and Sundays there are barbecues and fireworks. North of town, off Rte. 95 to the right on a fearsomely steep road; it's possible to take the cable car up from Rte. 95 (phone: 762-21300; fax: 762-21428). Very expensive.

Hacienda del Solar – This resort complex sprawls across some 80 acres of property, but still feels like a country inn. Its 22 elegant bungalows are named after female friends and relatives of the owner; "Isabel" is especially appealing for its tiled bathroom with a garden and skylight. There is a pool and a tennis court. Breakfast is served on the terrace; try the excellent *Ventana de Taxco* Italian restaurant for dinner (see *Eating Out*). A Modified American Plan is also available. Two miles (3 km) out of town on Rte. 95 (phone: 762-20323). Expensive.

Posada de la Misión – Decorated in colonial style, this 150-room inn offers comfortable lodgings, TV sets, heated swimming pool, Jacuzzi, shops, an inviting poolside restaurant and bar, and a tennis court. The Juan O'Gorman mural alongside the pool is an attraction on its own. Electronic chimes housed in two lovely towers on the property toll the quarter hour and play "Taxco de Mis Amores" four times a day: at 7 AM, 2 PM, 6 PM, and midnight. Rooms and bathrooms are on the small side, except for Nos. 39 and 27 and the newer section of 39 suites, which are exceptionally lovely but more expensive. Room price includes breakfast. 32 Cerro de la Misión, off Av. J. F. Kennedy, at the Mexico City entrance to the city (phone: 762-20063; fax: 762-22198). Expensive.

Agua Escondida – It may lack the charm of many of the older establishments, but it's right on the zocalo and rates high with young people. It has a pool and Ping-Pong table, restaurant, and parking. The rooms in back are farther removed from the discos on the zocalo. 4 Plaza Borda (phone: 762-20726; fax: 762-21306). Moderate.

Loma Linda – A cheerful, small place offering modest accommodations, it has 55 rooms, restaurant, bar, pool, and parking (no large cars). 52 Av. J. F. Kennedy (phone: 762-20206; fax: 762-25125). Moderate.

Santa Prisca – A favorite with repeat visitors, this old-fashioned downtown inn with two green courtyards and fountains has much charm and dignity. It has 40 comfortably furnished rooms, a bar, parking, and a lovely little restaurant, whose menu changes daily and includes homemade soup and other hearty fare for a low fixed price. Price includes breakfast. 1 Cena Obscuras (phone: 762-20080; fax: 762-21106). Moderate.

Victoria – This sprawling collection of 130 rooms extends over what was once the city's most lavish hacienda. Many of the rooms are a bit run-down, but what it lacks in modern amenities is more than compensated for by the personalized service and the home-cooked meals. Ask for a room on one of the upper floors of the estate to ensure that the hot water reaches you while it is still hot. Most of these rooms also have lovely balconies with a sensational view of the zocalo and the city. 5 Carlos J. Nibbi (phone: 762-20183). Moderate.

Los Arcos – A small gem, it was a convent back in 1620; it has 25 rooms and 3 two-level suites perfect for 4 people, and a congenial bar. The *Bugambillias* nightclub is located nearby as well. Just a block from the zocalo at 6 Juan Ruiz Alarcón (phone: 762-21836; fax: 762-23211). Inexpensive.

Posada de los Castillo – This small inn with only 15 rooms in the center of town is run by the famous silversmithing family. 3 Juan Ruiz Alarcón (phone: 762-21396). Inexpensive.

Posada las Palmas – Only 14 rooms and 10 bungalows, as well as a nice garden, pool, and parking. No credit cards accepted. Down the street from the post office at 1 Estacas (phone: 762-23177). Inexpensive.

EATING OUT: All the good hotels (see above) have restaurants of their own that serve adequate, if not outstanding, food. Expect to pay up to $50 for a meal for two at a spot listed in the expensive category; about $30 in moderate places; and under $15 in inexpensive ones. Wine, tax, and tips are extra. All restaurants accept MasterCard and Visa; a few also accept American Express. Unless otherwise noted, all restaurants are open daily.

La Pagaduría del Rey – Steaks, seafood, and French, Italian, and Mexican fare are served in a colonial setting; the views are extraordinary. Closed Mondays. Reservations advised on weekends. The menu is limited but varied. Cerro de Bermeja (phone: 762-23467). Expensive.

Toni's – Excellent prime ribs and lobster, along with a sensational view, make this a popular spot. Reservations advised on weekends. At the *Montetaxco* (phone: 762-21300). Expensive.

La Ventana de Taxco – There's a dramatic view of the city at night (the name means "window on Taxco") at this fine Italian eatery, which features guitar music nightly except Mondays during the high season. Reservations advised on weekends. *Hacienda del Solar,* Rte. 95, south of town (phone: 762-20587). Expensive.

Carrusel – A very popular place, it has pleasant service, good steaks, and generous portions. Reservations unnecessary. 8 Calle Cuauhtémoc (phone: 762-21655). Moderate.

Cielito Lindo – Considered a favorite among Taxcophiles, this place offers considerable charm and carefully prepared Mexican dishes, along with such American favorites as breaded veal cutlet and fried chicken, followed by lemon meringue pie. Reservations unnecessary. On the zocalo at 14 Plaza Borda (phone: 762-20603). Moderate.

La Hacienda – This 2-level eatery serves breakfast, lunch, and dinner. The Mexican platter reigns supreme here, enhanced by chilled mugs of beer. For dessert try

crêpes filled with homemade jam. Reservations unnecessary. 4 Calle Guillermo
Spratling and Plaza Borda (phone: 762-20663). Moderate.

Piccolo Mondo – Another pleasant spot at the *Montetaxco,* this one specializes in
parrilladas (a variety of meats grilled on a brazier at the table), and pizza baked
in a brick wood-burning oven. Reservations unnecessary. Rte. 95 (phone: 762-
21300). Moderate.

Sr. Costilla's – The name translates as "Mr. Chops," appropriate for an eatery
serving good steaks and chops. The mood at this branch of the popular Carlos
Anderson chain is lively and casual, with all sorts of baskets and hats hanging from
the ceiling and additional seating in the balcony. Reservations unnecessary. Upstairs at 1 Plaza Borda (phone: 762-23215). Moderate.

La Taberna – Run by the same family who owns the *Bora Bora* (below), this eatery
offers a more extensive menu featuring shrimp shish kebab, beef Stroganoff, crêpes,
salads, and pasta. There are table games, and the TV set airs major sports events
from the US. Reservations advised. 8 Benito Juárez (phone: 762-25226). Moderate.

Taxqueño – Another popular dining spot at the *Montetaxco,* this one specializes in
Mexican dishes. On Fridays and Saturdays, lunch and dinner are accompanied by
the lilting tropical sounds of a marimba. Reservations unnecessary. Rte. 95 (phone:
762-21300). Moderate.

Bora Bora – No South Seas rhythms and swaying palms here. In spite of the name,
the lure is good pizza and great people watching. Reservations unnecessary. Calle-
jón de las Delicias (phone: 762-21721). Inexpensive.

En route from Taxco – Continuing north along Route 95 there is a choice of
remaining on Route 95, the old mountain road, or taking Route 95-D, the toll
road, which goes around Cuernavaca and on to Mexico City. While Route 95-D
is much straighter, and consequently faster, we suggest Route 95, the more scenic
road with easy access to attractions such as Tehuixtla, the popular recreational
facilities at Lake Tequesquitengo, and the Xochicalco ruins. Farther on (50 miles/
80 km) is Cuernavaca, Mexico's oldest resort.

TEHUIXTLA: Take Route 95 north for 25 miles (40 km) to Puente de Ixtla; take the
unnumbered road south about 8 miles (12 km) to Tehuixtla and the home of *La
Fundación* bathing resort and spa, known as *Isstehuixtla* (less than a mile/1.6 km south
of town). Run by the Social Security Institute for Federal Employees, the resort is open
to the public. There is an admission fee and a charge for locker rentals, but you can
take advantage of the sulfur baths and swimming pools to your heart's content. There
are five pools in all, but the main one is a very deep swimming hole filled with waters
rising from the depths of the earth. A fast-flowing river runs through the property, with
a suspension bridge connecting the two banks. Swinging wildly as you walk across and
surrounded by tropical growth, the bridge is like an image from a childhood jungle
movie. This exotic atmosphere is carried even further by the poolside waiters who serve
you whole coconuts, chopping off the top to form a natural cup of cooling coconut milk.
There are snack stands and the very pleasant *La Fundación* restaurant, with such
specialties as *chiles relleños* (peppers stuffed with cheese or ground meat, and served
with tomato sauce) and *gorditos* (small tortillas lavished with sausage and green sauce).

A short walk across the bridge leads you to another restaurant, pool, and bar,
connected to *La Rivera* hotel (see *Best en Route*). It's not actually part of Tehuixtla,
but a friendly exchange back and forth is taken for granted. No English is spoken in
either place, but almost anything you might want can be indicated pretty easily with
smiles, shrugs, and pointing. The people of Tehuixtla are friendly and helpful.

Approximately 8 miles (12 km) north of Tehuixtla is Lake Tequesquitengo. On the northern tip of the lake is an unnumbered road leading to *Hacienda Vista Hermosa,* a beautiful recreational area for the whole family.

LAGUNA TEQUESQUITENGO (pronounced Tay-kays-kee-*ten*-go): Just about 27 miles (43 km) southeast of Cuernavaca, this natural lake is an increasingly popular recreation spot with Mexico City's water enthusiasts. There are motorboats and water skis for rent, as well as swimming, fishing, tennis courts, restaurants, hotels, guesthouses, snack bars, and tourists from every part of Mexico. Weekends tend to get a little hectic, but weekdays are simply lively, with fewer people trying to be in the same spot at once. One strange feature of this lake is that the water level rises and falls drastically, and in the middle are the remains of an Indian village that once stood aboveground. In 1820, the Indians were forced to move to the present location of Tequesquitengo, but the shoreline continues to rise and fall.

Continue on the unnumbered road from the northern tip of the lake for about 1 mile (1.6 km) to Jojutla de Juárez, where you'll find *Hacienda Vista Hermosa.*

HACIENDA VISTA HERMOSA: More than a luxury hotel, this is a resort spa created from the ruins of a colonial sugar mill. You can bring the whole family for swimming, tennis, bowling, horseback riding, or just sunning. There is open-air dining and a terrific Sunday brunch. Whether or not you are interested in staying overnight, it is a good place to spend an afternoon (see *Best en Route*).

En Route from Hacienda Vista Hermosa – Follow the road that leads 5 miles (8 km) back to the Route 95/Alpuyeca interchange. In Alpuyeca, the town church has some wonderful Indian murals. Follow Route 166, leading west 5½ miles (9 km), where you will see a sign to the right for the mysterious ruins just 7½ miles (12 km) ahead.

RUINAS XOCHICALCO (Xochicalco Ruins): Pronounced Zo-chee-*cahl*-co, the Nahuatl world meaning "house of flowers," the mounds of the site cover 6 square miles and lie 24 miles (38 km) southwest of Cuernavaca. There is a ball court, a palace, a honeycombed network of underground caves, passageways, and one restored pyramid that sits on the top of a rocky hill. The walls of this pyramidal structure are elaborately carved with figures of serpents and human beings thought to represent the priests of the temple. While there are elements suggesting Toltec origins, other aspects indicate Maya or Zapotec influence. Bas-relief designs are carved into the stone, and in one of the pyramids is a sunlit rooftop observatory used by Indian scientists to determine the date and time. Open daily from 8 AM to 5 PM.

En route from Xochicalco Ruins – Return to Alpuyeca and Route 95 and head north 24 miles (38 km) to Cuernavaca. Route 95 meets Route 95-D on the outskirts of Cuernavaca, where you can turn left onto Morelos, the main thoroughfare of this very beautiful city.

CUERNAVACA (pronounced Kwer-nah-*vah*-kah): Among the topics likely to be discussed when professional travelers congregate is which city in the world has the best climate. It might be one of those questions around which battle lines are drawn and ideological splits develop (ask two travel writers within earshot of one another to name the world's best beach, then sit back and watch the fur fly). There is an exception, however. For several centuries there has been one favorite with cognoscenti, from the Aztec kings and Hernán Cortés to hundreds of American and European expatriates who live here right now. That is Cuernavaca, with a name like poetry and a climate that is simply perfect. It is a weekend escape for middle class Mexico City residents and, like Paris, a place where good Americans go when they die — or just before that, if they are lucky.

Approximately 220 miles (352 km) north of Acapulco, Cuernavaca is Mexico's oldest resort and the capital of the state of Morelos. The Aztec named it Cuauhnahuac, "Place of the Whispering Trees." The Spanish found this word unpronounceable when they arrived in 1521, and promptly changed to Cuernavaca (cow's horn). The city was 1 of 30 awarded to Cortés by the Spanish king, and he chose it as his retirement home; unfortunately, he died in Spain in 1547 before he could return to it.

Small wonder he yearned for Cuernavaca. At 5,000 feet, the city has spring-like weather throughout most of the year; when Mexico City (at 7,200 feet) is plunged in cold rain, the swimming pools of Cuernavaca glitter in the sun. Among its natural water sources are a series of thermally heated springs and mineral waters, traditionally soothing for rheumatism and other ailments of the joints and incredibly relaxing and restorative to the spirit, even if one's joints are in perfect condition. Even in the pre-Columbian period, the Aztec came to Cuauhnahuac for mineral baths.

Despite its serene climate, Cuernavaca has been the scene of heavy political controversy since it was founded. The big sugar haciendas surrounding the city were first run by rich Spaniards, then after 1810, by equally rich Mexicans, many of whom lived in Europe and left the management of their lands to overseers, who treated the Indian laborers like slaves.

The 1910 Revolution brought to prominence Emiliano Zapata, who grew up in the nearby town of Cuautla. Zapata harbored a deep hatred for both the resident and absentee landlords, and his battle cry — "Land and Liberty and Death to the Hacendados!" — reflected the deeply rooted frustrations of the peasants. Zapata's ragtag Army of the South sacked and devastated every hacienda in the region, burning crops and razing buildings to the ground. When President Francisco I. Madero didn't immediately divide the land in Morelos into small portions for Zapata's Indians after the Revolution, Zapata broke with him. He joined forces with the flamboyant bandit Pancho Villa in 1914, during the occupation of Mexico City. But Zapata was not an educated man and found himself uncomfortable in the sophisticated city, and he soon came home. Too impractical for the rest of the politicians, he was trapped by federal troops and shot in April 1919. Greatly beloved by his followers, Zapata was the one true idealist in the Revolution. He never sought a penny for himself, only for his people. A true folk hero, Zapata's memory is revered as almost sacred in Cuernavaca.

When you visit Cuernavaca, you will undoubtedly be impressed by its flowers before you get any sense of its politics or history. Geraniums reach to rooftops; fuchsia and red and coral bougainvillea grow wild. The bluish lavender jacaranda and flaming poinciana tint the air with color. Stretching into the distance on the outskirts of town are fields of sugarcane, corn, beans, avocados, wheat, coffee, and peanuts. There also are groves of banana trees, mangoes, guavas, limes, and oranges. If you don't fall in love with Cuernavaca, you'll at least understand why so many people are fiercely attached to the place and why it generates such intense passion.

The best views of Cuernavaca are from Route 95, as you enter the town from Acapulco, and from the hills called Lomas de Cuernavaca, on either side of Route 95.

For some folk, Cuernavaca is a little too big for walking around, although it is only 4 short blocks between Palacio de Cortés (Cortés's Palace) and the Jardín Borda (Borda Gardens). There is a residential area south of the zocalo that is pleasant to drive around, since the gardens are not set behind walls, as in most Mexican homes.

The best information on Cuernavaca can be found at both the federal and state tourism offices. The former is at 2 Ignacio Comonfort (phone: 73-121815 or 73-125414); the latter is at 802 Morelos Sur (phone: 73-143920 or 73-143860).

This ancient city is unusual in that it has a double main plaza, or zocalo. One is Jardín Juárez (Garden of Juárez); the larger plaza is Jardín de los Héroes (Garden of Heroes). This is also one of the few towns where there is no church on the plaza. The government palace (statehouse) is here, though, and so are a number of sidewalk cafés. It's a favorite place for those who like to people watch and listen to lively band concerts (Thursdays, Saturdays, and Sundays). The mariachi bands that hang out around the plaza won't play without being paid. The zocalo is also frequented by vendors and poor people asking for coins.

At the corner of Hidalgo and Morelos is the Catedral de San Francisco (St. Francis Cathedral). Founded by Cortés in 1529, this is one of the oldest churches in Mexico. It was originally part of a Franciscan monastery, and during the colonial period it housed missionaries en route to the Far East via Acapulco. The interior of the church was renovated in 1959. In the process of restoration, a mural depicting the sacrifice of a Mexican saint, San Felipe de Jesús, and his fellow missionaries was uncovered. In the rear of the cathedral compound, the Chapel of the Third Order has sculptures by Indian artists. The Mariachi Mass at 11 AM and 7 PM on Sundays is famous all over Mexico, so if you want to hear the musicians or Bishop Luis Reynoso Cervantes, make sure you get here early.

Just across the street from the cathedral on Calle Morelos, visit the recently renovated Jardín Borda (Borda Gardens). This was the playground of former Mexican rulers Maximilian and Carlota, who would thoroughly approve of the restoration job done on the magnificent old mansion and the grounds. José de la Borda, who arrived in Mexico in 1716 and amassed a huge fortune in mining, died in Cuernavaca in 1778, leaving his grand estate to his son Manuel. Manuel invested a considerable amount of his inheritance in landscaping the estate's extensive gardens. Art exhibits and concerts are scheduled frequently. Open daily. Admission charge (phone: 73-140262).

On the southeast corner of the zocalo is the *Museo Cuauhnahuac* (originally Cortés's Palace). Intended by Hernán Cortés to be a fortress, this rather forbidding pile of stones was used for many years to house the state government offices. Now renovated, it has been transformed into a state museum. The highlights of the collection are the Diego Rivera murals depicting the history of the state of Morelos from the Spanish conquest to the Revolution. There are good views of the city from the terrace and roof. As was customary during the 16th century, the Spaniards invariably chose to build their most important structures on top of existing Aztec constructions, and here you can see the Tlauican pyramid, which was buried until renovation efforts discovered it. Closed Mondays. Admission charge (phone: 73-128171).

Near the railroad station, southeast of the market on Guerrero, is the Pyramid of Teopanzolco. The ruins of the pyramid — believed to date from the Aztec era — were discovered during the Revolution of 1910, when cannon mounted on a hillside shook loose the soil. Closed Mondays. Admission charge.

In the *Casino de la Selva* hotel (Vicente Guerrero) are the Siqueiros Murals. Among the largest murals ever painted, these depict events from local history. David Alfaro Siqueiros is one of Mexico's three most famous artists — the other two are José Clemente Orozco and Diego Rivera. The work is characterized by intense, bright colors; bold forms; and a sympathetic portrayal of social problems (phone: 73-124700).

Not too far away, on Morelos in front of the cathedral is Casa Municipal de la Plástica y la Cultura, in City Hall. The murals on the second floor depict Aztec rituals and scenes from the life of Maximilian and Carlota in Mexico. Among the most striking are the depiction of Maximilian and the beautiful Indian woman purported to be one of his love interests, and that of Carlota pleading with Benito Juárez for Maximilian's life. Gallery exhibits change regularly. Open weekdays (phone: 73-185748).

About 1 mile (1.6 km) west of downtown is Salto de San Antón. A scenic waterfall cascades over a 100-foot-high ravine set in a pretty, landscaped area. At the top of the hill, you can buy local pottery. Be sure to bargain for the best price.

Another place of interest is the *Casa Museo Robert Brady* (Robert Brady Museum and Home). An expatriate American artist, Brady moved to Cuernavaca in 1961 and purchased La Casa de la Torre (the Tower House), originally part of a Franciscan convent built in the first half of the 16th century. Brady lived and worked in Cuernavaca until his death in 1986, amassing a collection of more than 1,300 Mexican and foreign works of art, pre-Columbian figures, Mexican colonial pieces, and fine examples of crafts from Mexico and many other parts of the world. The house's wildly colorful rooms and the unusual arrangement of its contents are exactly as Brady left them. Open Thursdays and Fridays from 10 AM to 2 PM and from 4 to 6 PM, and on Saturdays from 10 AM to 2 PM. Admission charge includes a guided tour, by appointment only (phone: 73-121136).

Also don't miss the *Museo de la Herbolaria* (Herb Museum; at 200 Matamoros). Known as El Olvido, this was Maximilian's refuge from court etiquette, political intrigue, and (they say) his wife, Carlota. In addition to the herb gardens and a museum of "traditional" medicine, the *Society of Friends of the Ethnobotanical Gardens* also runs a small shop, where they sell arts and crafts and naturally grown products. Closed Mondays. No admission charge (phone: 73-123108).

A wild-animal park with more than 100 species of birds and animals from all over the world, *Zoofari* (about 35 miles/56 km from Cuernavaca on the Carr. Federal — Rte. 95 — to Taxco, just past Huajintlán) must be visited by car since the animals roam free. There is also a restaurant, a handicrafts shop, a wide selection of pets for sale, rides on ponies and dwarf mules, and clean restrooms. Open daily. Admission charge.

Chapultepec Park, Cuernavaca's playground (Plan de Ayala and the 95-D interchange), recently had a complete face-lift. Spring-fed canals wind through 500 acres of lush tropical gardens, and vestiges of a 16th-century aqueduct built by Cortés outline the hills. There is also a miniature train, an aviary, a lake where rowboats can be rented, children's games, a dolphin show, and a planetarium. Closed Mondays.

About 35 miles (56 km) east of Cuernavaca, Oaxtepec is a vacation and convention center that was formerly the site of Montezuma's botanical gardens. In 1604, the Hospital of Santa Cruz was established here so that people could benefit from the curative waters. The hospital attracted people from as far away as Peru during its 200 years in operation. You can see the ruins of the hospital and the botanical gardens. There is also a recreation area with swimming pool, playgrounds, athletic fields, housing, and dining facilities. Two miles (3 km) away in Las Estacas — just off the road to Cuautla — there is a circular pool with a constant rolling, frothing, bubble of water at its center. It's wonderful to swim in. Take the Mexico City–Cuautla toll road (Carr. de Cuota) to the Yautepec cutoff and follow signs to Tlaltizapan. For information, call Tlaltizapan 31. A short distance south of Oaxtepec, at Cocoyoc, there's a sugar hacienda that has been turned into a fine resort hotel called *Hacienda Cocoyoc;* see *Best en Route* for details.

Cuernavaca is not particularly noted for any indigenous crafts, although the residents do make cane furniture (usually unvarnished), straw hats, and *huaraches* (sandals). There is also a big local market that sells food, household items, and clothing. This is the best place for hunting down local arts and crafts. To find the market, use the zocalo as a starting point and walk 5 blocks north on Guerrero. When you come to the footbridge crossing a ravine, turn right and you'll be at the market. Although it's not a bargain hunter's paradise, there are artisans' stalls next to the *Museo Cuauhnahuac.* There is an arcade with well-made crafts at the *Casino de la Selva* and an exclusive shopping center at Plaza los Arcos, 501 Plan de Ayala.

Aries–Casa de las Campanas – For leather goods and designer clothing. 2 Comonfort (phone: 73-126662).

Bio-Art – An impressive selection of handicrafts, textiles, and decorative objects. Corner of Díaz Ordaz Blvd. and Alta Tensión (phone: 73-141458).

Carlota – Artwork by local artists, antiques, gifts, and wearable art. *Hotel Maximilian's,* 125 Galeana (phone: 73-122713).

Cerámica de Cuernavaca – Hand-painted dinnerware and objets d'art. 708 Plan de Ayala (phone: 73-156631).

Cerámica Santa María – More hand-painted dinnerware and objets d'art. 900 Zapata (phone: 73-130670).

Con Angel – Only angels are displayed in a showroom in Patricia Garita's spectacular colonial-style home. They're made from clay, tin, copper, porcelain, glass, and papier-mâché. It's heavenly. Open Wednesdays through Saturdays, by appointment only. 410 Calle San Jerónimo (phone: 73-132208).

Galería Yitzel – Across the street from *Bio-Art,* this gallery displays traditional and contemporary Mexican art, including sculptures by Victor Hugo Castañeda and watercolors by Robert Turu. Díaz Ordaz Blvd. and Alta Tensión (phone: 73-189925).

Girasol – A stunning collection of Mexican-inspired clothes for women. Across the street from *Bio-Art,* at the corner of Díaz Ordaz Blvd. and Alta Tensión (phone: 73-182796).

Harms Joyeros – Unique jewelry and an exceptional collection of handicrafts, beautifully displayed. A few doors down from *Posada Las Mañanitas.* 12 Ricardo Linares (phone: 73-124243).

Materials Coloniales – If you've admired the tiles in colonial inns throughout Mexico, you may buy some of your own at this shop. 2026 Plan de Ayala (phone: 73-151270).

Mieke's Bodega – Mexican antiques and reproductions of antiques, as well as ceramics, furniture, lamps, and carved doors, are attractively displayed. 5 Calle del Sol, in the Jardines de Cuernavaca area (phone: 73-157232).

La Palomita Blanca – Marie Dowling, a very lovely and friendly lady, has antiques and art on consignment here. 6 Zempoala, in the Cuauhnahuac area (phone: 73-156308).

Sports enthusiasts will favor Cuernavaca and its environs. For golfers, Cuernavaca offers several choices. *Los Tabachines Club de Golf* (phone: 73-143999) is the site of the annual *Rolex Golf Tournament* in January, and *San Gaspar* (phone: 73-194404) has a 280-yard practice tee and an 18-hole, par 72 course. *Los Tabachines* also has tennis courts and swimming pools. Guest privileges can be arranged through most Cuernavaca hotels. Other Cuernavaca golf clubs are *Club de Golf Santa Fe* (phone: 73-912011) on the Mexico–Acapulco toll road, near the Alpuyeca exit; *Club de Golf Cuernavaca* (1 Calle Plutarco Elías Calles; phone: 73-184927), the town's oldest and most beautiful course; and *Hacienda Cocoyoc* (phone: 73-522000; see *Best en Route*).

If tennis is your game, the *Villa Internacional de Tenis* (702 Chalma, Lomas de Atzingo; phone: 73-130829 or 73-170611) has 10 clay courts; *Clarion Cuernavaca Racquet Club* (100 Francisco Villa; phone: 73-112067) has 9 courts; *Cuernavaca Track* (715 Calle Domingo Diez; phone: 73-132377) has 6 clay courts. *Tennis Palace* (903 Paseo del Conquistador; phone: 73-136500) has 5 courts. Consult your hotel about obtaining a visitor's card to private tennis clubs.

After dark on weekends, Cuernavaca is a fairly lively place. *Barbazul* (10 Prado; phone: 73-139092), which means "Bluebeard," is one of the top discos, along with *Marjaba* (1000 Sonora; phone: 73-162826). Other favorites are *Ta'izz* (50 Bajada de Chapultepec; phone: 73-154060) and *Mambo* at the *Casino de la Selva* (phone: 73-124700). *Los Quetzales,* in the *Villa del Conquistador* (phone: 73-131055), has a piano bar as well as a restaurant, and *La Cueva* at the *Casino de la Selva* (phone: 73-124700) has live music Fridays and Saturdays from 10 PM on and a flamenco show Thursdays through Saturdays.

BEST EN ROUTE

CHECKING IN: Most hotels along this route are small, with large, beautiful gardens set behind high walls. Most have heated swimming pools, too. It's a good idea to make reservations at least a week in advance. Considering the high quality of accommodations, the prices are quite reasonable. Expect to pay $120 to $130 for a double room at places described as very expensive; $60 to $80 at the places listed as expensive; $50 in the moderate category; and $40 or less at the inexpensive inns.

TEHUIXTLA

La Rivera – Adjacent to the famous bathing resort of *Isstehuixtla,* the rooms and cottages of this 36-unit hotel are scattered over spacious riverfront grounds. There is a restaurant, bar, and a swimming pool, and though the popular resort is patronized mainly by Mexicans, foreign visitors are more than welcome. Off Rte. 95, southeast of the Alpuyeca interchange or the Vista Hermosa–Tequesquitengo cutoff, about 3 miles (5 km) south of Lake Tequesquitengo (phone: request assistance from operator No. 23 in Tehuixtla). Inexpensive.

JOJUTLA DE JUÁREZ

Hacienda Vista Hermosa – Built over 400 years ago, this grand estate — once a sugarcane mill — is now a lovely resort offering swimming, tennis, bowling, and horseback riding — and a fine restaurant, especially good for Sunday dinner. There is a bar and alfresco dining. Colonial-style furnishings fill the 100 available units. About 30 miles (48 km) southeast of Cuernavaca, off the Alpuyeca interchange (phone: 734-70492; 5-535-0777 in Mexico City; 800-421-0767 in the US). Moderate.

CUERNAVACA

Clarion Cuernavaca Racquet Club – A posh playground for the Beautiful People. Those accustomed to the finer things in life can use the club's 9 tennis courts, swim in the pool, and dine well. Truly lovely. 100 Francisco Villa (phone: 73-112067 or 73-112373; 800-221-2222 in the US; fax: 73-175483). Very expensive.

Las Mañanitas – Several fireplaces and an elegant colonial decor distinguish this 2-room, 20-suite inn. It's also known for its exquisite gardens, which have peacocks, cranes, flamingos, and parrots in residence. Facilities include a heated swimming pool, cocktail lounge, and a fine dining room. No credit cards accepted. 107 Ricardo Linares (phone: 73-124646; fax: 73-183672). Very expensive.

Villa Bejar – Antique cars transport guests and their luggage to the 25 deluxe suites, including 2 nuptial suites and a presidential suite, each with its own private garden. A lovely pool, tennis, boutiques, spacious gardens, impeccable service, and a good restaurant and bar with nightly entertainment make this place a favorite getaway for wealthy Mexicans. 2350 Domingo Diez (phone: 73-174811 or 73-175000; fax: 73-174953). Very expensive.

Le Château René – The management of one of Cuernavaca's best restaurants (see *Eating Out*) also runs this colonial-style hotel with 12 suites, each of which is equipped with a color TV set and its own terrace overlooking a lovely garden and pool. 11 Calz. de los Reyes (phone: 73-172300 or 73-172350; fax: 73-172401). Expensive.

Hacienda Cocoyoc – A restored 16th-century hacienda about 30 minutes from downtown Cuernavaca, it offers a 9-hole golf course, as well as access to an 18-hole course, not to mention horses, tennis, 2 large pools, and 5 restaurants. In addition to the 261 rooms, there are 28 deluxe rooms and 25 master suites, each with private pool. American Plan available. Popular for meetings and conventions. Cuautla Hwy. (phone: 73-562211; 5-550-6480 in Mexico City; fax: 73-70488). Expensive.

Hacienda de Cortés – Built as a retirement home for the conqueror, this 420-year-old plantation now has 22 suites, plus lovely gardens, a pool, a Jacuzzi, and a good restaurant with live music. 90 Plaza Kennedy, Atlacomulco (phone: 73-158844 or 73-150035; fax: 73-160867). Expensive.

Hacienda Vista Hermosa – This 102-room hacienda-style place attracts tour groups and hordes of day-trippers on Sundays, but can be quite delightful mid-week. It has a pool, tennis court, squash, horseback riding, jogging track, disco, and restaurant. About 15 miles (24 km) south of Cuernavaca in Tequesquitengo (phone: 734-70492 in Tequesquitengo or 5-535-0107 in Mexico City; fax: 73-70488). Expensive.

Hostería las Quintas – On spacious grounds, this dignified, colonial establishment has 15 rooms and 33 junior suites, some with terraces and some with fireplaces. There is a heated swimming pool, a restaurant, and a cocktail lounge. 107 Díaz Ordaz (phone: 73-183949). Expensive.

Maximilian's – Twenty-nine of its 62 cozy suites have fireplaces, and all have a telephone plus cable TV that picks up US channels. Facilities include a large garden, 2 heated pools, piano bar (open Thursdays through Saturdays), friendly service, and a fine restaurant specializing in international dishes (see *Eating Out*). 125 Galeana, Colonia Acapantzingo (phone: 73-182010; fax: 73-122152). Expensive.

Del Prado Cuernavaca – Rather large by Cuernavaca standards, it has 200 rooms, spacious garden, pool, 4 tennis courts, social activities for adults and children, restaurant, bar, and snack bar. 58 Nardo (phone: 73-174000; fax: 73-174155). Expensive.

Posada Primavera – On a hill overlooking Cuernavaca, this property offers a heated swimming pool, color TV sets, restaurant, bar, and nightclub. 20 rooms and 8 suites. 57 Av. Paseo del Conquistador (phone: 73-138420; fax: 73-138853). Moderate.

Posada San Angelo – A colonial inn with 17 rooms, it has a heated swimming pool, lovely gardens, TV sets in the rooms and satellite TV in the lobby, and a good dining room. 100 Cerrada de la Selva (phone: 73-141325; fax: 73-126604). Moderate.

Villa Internacional de Tenis – There are 10 tennis courts for the 14 luxurious suites at this lovely resort. Spacious gardens, a large pool, satellite TV, and a restaurant are among the other amenities. Suite rate includes up to two adults and two children under 15. 702 Chalma, Lomas de Atzingo (phone: 73-130829 or 73-170611; fax: 73-173717). Moderate.

Villa Vegetariana – It's a vegetarian health spa with 38 rooms, gym, aerobics classes, massage, sauna, squash, tennis, Ping-Pong, and a pool. Rate includes all meals, treatments, and use of all facilities. Mailing address: 114 Pino, Santa María Ahuacatitlán, Apdo. 1228 (phone: 73-131044). Moderate.

Vista Hermosa – This cozy inn, built around a charming patio, has a heated pool and wading pool, restaurant, and bar. Río Pánuco and Papaloapan (phone: 73-153049 or 73-152374). Moderate.

Casino de la Selva – Popular with families as well as a younger crowd, this 230-room resort hotel offers many amenities, including a cinema, bowling alley, swimming pools, disco, restaurant, and bar. Vicente Guerrero (phone: 73-124700; fax: 73-189624). Moderate to inexpensive.

Posada Jacarandas – The 85 rooms in this inn are set in spacious, manicured gardens and most have porches; there is also a Love Nest suite built high up in a tree. Meals are served on an enclosed terrace overlooking the gardens, blooming with roses, bougainvillea, mangoes, tulips, orchids, and, of course, jacaranda trees. Two tennis courts and swimming pools provide diversion. Rooms and dining facilities are separate for guests with children and those without. 805 Cuauhtémoc (phone: 73-157777; fax: 73-157888). Inexpensive.

Posada de Xochiquetzal – Americans run this 16-room colonial hotel, which has a lovely dining room with fireplace, a large garden, and a pool. 200 Calle Leyva (phone: 73-185767 or 73-120220). Inexpensive.

Quinta las Flores – All 25 rooms overlook a charming garden. There is also a terrace spacious enough to accommodate the hotel's pool and dining room. Meals are family-style, and breakfast is included in the price. 210 Tlaquepaque (phone: 73-141244 or 73-125769; fax: 73-123751). Inexpensive.

Villa del Conquistador – This 39-room hostelry has a spectacular view of Cuernavaca, as well as a heated pool, tennis, squash, miniature golf, 2 restaurants, and a bar with live entertainment. 134 Paseo del Conquistador (phone: 73-131055; 5-516-0483 in Mexico City; fax: 73-132365). Inexpensive.

EATING OUT: Cuernavaca has interesting restaurants offering a wide variety of international dishes. *Huitlacoche* (a corn fungus with a delicate mushroom flavor) is popular and is prepared in a variety of ways. All the expensive hotels listed in *Best en Route* have dining rooms rated among the best in town. Expect to pay up to $50 for a meal for two at one of the places we've listed as expensive; $25 to $30 in the moderate category; and about $20 or less in inexpensive spots. Prices don't include tips, wine, or drinks. Most restaurants accept MasterCard and Visa; a few also accept American Express and Diners Club.

Casa del Campo – A lovely colonial home, it has been converted into one of Cuernavaca's most successful dining places. Tables are arranged on the delightful horseshoe-shaped balcony, and drinks are served in the garden. *Camarónes amorosos* (shrimp baked in a white sauce and served in a puff pastry shell) and the *Princesa Verde* (almond cake filled with raspberry jam) are two major reasons for the growing popularity of this place. Open daily. Reservations advised. 101 Abasolo (phone: 73-182635 or 73-182689). Expensive.

Château du Lac – Set on the shores of Lake Tequesquitengo, about 33 miles (53 km) from Cuernavaca, this excellent French eatery is owned by Ghislaine and Phillip Mercier, who are always on hand to preside over the kitchen and to see that everything runs smoothly. Open Fridays, Saturdays, and Sundays from 1 to 11 PM. Reservations advised. Km 10, Circuito Lake Tequesquitengo (phone: 734-70173). Expensive.

Ma Maison – French cooking techniques are blended with Mexican ingredients, creating such delicacies as filet of sea bass stuffed with *huitlacoche* and a pâté of smoked trout. Open daily. Reservations advised. 58 Francisco Villa (phone: 73-131435). Expensive.

Las Mañanitas – Perhaps the best restaurant in town, the international menu featured at this lovely spot is complemented by fine service and seating on the terrace and in the garden. Open daily. Reservations advised. No credit cards accepted. 107 Ricardo Linares (phone: 73-124646). Expensive.

Sumiya – The late heiress Barbara Hutton's former Japanese palace is now a restaurant. The menu is international, including tempura and sashimi, and the setting is magnificent. Closed Mondays. Reservations advised. In Juitepec, 3 miles (5 km) past the CIVAC exit on the Acapulco highway (phone: 73-190622 or 73-190242; fax: 73-190622). Expensive.

Allegro – At the *Posada de Xochiquetzal,* this place serves northern Italian specialties. Diners may sit outdoors on a patio overlooking a garden. Open daily. Reservations advised. 200 Calle Leyva (phone: 73-185767 or 73-120220). Moderate.

Le Château René – Housed in a venerable mansion, it offers French and Swiss dishes that are well prepared and thoughtfully served. Open daily. Reservations advised. 11 Calz. de los Reyes (phone: 73-172300). Moderate.

Hacienda de Cortés – Favored by Cuernavaca regulars, this place has an international menu, excellent service, and the romantic setting of a converted hacienda. Open daily. Reservations advised. 90 Plaza Kennedy, Atlacomulco district (phone: 73-158844 or 73-150035). Moderate.

Harry's Grill – A lively crowd gathers at this link in the ubiquitous Carlos Anderson chain of restaurants for barbecued chicken and ribs. Open daily. Reservations advised. 3 Gutenberg (phone: 73-127679). Moderate.

India Bonita – Operating for more than 40 years, this unassuming *fonda* (inn) has a reputation as one of the best restaurants in town for Mexican fare. Closed Mondays. No reservations. 6-B Morrow (phone: 73-121266). Moderate.

Maximilian's – Fine international and Mexican cooking are specialties here. Ask for the *huitlacoche* pâté, which is divine. American-style dishes are also available. Open daily. Reservations advised. 125 Galeana, Colonia Acapantzingo district (phone: 73-123478). Moderate.

Las Quintas – Although the menu here is not especially creative, select dishes — especially the stuffed peppers and *huitlacoche* crêpes — are well prepared. Open daily. Reservations advised. *Hostería las Quintas,* 107 Díaz Ordaz (phone: 73-183949). Moderate.

Vienes – It's not fancy, but the food is excellent. Try the steak tartare and the lovely, soufflé-like Austrian dessert called *Salzburger nockerl.* Closed Tuesdays. Reservations advised. 4 Lerdo de Tejada, a block from the zocalo (phone: 73-120217). Moderate.

VIP's – A gringo-style eatery with a wide selection of American and Mexican dishes. Good waffles. Open daily. No reservations. 9 Blvd. Juárez (phone: 73-128342). Moderate to inexpensive.

La Parroquia – This Mexican-sounding spot dishes up mostly Middle Eastern meals. If you're addicted to souvlaki, shish kebab, and hummus, this place is for you. Other ethnic specialties served, too. Open daily. Reservations unnecessary. On the zocalo (phone: 73-125400). Inexpensive.

Los Pasteles del Vienes – Just a few steps away from — and owned by — *Vienes,* this is a nice place for pastries and European-style snacks. Open daily. Reservations unnecessary. Lerdo de Tejada and Comonfort (phone: 73-143404). Inexpensive.

Playa Dorada – Absolutely no atmosphere, but perfectly prepared fish and shellfish at reasonable prices. Open daily. Reservations unnecessary. 33 Morelos Sur (phone: 73-143633). Inexpensive.

Vivaldi – This has become one of the most popular spots in Cuernavaca. Tasty European-style food and pastries are served in a delightful converted house across the street from the parking lot of the *Superama la Selva.* Diners can choose between indoor and garden seating; taped classical music provides a soothing background. Open daily. No reservations. 102 Calle Pericón (phone: 73-180122). Inexpensive.

■ **Note:** Along the Boulevard Plan de Ayala, one taco stand after another serves a very broad variety of traditional (and delicious) tacos, evenings after 7 PM.

En route from Cuernavaca – Follow Route 95, the old mountain road, north to Mexico City. The mountain drive is fairly narrow, but the road is well maintained, and the views scenic and truly beautiful. When passing through Tres Cumbres, also referred to as Tres Marías, a small lumber town that looks out over the valleys of Mexico and Cuernavaca, take an interesting side trip to Lagunas de Zempoala. Veer west, leaving Route 95, and drive 8 miles (13 km) on a winding paved road.

LAGUNAS DE ZEMPOALA: Known to the Indians as "Lakes of the Windy Place," these seven small bodies of water are more than 9,000 feet above sea level. Each is very beautiful and kept well stocked with trout, but don't get any ideas about casting rod and reel. Fishing is strictly forbidden. Part of a national park, the lakes are set amidst pine woods and offer lovely picnic areas. Note that camping has now been prohibited because of the danger presented by *banditos*. Take along a jacket or heavy sweater; it gets quite cool here, particularly after sunset. Weekends tend to get crowded, but weekdays are quiet, peaceful, and an idyllic contrast to the modern bustle of Mexico City, less than 2 hours away. The local craftspeople are famous for their varnished wood furniture and lamps made from tree trunks.

En route from Lagunas de Zempoala – Returning to the main highway, follow Route 95-D south toward Tepoztlán, another worthwhile side trip.

TEPOZTLÁN: On Route 95-D you can catch the first glimpse of what is to come farther down the road: a lookout with an amazingly clear view of Popocatépetl and Ixtaccíhuatl, the snow-topped volcanoes that command the surrounding countryside and are visible from three states. After La Pera, a pear-shaped curve on the Cuernavaca highway, take the Cuautla turnoff, Route 115-D, to Tepoztlán, a beautiful Indian village set among the mountains in a lush, green vale. The predominant language is Nahuatl, the customs are ancient, but it is a town prepared to deal with tourists quite happily. A stately hotel, *Posada del Tepozteco,* overlooks the village and has a great view (see *Best en Route*). The marketplace is an outdoor area where, once a week, produce and household wares are spread out on the ground beneath cloth sunshades.

The streets in town are a picturesque network of steep and winding cobblestones, but the most unique and interesting sites in Tepoztlán are the temples and pyramid structures that stand on the mountain peak 1,200 feet above the town. The most famous, the Shrine of Tepozteco, was dedicated to Tepoztecatl, god of pulque, a popular alcoholic beverage fermented from the sap of the maguey plant, a member of the cactus family. There is a steep climb through the thin mountain air to the pyramid base of this shrine. A narrow stairway on the western side leads up to the inner shrine, where the walls are covered with bold-relief hieroglyphs. Though the trip up is strenuous, the view from the heights is awe-inspiring.

An archaeological museum in one of the town's old convent buildings of the 16th century has an interesting collection of pre-Hispanic art and of objects that will give you a full sense of the lives of the people who worshiped at the shrine. Although Christianity did not take hold here as in larger, more colonialized areas, the Dominicans did attempt to convert the Indians; they built the convent in 1559. The structure is huge, and for visitors who speak Spanish, there is a guided tour filled with tales of all the convent's incarnations, from the 16th-century destruction of native idols to early-20th-century revolutionary army barracks. Ask for *"el convento."*

At a fiesta on September 8, the whole town honors Tepoztecatl's connection with pulque by getting drunk. One other unusual festival is held annually on the 3 days before *Ash Wednesday,* when the men of the area dance the *brincos,* or jumps, an ancient Aztec movement performed in conquistador costumes, beards, wigs, and masks.

En route from Tepoztlán – Retrace your steps to the Cuautla interchange. If you prefer, continue on Route 95-D, which will provide a much faster drive into Mexico City. At this point, you're some 10,000 feet above sea level. Approaching Mexico City, you'll notice many white billboards warning motorists of the smog-control program now in effect. Depending on their license plate number, motorists are banned from driving on certain days. So take note: There is an $80 fine plus a 24-hour confiscation of your vehicle if you violate this regulation.

Upon entering the Federal District, you'll pass the Olympic Village on the left, now a housing project. The highway takes you into the city center via Periférico through Chapultepec Park to Paseo de la Reforma, the main avenue in Mexico City. For more information on Mexico City, see *Birnbaum's Mexico 1993.*

BEST EN ROUTE

TEPOZTLÁN

In Tepoztlán expect to pay $50 for a double room at the place described as moderate; $40 or less at the inexpensive one.

Posada del Tepozteco – Set on a hill overlooking the village of Tepoztlán, this lovely, old, remodeled colonial-style inn has 8 rooms and 5 suites. Facilities include 2 pools, extensive gardens, a fine dining room (try to get a window seat for an outstanding view of the surrounding valley and mountain peaks), and a bar. 3 Calle del Paraíso (phone: 739-50010 or 739-50323). Moderate.

Tepoztlán – Not much character but comfortable, offering 36 rooms, 2 suites with Jacuzzis, a restaurant-bar, and heated pool. On weekends the hotel fills up with families and gets quite noisy. At the entrance to town, at 6 Calle del Industrias (phone: 739-50522 or 739-50503). Inexpensive.

INDEX

Index